THE ONE

TRUE

SECRET

TO

ANTI-RACISM

This Book was written by Curtis Smith
It's my take on race and how stupid thinking of ourselfs as anything other than human, regardless of color makes no sense.

TO BE ANTI-RACIST YOU MUST UNDERSTAND THE THERE IS ONLY ONE RACE, HUMAN. EVERYTHING ELSE IS BULLSHIT, TO MAKE SOME FEEL INFERIOR OR SUPERIOR. ITS JUST THAT SIMPLE, NOW STOP BEING A DUMBASS AND WORK TO BE A BETTER HUMAN.

TO BE ANTI-RACIST YOU MUST UNDERSTAND THE THERE IS ONLY ONE RACE, HUMAN. EVERYTHING ELSE IS BULLSHIT, TO MAKE SOME FEEL INFERIOR OR SUPERIOR. ITS JUST THAT SIMPLE, NOW STOP BEING A DUMBASS AND WORK TO BE A BETTER HUMAN.

TO BE ANTI-RACIST YOU MUST UNDERSTAND THE THERE IS ONLY ONE RACE, HUMAN. EVERYTHING ELSE IS BULLSHIT, TO MAKE SOME FEEL INFERIOR OR SUPERIOR. ITS JUST THAT SIMPLE, NOW STOP BEING A DUMBASS AND WORK TO BE A BETTER HUMAN.

TO BE ANTI-RACIST YOU MUST UNDERSTAND THE THERE IS ONLY ONE RACE, HUMAN. EVERYTHING ELSE IS BULLSHIT, TO MAKE SOME FEEL INFERIOR OR SUPERIOR. ITS JUST THAT SIMPLE, NOW STOP BEING A DUMBASS AND WORK TO BE A BETTER HUMAN.

TO BE ANTI-RACIST YOU MUST UNDERSTAND THE THERE IS ONLY ONE RACE, HUMAN. EVERYTHING ELSE IS BULLSHIT, TO MAKE SOME FEEL INFERIOR OR SUPERIOR. ITS JUST THAT SIMPLE, NOW STOP BEING A DUMBASS AND WORK TO BE A BETTER HUMAN.

TO BE ANTI-RACIST YOU MUST UNDERSTAND THE THERE IS ONLY ONE RACE, HUMAN. EVERYTHING ELSE IS BULLSHIT, TO MAKE SOME FEEL INFERIOR OR SUPERIOR. ITS JUST THAT SIMPLE, NOW STOP BEING A DUMBASS AND WORK TO BE A BETTER HUMAN.

TO BE ANTI-RACIST YOU MUST UNDERSTAND THE THERE IS ONLY ONE RACE, HUMAN. EVERYTHING ELSE IS BULLSHIT, TO MAKE SOME FEEL INFERIOR OR SUPERIOR. ITS JUST THAT SIMPLE, NOW STOP BEING A DUMBASS AND WORK TO BE A BETTER HUMAN.

TO BE ANTI-RACIST YOU MUST UNDERSTAND THE THERE IS ONLY ONE RACE, HUMAN. EVERYTHING ELSE IS BULLSHIT, TO MAKE SOME FEEL INFERIOR OR SUPERIOR. ITS JUST THAT SIMPLE, NOW STOP BEING A DUMBASS AND WORK TO BE A BETTER HUMAN.

TO BE ANTI-RACIST YOU MUST UNDERSTAND THE THERE IS ONLY ONE RACE, HUMAN. EVERYTHING ELSE IS BULLSHIT, TO MAKE SOME FEEL INFERIOR OR SUPERIOR. ITS JUST THAT SIMPLE, NOW STOP BEING A DUMBASS AND WORK TO BE A BETTER HUMAN.

TO BE ANTI-RACIST YOU MUST UNDERSTAND THE THERE IS ONLY ONE RACE, HUMAN. EVERYTHING ELSE IS BULLSHIT, TO MAKE SOME FEEL INFERIOR OR SUPERIOR. ITS JUST THAT SIMPLE, NOW STOP BEING A DUMBASS AND WORK TO BE A BETTER HUMAN.

JUST THAT SIMPLE, NOW STOP BEING A DUMBASS AND WORK TO BE A BETTER HUMAN.

TO BE ANTI-RACIST YOU MUST UNDERSTAND THE THERE IS ONLY ONE RACE, HUMAN. EVERYTHING ELSE IS BULLSHIT, TO MAKE SOME FEEL INFERIOR OR SUPERIOR. ITS JUST THAT SIMPLE, NOW STOP BEING A DUMBASS AND WORK TO BE A BETTER HUMAN.

TO BE ANTI-RACIST YOU MUST UNDERSTAND THE THERE IS ONLY ONE RACE, HUMAN. EVERYTHING ELSE IS BULLSHIT, TO MAKE SOME FEEL INFERIOR OR SUPERIOR. ITS JUST THAT SIMPLE, NOW STOP BEING A DUMBASS AND WORK TO BE A BETTER HUMAN.

TO BE ANTI-RACIST YOU MUST UNDERSTAND THE THERE IS ONLY ONE RACE, HUMAN. EVERYTHING ELSE IS BULLSHIT, TO MAKE SOME FEEL INFERIOR OR SUPERIOR. ITS JUST THAT SIMPLE, NOW STOP BEING A DUMBASS AND WORK TO BE A BETTER HUMAN.

TO BE ANTI-RACIST YOU MUST UNDERSTAND THE THERE IS ONLY ONE RACE, HUMAN. EVERYTHING ELSE IS BULLSHIT, TO MAKE SOME FEEL INFERIOR OR SUPERIOR. ITS JUST THAT SIMPLE, NOW STOP BEING A DUMBASS AND WORK TO BE A BETTER HUMAN.

TO BE ANTI-RACIST YOU MUST UNDERSTAND THE THERE IS ONLY ONE RACE, HUMAN. EVERYTHING ELSE IS BULLSHIT, TO MAKE SOME FEEL INFERIOR OR SUPERIOR. ITS JUST THAT SIMPLE, NOW STOP BEING A DUMBASS AND WORK TO BE A BETTER HUMAN.

TO BE ANTI-RACIST YOU MUST UNDERSTAND THE THERE IS ONLY ONE RACE, HUMAN. EVERYTHING ELSE IS BULLSHIT, TO MAKE SOME FEEL INFERIOR OR SUPERIOR. ITS JUST THAT SIMPLE, NOW STOP BEING A DUMBASS AND WORK TO BE A BETTER HUMAN.

TO BE ANTI-RACIST YOU MUST UNDERSTAND THE THERE IS ONLY ONE RACE, HUMAN. EVERYTHING ELSE IS BULLSHIT, TO MAKE SOME FEEL INFERIOR OR SUPERIOR. ITS JUST THAT SIMPLE, NOW STOP BEING A DUMBASS AND WORK TO BE A BETTER HUMAN.

TO BE ANTI-RACIST YOU MUST UNDERSTAND THE THERE IS ONLY ONE RACE, HUMAN. EVERYTHING ELSE IS BULLSHIT, TO MAKE SOME FEEL INFERIOR OR SUPERIOR. ITS JUST THAT SIMPLE, NOW STOP BEING A DUMBASS AND WORK TO BE A BETTER HUMAN.

TO BE ANTI-RACIST YOU MUST UNDERSTAND THE THERE IS ONLY ONE RACE, HUMAN. EVERYTHING ELSE IS BULLSHIT, TO MAKE SOME FEEL INFERIOR OR SUPERIOR. ITS JUST THAT SIMPLE, NOW STOP BEING A DUMBASS AND WORK TO BE A BETTER HUMAN.

TO BE ANTI-RACIST YOU MUST UNDERSTAND THE THERE IS ONLY ONE RACE, HUMAN. EVERYTHING ELSE IS BULLSHIT, TO MAKE SOME FEEL INFERIOR OR SUPERIOR. ITS

TO BE ANTI-RACIST YOU MUST UNDERSTAND THE THERE IS ONLY ONE RACE, HUMAN. EVERYTHING ELSE IS BULLSHIT, TO MAKE SOME FEEL INFERIOR OR SUPERIOR. ITS JUST THAT SIMPLE, NOW STOP BEING A DUMBASS AND WORK TO BE A BETTER HUMAN.

TO BE ANTI-RACIST YOU MUST UNDERSTAND THE THERE IS ONLY ONE RACE, HUMAN. EVERYTHING ELSE IS BULLSHIT, TO MAKE SOME FEEL INFERIOR OR SUPERIOR. ITS JUST THAT SIMPLE, NOW STOP BEING A DUMBASS AND WORK TO BE A BETTER HUMAN.

TO BE ANTI-RACIST YOU MUST UNDERSTAND THE THERE IS ONLY ONE RACE, HUMAN. EVERYTHING ELSE IS BULLSHIT, TO MAKE SOME FEEL INFERIOR OR SUPERIOR. ITS JUST THAT SIMPLE, NOW STOP BEING A DUMBASS AND WORK TO BE A BETTER HUMAN.

TO BE ANTI-RACIST YOU MUST UNDERSTAND THE THERE IS ONLY ONE RACE, HUMAN. EVERYTHING ELSE IS BULLSHIT, TO MAKE SOME FEEL INFERIOR OR SUPERIOR. ITS JUST THAT SIMPLE, NOW STOP BEING A DUMBASS AND WORK TO BE A BETTER HUMAN.

TO BE ANTI-RACIST YOU MUST UNDERSTAND THE THERE IS ONLY ONE RACE, HUMAN. EVERYTHING ELSE IS BULLSHIT, TO MAKE SOME FEEL INFERIOR OR SUPERIOR. ITS JUST THAT SIMPLE, NOW STOP BEING A DUMBASS AND WORK TO BE A BETTER HUMAN.

TO BE ANTI-RACIST YOU MUST UNDERSTAND THE THERE IS ONLY ONE RACE, HUMAN. EVERYTHING ELSE IS BULLSHIT, TO MAKE SOME FEEL INFERIOR OR SUPERIOR. ITS JUST THAT SIMPLE, NOW STOP BEING A DUMBASS AND WORK TO BE A BETTER HUMAN.

TO BE ANTI-RACIST YOU MUST UNDERSTAND THE THERE IS ONLY ONE RACE, HUMAN. EVERYTHING ELSE IS BULLSHIT, TO MAKE SOME FEEL INFERIOR OR SUPERIOR. ITS JUST THAT SIMPLE, NOW STOP BEING A DUMBASS AND WORK TO BE A BETTER HUMAN.

TO BE ANTI-RACIST YOU MUST UNDERSTAND THE THERE IS ONLY ONE RACE, HUMAN. EVERYTHING ELSE IS BULLSHIT, TO MAKE SOME FEEL INFERIOR OR SUPERIOR. ITS JUST THAT SIMPLE, NOW STOP BEING A DUMBASS AND WORK TO BE A BETTER HUMAN.

TO BE ANTI-RACIST YOU MUST UNDERSTAND THE THERE IS ONLY ONE RACE, HUMAN. EVERYTHING ELSE IS BULLSHIT, TO MAKE SOME FEEL INFERIOR OR SUPERIOR. ITS JUST THAT SIMPLE, NOW STOP BEING A DUMBASS AND WORK TO BE A BETTER HUMAN.

TO BE ANTI-RACIST YOU MUST UNDERSTAND THE THERE IS ONLY ONE RACE, HUMAN. EVERYTHING ELSE IS BULLSHIT, TO MAKE SOME FEEL INFERIOR OR SUPERIOR. ITS JUST THAT SIMPLE, NOW STOP BEING A DUMBASS AND WORK TO BE A BETTER HUMAN.

TO BE ANTI-RACIST YOU MUST UNDERSTAND THE THERE IS ONLY ONE RACE, HUMAN. EVERYTHING ELSE IS BULLSHIT, TO MAKE SOME FEEL INFERIOR OR SUPERIOR. ITS JUST THAT SIMPLE, NOW STOP BEING A DUMBASS AND WORK TO BE A BETTER HUMAN.

JUST THAT SIMPLE, NOW STOP BEING A DUMBASS AND WORK TO BE A BETTER HUMAN.

TO BE ANTI-RACIST YOU MUST UNDERSTAND THE THERE IS ONLY ONE RACE, HUMAN. EVERYTHING ELSE IS BULLSHIT, TO MAKE SOME FEEL INFERIOR OR SUPERIOR. ITS JUST THAT SIMPLE, NOW STOP BEING A DUMBASS AND WORK TO BE A BETTER HUMAN.

TO BE ANTI-RACIST YOU MUST UNDERSTAND THE THERE IS ONLY ONE RACE, HUMAN. EVERYTHING ELSE IS BULLSHIT, TO MAKE SOME FEEL INFERIOR OR SUPERIOR. ITS JUST THAT SIMPLE, NOW STOP BEING A DUMBASS AND WORK TO BE A BETTER HUMAN.

TO BE ANTI-RACIST YOU MUST UNDERSTAND THE THERE IS ONLY ONE RACE, HUMAN. EVERYTHING ELSE IS BULLSHIT, TO MAKE SOME FEEL INFERIOR OR SUPERIOR. ITS JUST THAT SIMPLE, NOW STOP BEING A DUMBASS AND WORK TO BE A BETTER HUMAN.

TO BE ANTI-RACIST YOU MUST UNDERSTAND THE THERE IS ONLY ONE RACE, HUMAN. EVERYTHING ELSE IS BULLSHIT, TO MAKE SOME FEEL INFERIOR OR SUPERIOR. ITS JUST THAT SIMPLE, NOW STOP BEING A DUMBASS AND WORK TO BE A BETTER HUMAN.

TO BE ANTI-RACIST YOU MUST UNDERSTAND THE THERE IS ONLY ONE RACE, HUMAN. EVERYTHING ELSE IS BULLSHIT, TO MAKE SOME FEEL INFERIOR OR SUPERIOR. ITS JUST THAT SIMPLE, NOW STOP BEING A DUMBASS AND WORK TO BE A BETTER HUMAN.

TO BE ANTI-RACIST YOU MUST UNDERSTAND THE THERE IS ONLY ONE RACE, HUMAN. EVERYTHING ELSE IS BULLSHIT, TO MAKE SOME FEEL INFERIOR OR SUPERIOR. ITS JUST THAT SIMPLE, NOW STOP BEING A DUMBASS AND WORK TO BE A BETTER HUMAN.

TO BE ANTI-RACIST YOU MUST UNDERSTAND THE THERE IS ONLY ONE RACE, HUMAN. EVERYTHING ELSE IS BULLSHIT, TO MAKE SOME FEEL INFERIOR OR SUPERIOR. ITS JUST THAT SIMPLE, NOW STOP BEING A DUMBASS AND WORK TO BE A BETTER HUMAN.

TO BE ANTI-RACIST YOU MUST UNDERSTAND THE THERE IS ONLY ONE RACE, HUMAN. EVERYTHING ELSE IS BULLSHIT, TO MAKE SOME FEEL INFERIOR OR SUPERIOR. ITS JUST THAT SIMPLE, NOW STOP BEING A DUMBASS AND WORK TO BE A BETTER HUMAN.

TO BE ANTI-RACIST YOU MUST UNDERSTAND THE THERE IS ONLY ONE RACE, HUMAN. EVERYTHING ELSE IS BULLSHIT, TO MAKE SOME FEEL INFERIOR OR SUPERIOR. ITS JUST THAT SIMPLE, NOW STOP BEING A DUMBASS AND WORK TO BE A BETTER HUMAN.

TO BE ANTI-RACIST YOU MUST UNDERSTAND THE THERE IS ONLY ONE RACE, HUMAN. EVERYTHING ELSE IS BULLSHIT, TO MAKE SOME FEEL INFERIOR OR SUPERIOR, ITS

TO BE ANTI-RACIST YOU MUST UNDERSTAND THE THERE IS ONLY ONE RACE, HUMAN. EVERYTHING ELSE IS BULLSHIT, TO MAKE SOME FEEL INFERIOR OR SUPERIOR. ITS JUST THAT SIMPLE, NOW STOP BEING A DUMBASS AND WORK TO BE A BETTER HUMAN.

TO BE ANTI-RACIST YOU MUST UNDERSTAND THE THERE IS ONLY ONE RACE, HUMAN. EVERYTHING ELSE IS BULLSHIT, TO MAKE SOME FEEL INFERIOR OR SUPERIOR. ITS JUST THAT SIMPLE, NOW STOP BEING A DUMBASS AND WORK TO BE A BETTER HUMAN.

TO BE ANTI-RACIST YOU MUST UNDERSTAND THE THERE IS ONLY ONE RACE, HUMAN. EVERYTHING ELSE IS BULLSHIT, TO MAKE SOME FEEL INFERIOR OR SUPERIOR. ITS JUST THAT SIMPLE, NOW STOP BEING A DUMBASS AND WORK TO BE A BETTER HUMAN.

TO BE ANTI-RACIST YOU MUST UNDERSTAND THE THERE IS ONLY ONE RACE, HUMAN. EVERYTHING ELSE IS BULLSHIT, TO MAKE SOME FEEL INFERIOR OR SUPERIOR. ITS JUST THAT SIMPLE, NOW STOP BEING A DUMBASS AND WORK TO BE A BETTER HUMAN.

TO BE ANTI-RACIST YOU MUST UNDERSTAND THE THERE IS ONLY ONE RACE, HUMAN. EVERYTHING ELSE IS BULLSHIT, TO MAKE SOME FEEL INFERIOR OR SUPERIOR. ITS JUST THAT SIMPLE, NOW STOP BEING A DUMBASS AND WORK TO BE A BETTER HUMAN.

TO BE ANTI-RACIST YOU MUST UNDERSTAND THE THERE IS ONLY ONE RACE, HUMAN. EVERYTHING ELSE IS BULLSHIT, TO MAKE SOME FEEL INFERIOR OR SUPERIOR. ITS JUST THAT SIMPLE, NOW STOP BEING A DUMBASS AND WORK TO BE A BETTER HUMAN.

TO BE ANTI-RACIST YOU MUST UNDERSTAND THE THERE IS ONLY ONE RACE, HUMAN. EVERYTHING ELSE IS BULLSHIT, TO MAKE SOME FEEL INFERIOR OR SUPERIOR. ITS JUST THAT SIMPLE, NOW STOP BEING A DUMBASS AND WORK TO BE A BETTER HUMAN.

TO BE ANTI-RACIST YOU MUST UNDERSTAND THE THERE IS ONLY ONE RACE, HUMAN. EVERYTHING ELSE IS BULLSHIT, TO MAKE SOME FEEL INFERIOR OR SUPERIOR. ITS JUST THAT SIMPLE, NOW STOP BEING A DUMBASS AND WORK TO BE A BETTER HUMAN.

TO BE ANTI-RACIST YOU MUST UNDERSTAND THE THERE IS ONLY ONE RACE, HUMAN. EVERYTHING ELSE IS BULLSHIT, TO MAKE SOME FEEL INFERIOR OR SUPERIOR. ITS JUST THAT SIMPLE, NOW STOP BEING A DUMBASS AND WORK TO BE A BETTER HUMAN.

TO BE ANTI-RACIST YOU MUST UNDERSTAND THE THERE IS ONLY ONE RACE, HUMAN. EVERYTHING ELSE IS BULLSHIT, TO MAKE SOME FEEL INFERIOR OR SUPERIOR. ITS JUST THAT SIMPLE, NOW STOP BEING A DUMBASS AND WORK TO BE A BETTER HUMAN.

TO BE ANTI-RACIST YOU MUST UNDERSTAND THE THERE IS ONLY ONE RACE, HUMAN. EVERYTHING ELSE IS BULLSHIT, TO MAKE SOME FEEL INFERIOR OR SUPERIOR. ITS JUST THAT SIMPLE, NOW STOP BEING A DUMBASS AND WORK TO BE A BETTER HUMAN.

JUST THAT SIMPLE, NOW STOP BEING A DUMBASS AND WORK TO BE A BETTER HUMAN.

TO BE ANTI-RACIST YOU MUST UNDERSTAND THE THERE IS ONLY ONE RACE, HUMAN. EVERYTHING ELSE IS BULLSHIT, TO MAKE SOME FEEL INFERIOR OR SUPERIOR. ITS JUST THAT SIMPLE, NOW STOP BEING A DUMBASS AND WORK TO BE A BETTER HUMAN.

TO BE ANTI-RACIST YOU MUST UNDERSTAND THE THERE IS ONLY ONE RACE, HUMAN. EVERYTHING ELSE IS BULLSHIT, TO MAKE SOME FEEL INFERIOR OR SUPERIOR. ITS JUST THAT SIMPLE, NOW STOP BEING A DUMBASS AND WORK TO BE A BETTER HUMAN.

TO BE ANTI-RACIST YOU MUST UNDERSTAND THE THERE IS ONLY ONE RACE, HUMAN. EVERYTHING ELSE IS BULLSHIT, TO MAKE SOME FEEL INFERIOR OR SUPERIOR. ITS JUST THAT SIMPLE, NOW STOP BEING A DUMBASS AND WORK TO BE A BETTER HUMAN.

TO BE ANTI-RACIST YOU MUST UNDERSTAND THE THERE IS ONLY ONE RACE, HUMAN. EVERYTHING ELSE IS BULLSHIT, TO MAKE SOME FEEL INFERIOR OR SUPERIOR. ITS JUST THAT SIMPLE, NOW STOP BEING A DUMBASS AND WORK TO BE A BETTER HUMAN.

TO BE ANTI-RACIST YOU MUST UNDERSTAND THE THERE IS ONLY ONE RACE, HUMAN. EVERYTHING ELSE IS BULLSHIT, TO MAKE SOME FEEL INFERIOR OR SUPERIOR. ITS JUST THAT SIMPLE, NOW STOP BEING A DUMBASS AND WORK TO BE A BETTER HUMAN.

TO BE ANTI-RACIST YOU MUST UNDERSTAND THE THERE IS ONLY ONE RACE, HUMAN. EVERYTHING ELSE IS BULLSHIT, TO MAKE SOME FEEL INFERIOR OR SUPERIOR. ITS JUST THAT SIMPLE, NOW STOP BEING A DUMBASS AND WORK TO BE A BETTER HUMAN.

TO BE ANTI-RACIST YOU MUST UNDERSTAND THE THERE IS ONLY ONE RACE, HUMAN. EVERYTHING ELSE IS BULLSHIT, TO MAKE SOME FEEL INFERIOR OR SUPERIOR. ITS JUST THAT SIMPLE, NOW STOP BEING A DUMBASS AND WORK TO BE A BETTER HUMAN.

TO BE ANTI-RACIST YOU MUST UNDERSTAND THE THERE IS ONLY ONE RACE, HUMAN. EVERYTHING ELSE IS BULLSHIT, TO MAKE SOME FEEL INFERIOR OR SUPERIOR. ITS JUST THAT SIMPLE, NOW STOP BEING A DUMBASS AND WORK TO BE A BETTER HUMAN.

TO BE ANTI-RACIST YOU MUST UNDERSTAND THE THERE IS ONLY ONE RACE, HUMAN. EVERYTHING ELSE IS BULLSHIT, TO MAKE SOME FEEL INFERIOR OR SUPERIOR. ITS

TO BE ANTI-RACIST YOU MUST UNDERSTAND THE THERE IS ONLY ONE RACE, HUMAN. EVERYTHING ELSE IS BULLSHIT, TO MAKE SOME FEEL INFERIOR OR SUPERIOR. ITS JUST THAT SIMPLE, NOW STOP BEING A DUMBASS AND WORK TO BE A BETTER HUMAN.

TO BE ANTI-RACIST YOU MUST UNDERSTAND THE THERE IS ONLY ONE RACE, HUMAN. EVERYTHING ELSE IS BULLSHIT, TO MAKE SOME FEEL INFERIOR OR SUPERIOR. ITS JUST THAT SIMPLE, NOW STOP BEING A DUMBASS AND WORK TO BE A BETTER HUMAN.

TO BE ANTI-RACIST YOU MUST UNDERSTAND THE THERE IS ONLY ONE RACE, HUMAN. EVERYTHING ELSE IS BULLSHIT, TO MAKE SOME FEEL INFERIOR OR SUPERIOR. ITS JUST THAT SIMPLE, NOW STOP BEING A DUMBASS AND WORK TO BE A BETTER HUMAN.

TO BE ANTI-RACIST YOU MUST UNDERSTAND THE THERE IS ONLY ONE RACE, HUMAN. EVERYTHING ELSE IS BULLSHIT, TO MAKE SOME FEEL INFERIOR OR SUPERIOR. ITS JUST THAT SIMPLE, NOW STOP BEING A DUMBASS AND WORK TO BE A BETTER HUMAN.

TO BE ANTI-RACIST YOU MUST UNDERSTAND THE THERE IS ONLY ONE RACE, HUMAN. EVERYTHING ELSE IS BULLSHIT, TO MAKE SOME FEEL INFERIOR OR SUPERIOR. ITS JUST THAT SIMPLE, NOW STOP BEING A DUMBASS AND WORK TO BE A BETTER HUMAN.

TO BE ANTI-RACIST YOU MUST UNDERSTAND THE THERE IS ONLY ONE RACE, HUMAN. EVERYTHING ELSE IS BULLSHIT, TO MAKE SOME FEEL INFERIOR OR SUPERIOR. ITS JUST THAT SIMPLE, NOW STOP BEING A DUMBASS AND WORK TO BE A BETTER HUMAN.

TO BE ANTI-RACIST YOU MUST UNDERSTAND THE THERE IS ONLY ONE RACE, HUMAN. EVERYTHING ELSE IS BULLSHIT, TO MAKE SOME FEEL INFERIOR OR SUPERIOR. ITS JUST THAT SIMPLE, NOW STOP BEING A DUMBASS AND WORK TO BE A BETTER HUMAN.

TO BE ANTI-RACIST YOU MUST UNDERSTAND THE THERE IS ONLY ONE RACE, HUMAN. EVERYTHING ELSE IS BULLSHIT, TO MAKE SOME FEEL INFERIOR OR SUPERIOR. ITS JUST THAT SIMPLE, NOW STOP BEING A DUMBASS AND WORK TO BE A BETTER HUMAN.

TO BE ANTI-RACIST YOU MUST UNDERSTAND THE THERE IS ONLY ONE RACE, HUMAN. EVERYTHING ELSE IS BULLSHIT, TO MAKE SOME FEEL INFERIOR OR SUPERIOR. ITS JUST THAT SIMPLE, NOW STOP BEING A DUMBASS AND WORK TO BE A BETTER HUMAN.

TO BE ANTI-RACIST YOU MUST UNDERSTAND THE THERE IS ONLY ONE RACE, HUMAN. EVERYTHING ELSE IS BULLSHIT, TO MAKE SOME FEEL INFERIOR OR SUPERIOR. ITS JUST THAT SIMPLE, NOW STOP BEING A DUMBASS AND WORK TO BE A BETTER HUMAN.

TO BE ANTI-RACIST YOU MUST UNDERSTAND THE THERE IS ONLY ONE RACE, HUMAN. EVERYTHING ELSE IS BULLSHIT, TO MAKE SOME FEEL INFERIOR OR SUPERIOR. ITS JUST THAT SIMPLE, NOW STOP BEING A DUMBASS AND WORK TO BE A BETTER HUMAN.

JUST THAT SIMPLE, NOW STOP BEING A DUMBASS AND WORK TO BE A BETTER HUMAN.

TO BE ANTI-RACIST YOU MUST UNDERSTAND THE THERE IS ONLY ONE RACE, HUMAN. EVERYTHING ELSE IS BULLSHIT, TO MAKE SOME FEEL INFERIOR OR SUPERIOR. ITS JUST THAT SIMPLE, NOW STOP BEING A DUMBASS AND WORK TO BE A BETTER HUMAN.

TO BE ANTI-RACIST YOU MUST UNDERSTAND THE THERE IS ONLY ONE RACE, HUMAN. EVERYTHING ELSE IS BULLSHIT, TO MAKE SOME FEEL INFERIOR OR SUPERIOR. ITS JUST THAT SIMPLE, NOW STOP BEING A DUMBASS AND WORK TO BE A BETTER HUMAN.

TO BE ANTI-RACIST YOU MUST UNDERSTAND THE THERE IS ONLY ONE RACE, HUMAN. EVERYTHING ELSE IS BULLSHIT, TO MAKE SOME FEEL INFERIOR OR SUPERIOR. ITS JUST THAT SIMPLE, NOW STOP BEING A DUMBASS AND WORK TO BE A BETTER HUMAN.

TO BE ANTI-RACIST YOU MUST UNDERSTAND THE THERE IS ONLY ONE RACE, HUMAN. EVERYTHING ELSE IS BULLSHIT, TO MAKE SOME FEEL INFERIOR OR SUPERIOR. ITS JUST THAT SIMPLE, NOW STOP BEING A DUMBASS AND WORK TO BE A BETTER HUMAN.

TO BE ANTI-RACIST YOU MUST UNDERSTAND THE THERE IS ONLY ONE RACE, HUMAN. EVERYTHING ELSE IS BULLSHIT, TO MAKE SOME FEEL INFERIOR OR SUPERIOR. ITS JUST THAT SIMPLE, NOW STOP BEING A DUMBASS AND WORK TO BE A BETTER HUMAN.

TO BE ANTI-RACIST YOU MUST UNDERSTAND THE THERE IS ONLY ONE RACE, HUMAN. EVERYTHING ELSE IS BULLSHIT, TO MAKE SOME FEEL INFERIOR OR SUPERIOR. ITS JUST THAT SIMPLE, NOW STOP BEING A DUMBASS AND WORK TO BE A BETTER HUMAN.

TO BE ANTI-RACIST YOU MUST UNDERSTAND THE THERE IS ONLY ONE RACE, HUMAN. EVERYTHING ELSE IS BULLSHIT, TO MAKE SOME FEEL INFERIOR OR SUPERIOR. ITS JUST THAT SIMPLE, NOW STOP BEING A DUMBASS AND WORK TO BE A BETTER HUMAN.

TO BE ANTI-RACIST YOU MUST UNDERSTAND THE THERE IS ONLY ONE RACE, HUMAN. EVERYTHING ELSE IS BULLSHIT, TO MAKE SOME FEEL INFERIOR OR SUPERIOR. ITS JUST THAT SIMPLE, NOW STOP BEING A DUMBASS AND WORK TO BE A BETTER HUMAN.

TO BE ANTI-RACIST YOU MUST UNDERSTAND THE THERE IS ONLY ONE RACE, HUMAN. EVERYTHING ELSE IS BULLSHIT, TO MAKE SOME FEEL INFERIOR OR SUPERIOR. ITS JUST THAT SIMPLE, NOW STOP BEING A DUMBASS AND WORK TO BE A BETTER HUMAN.

TO BE ANTI-RACIST YOU MUST UNDERSTAND THE THERE IS ONLY ONE RACE, HUMAN. EVERYTHING ELSE IS BULLSHIT, TO MAKE SOME FEEL INFERIOR OR SUPERIOR. ITS

TO BE ANTI-RACIST YOU MUST UNDERSTAND THE THERE IS ONLY ONE RACE, HUMAN. EVERYTHING ELSE IS BULLSHIT, TO MAKE SOME FEEL INFERIOR OR SUPERIOR. ITS JUST THAT SIMPLE, NOW STOP BEING A DUMBASS AND WORK TO BE A BETTER HUMAN.

TO BE ANTI-RACIST YOU MUST UNDERSTAND THE THERE IS ONLY ONE RACE, HUMAN. EVERYTHING ELSE IS BULLSHIT, TO MAKE SOME FEEL INFERIOR OR SUPERIOR. ITS JUST THAT SIMPLE, NOW STOP BEING A DUMBASS AND WORK TO BE A BETTER HUMAN.

TO BE ANTI-RACIST YOU MUST UNDERSTAND THE THERE IS ONLY ONE RACE, HUMAN. EVERYTHING ELSE IS BULLSHIT, TO MAKE SOME FEEL INFERIOR OR SUPERIOR. ITS JUST THAT SIMPLE, NOW STOP BEING A DUMBASS AND WORK TO BE A BETTER HUMAN.

TO BE ANTI-RACIST YOU MUST UNDERSTAND THE THERE IS ONLY ONE RACE, HUMAN. EVERYTHING ELSE IS BULLSHIT, TO MAKE SOME FEEL INFERIOR OR SUPERIOR. ITS JUST THAT SIMPLE, NOW STOP BEING A DUMBASS AND WORK TO BE A BETTER HUMAN.

TO BE ANTI-RACIST YOU MUST UNDERSTAND THE THERE IS ONLY ONE RACE, HUMAN. EVERYTHING ELSE IS BULLSHIT, TO MAKE SOME FEEL INFERIOR OR SUPERIOR. ITS JUST THAT SIMPLE, NOW STOP BEING A DUMBASS AND WORK TO BE A BETTER HUMAN.

TO BE ANTI-RACIST YOU MUST UNDERSTAND THE THERE IS ONLY ONE RACE, HUMAN. EVERYTHING ELSE IS BULLSHIT, TO MAKE SOME FEEL INFERIOR OR SUPERIOR. ITS JUST THAT SIMPLE, NOW STOP BEING A DUMBASS AND WORK TO BE A BETTER HUMAN.

TO BE ANTI-RACIST YOU MUST UNDERSTAND THE THERE IS ONLY ONE RACE, HUMAN. EVERYTHING ELSE IS BULLSHIT, TO MAKE SOME FEEL INFERIOR OR SUPERIOR. ITS JUST THAT SIMPLE, NOW STOP BEING A DUMBASS AND WORK TO BE A BETTER HUMAN.

TO BE ANTI-RACIST YOU MUST UNDERSTAND THE THERE IS ONLY ONE RACE, HUMAN. EVERYTHING ELSE IS BULLSHIT, TO MAKE SOME FEEL INFERIOR OR SUPERIOR. ITS JUST THAT SIMPLE, NOW STOP BEING A DUMBASS AND WORK TO BE A BETTER HUMAN.

TO BE ANTI-RACIST YOU MUST UNDERSTAND THE THERE IS ONLY ONE RACE, HUMAN. EVERYTHING ELSE IS BULLSHIT, TO MAKE SOME FEEL INFERIOR OR SUPERIOR. ITS JUST THAT SIMPLE, NOW STOP BEING A DUMBASS AND WORK TO BE A BETTER HUMAN.

TO BE ANTI-RACIST YOU MUST UNDERSTAND THE THERE IS ONLY ONE RACE, HUMAN. EVERYTHING ELSE IS BULLSHIT, TO MAKE SOME FEEL INFERIOR OR SUPERIOR. ITS JUST THAT SIMPLE, NOW STOP BEING A DUMBASS AND WORK TO BE A BETTER HUMAN.

TO BE ANTI-RACIST YOU MUST UNDERSTAND THE THERE IS ONLY ONE RACE, HUMAN. EVERYTHING ELSE IS BULLSHIT, TO MAKE SOME FEEL INFERIOR OR SUPERIOR. ITS JUST THAT SIMPLE, NOW STOP BEING A DUMBASS AND WORK TO BE A BETTER HUMAN.

JUST THAT SIMPLE, NOW STOP BEING A DUMBASS AND WORK TO BE A BETTER HUMAN.

TO BE ANTI-RACIST YOU MUST UNDERSTAND THE THERE IS ONLY ONE RACE, HUMAN. EVERYTHING ELSE IS BULLSHIT, TO MAKE SOME FEEL INFERIOR OR SUPERIOR. ITS JUST THAT SIMPLE, NOW STOP BEING A DUMBASS AND WORK TO BE A BETTER HUMAN.

TO BE ANTI-RACIST YOU MUST UNDERSTAND THE THERE IS ONLY ONE RACE, HUMAN. EVERYTHING ELSE IS BULLSHIT, TO MAKE SOME FEEL INFERIOR OR SUPERIOR. ITS JUST THAT SIMPLE, NOW STOP BEING A DUMBASS AND WORK TO BE A BETTER HUMAN.

TO BE ANTI-RACIST YOU MUST UNDERSTAND THE THERE IS ONLY ONE RACE, HUMAN. EVERYTHING ELSE IS BULLSHIT, TO MAKE SOME FEEL INFERIOR OR SUPERIOR. ITS JUST THAT SIMPLE, NOW STOP BEING A DUMBASS AND WORK TO BE A BETTER HUMAN.

TO BE ANTI-RACIST YOU MUST UNDERSTAND THE THERE IS ONLY ONE RACE, HUMAN. EVERYTHING ELSE IS BULLSHIT, TO MAKE SOME FEEL INFERIOR OR SUPERIOR. ITS JUST THAT SIMPLE, NOW STOP BEING A DUMBASS AND WORK TO BE A BETTER HUMAN.

TO BE ANTI-RACIST YOU MUST UNDERSTAND THE THERE IS ONLY ONE RACE, HUMAN. EVERYTHING ELSE IS BULLSHIT, TO MAKE SOME FEEL INFERIOR OR SUPERIOR. ITS JUST THAT SIMPLE, NOW STOP BEING A DUMBASS AND WORK TO BE A BETTER HUMAN.

TO BE ANTI-RACIST YOU MUST UNDERSTAND THE THERE IS ONLY ONE RACE, HUMAN. EVERYTHING ELSE IS BULLSHIT, TO MAKE SOME FEEL INFERIOR OR SUPERIOR. ITS JUST THAT SIMPLE, NOW STOP BEING A DUMBASS AND WORK TO BE A BETTER HUMAN.

TO BE ANTI-RACIST YOU MUST UNDERSTAND THE THERE IS ONLY ONE RACE, HUMAN. EVERYTHING ELSE IS BULLSHIT, TO MAKE SOME FEEL INFERIOR OR SUPERIOR. ITS JUST THAT SIMPLE, NOW STOP BEING A DUMBASS AND WORK TO BE A BETTER HUMAN.

TO BE ANTI-RACIST YOU MUST UNDERSTAND THE THERE IS ONLY ONE RACE, HUMAN. EVERYTHING ELSE IS BULLSHIT, TO MAKE SOME FEEL INFERIOR OR SUPERIOR. ITS JUST THAT SIMPLE, NOW STOP BEING A DUMBASS AND WORK TO BE A BETTER HUMAN.

TO BE ANTI-RACIST YOU MUST UNDERSTAND THE THERE IS ONLY ONE RACE, HUMAN. EVERYTHING ELSE IS BULLSHIT, TO MAKE SOME FEEL INFERIOR OR SUPERIOR. ITS

TO BE ANTI-RACIST YOU MUST UNDERSTAND THE THERE IS ONLY ONE RACE, HUMAN. EVERYTHING ELSE IS BULLSHIT, TO MAKE SOME FEEL INFERIOR OR SUPERIOR. ITS JUST THAT SIMPLE, NOW STOP BEING A DUMBASS AND WORK TO BE A BETTER HUMAN.

TO BE ANTI-RACIST YOU MUST UNDERSTAND THE THERE IS ONLY ONE RACE, HUMAN. EVERYTHING ELSE IS BULLSHIT, TO MAKE SOME FEEL INFERIOR OR SUPERIOR. ITS JUST THAT SIMPLE, NOW STOP BEING A DUMBASS AND WORK TO BE A BETTER HUMAN.

TO BE ANTI-RACIST YOU MUST UNDERSTAND THE THERE IS ONLY ONE RACE, HUMAN. EVERYTHING ELSE IS BULLSHIT, TO MAKE SOME FEEL INFERIOR OR SUPERIOR. ITS JUST THAT SIMPLE, NOW STOP BEING A DUMBASS AND WORK TO BE A BETTER HUMAN.

TO BE ANTI-RACIST YOU MUST UNDERSTAND THE THERE IS ONLY ONE RACE, HUMAN. EVERYTHING ELSE IS BULLSHIT, TO MAKE SOME FEEL INFERIOR OR SUPERIOR. ITS JUST THAT SIMPLE, NOW STOP BEING A DUMBASS AND WORK TO BE A BETTER HUMAN.

TO BE ANTI-RACIST YOU MUST UNDERSTAND THE THERE IS ONLY ONE RACE, HUMAN. EVERYTHING ELSE IS BULLSHIT, TO MAKE SOME FEEL INFERIOR OR SUPERIOR. ITS JUST THAT SIMPLE, NOW STOP BEING A DUMBASS AND WORK TO BE A BETTER HUMAN.

TO BE ANTI-RACIST YOU MUST UNDERSTAND THE THERE IS ONLY ONE RACE, HUMAN. EVERYTHING ELSE IS BULLSHIT, TO MAKE SOME FEEL INFERIOR OR SUPERIOR. ITS JUST THAT SIMPLE, NOW STOP BEING A DUMBASS AND WORK TO BE A BETTER HUMAN.

TO BE ANTI-RACIST YOU MUST UNDERSTAND THE THERE IS ONLY ONE RACE, HUMAN. EVERYTHING ELSE IS BULLSHIT, TO MAKE SOME FEEL INFERIOR OR SUPERIOR. ITS JUST THAT SIMPLE, NOW STOP BEING A DUMBASS AND WORK TO BE A BETTER HUMAN.

TO BE ANTI-RACIST YOU MUST UNDERSTAND THE THERE IS ONLY ONE RACE, HUMAN. EVERYTHING ELSE IS BULLSHIT, TO MAKE SOME FEEL INFERIOR OR SUPERIOR. ITS JUST THAT SIMPLE, NOW STOP BEING A DUMBASS AND WORK TO BE A BETTER HUMAN.

TO BE ANTI-RACIST YOU MUST UNDERSTAND THE THERE IS ONLY ONE RACE, HUMAN. EVERYTHING ELSE IS BULLSHIT, TO MAKE SOME FEEL INFERIOR OR SUPERIOR. ITS JUST THAT SIMPLE, NOW STOP BEING A DUMBASS AND WORK TO BE A BETTER HUMAN.

TO BE ANTI-RACIST YOU MUST UNDERSTAND THE THERE IS ONLY ONE RACE, HUMAN. EVERYTHING ELSE IS BULLSHIT, TO MAKE SOME FEEL INFERIOR OR SUPERIOR. ITS JUST THAT SIMPLE, NOW STOP BEING A DUMBASS AND WORK TO BE A BETTER HUMAN.

TO BE ANTI-RACIST YOU MUST UNDERSTAND THE THERE IS ONLY ONE RACE, HUMAN. EVERYTHING ELSE IS BULLSHIT, TO MAKE SOME FEEL INFERIOR OR SUPERIOR. ITS JUST THAT SIMPLE, NOW STOP BEING A DUMBASS AND WORK TO BE A BETTER HUMAN.

JUST THAT SIMPLE, NOW STOP BEING A DUMBASS AND WORK TO BE A BETTER
HUMAN.

TO BE ANTI-RACIST YOU MUST UNDERSTAND THE THERE IS ONLY ONE RACE, HUMAN.
EVERYTHING ELSE IS BULLSHIT, TO MAKE SOME FEEL INFERIOR OR SUPERIOR. ITS
JUST THAT SIMPLE, NOW STOP BEING A DUMBASS AND WORK TO BE A BETTER
HUMAN.

TO BE ANTI-RACIST YOU MUST UNDERSTAND THE THERE IS ONLY ONE RACE, HUMAN.
EVERYTHING ELSE IS BULLSHIT, TO MAKE SOME FEEL INFERIOR OR SUPERIOR. ITS
JUST THAT SIMPLE, NOW STOP BEING A DUMBASS AND WORK TO BE A BETTER
HUMAN.

TO BE ANTI-RACIST YOU MUST UNDERSTAND THE THERE IS ONLY ONE RACE, HUMAN.
EVERYTHING ELSE IS BULLSHIT, TO MAKE SOME FEEL INFERIOR OR SUPERIOR. ITS
JUST THAT SIMPLE, NOW STOP BEING A DUMBASS AND WORK TO BE A BETTER
HUMAN.

TO BE ANTI-RACIST YOU MUST UNDERSTAND THE THERE IS ONLY ONE RACE, HUMAN.
EVERYTHING ELSE IS BULLSHIT, TO MAKE SOME FEEL INFERIOR OR SUPERIOR. ITS
JUST THAT SIMPLE, NOW STOP BEING A DUMBASS AND WORK TO BE A BETTER
HUMAN.

TO BE ANTI-RACIST YOU MUST UNDERSTAND THE THERE IS ONLY ONE RACE, HUMAN.
EVERYTHING ELSE IS BULLSHIT, TO MAKE SOME FEEL INFERIOR OR SUPERIOR. ITS
JUST THAT SIMPLE, NOW STOP BEING A DUMBASS AND WORK TO BE A BETTER
HUMAN.

TO BE ANTI-RACIST YOU MUST UNDERSTAND THE THERE IS ONLY ONE RACE, HUMAN.
EVERYTHING ELSE IS BULLSHIT, TO MAKE SOME FEEL INFERIOR OR SUPERIOR. ITS
JUST THAT SIMPLE, NOW STOP BEING A DUMBASS AND WORK TO BE A BETTER
HUMAN.

TO BE ANTI-RACIST YOU MUST UNDERSTAND THE THERE IS ONLY ONE RACE, HUMAN.
EVERYTHING ELSE IS BULLSHIT, TO MAKE SOME FEEL INFERIOR OR SUPERIOR. ITS
JUST THAT SIMPLE, NOW STOP BEING A DUMBASS AND WORK TO BE A BETTER
HUMAN.

TO BE ANTI-RACIST YOU MUST UNDERSTAND THE THERE IS ONLY ONE RACE, HUMAN.
EVERYTHING ELSE IS BULLSHIT, TO MAKE SOME FEEL INFERIOR OR SUPERIOR. ITS
JUST THAT SIMPLE, NOW STOP BEING A DUMBASS AND WORK TO BE A BETTER
HUMAN.

TO BE ANTI-RACIST YOU MUST UNDERSTAND THE THERE IS ONLY ONE RACE, HUMAN.
EVERYTHING ELSE IS BULLSHIT, TO MAKE SOME FEEL INFERIOR OR SUPERIOR. ITS
JUST THAT SIMPLE, NOW STOP BEING A DUMBASS AND WORK TO BE A BETTER
HUMAN.

TO BE ANTI-RACIST YOU MUST UNDERSTAND THE THERE IS ONLY ONE RACE, HUMAN.
EVERYTHING ELSE IS BULLSHIT, TO MAKE SOME FEEL INFERIOR OR SUPERIOR. ITS

TO BE ANTI-RACIST YOU MUST UNDERSTAND THE THERE IS ONLY ONE RACE, HUMAN. EVERYTHING ELSE IS BULLSHIT, TO MAKE SOME FEEL INFERIOR OR SUPERIOR. ITS JUST THAT SIMPLE, NOW STOP BEING A DUMBASS AND WORK TO BE A BETTER HUMAN.

TO BE ANTI-RACIST YOU MUST UNDERSTAND THE THERE IS ONLY ONE RACE, HUMAN. EVERYTHING ELSE IS BULLSHIT, TO MAKE SOME FEEL INFERIOR OR SUPERIOR. ITS JUST THAT SIMPLE, NOW STOP BEING A DUMBASS AND WORK TO BE A BETTER HUMAN.

TO BE ANTI-RACIST YOU MUST UNDERSTAND THE THERE IS ONLY ONE RACE, HUMAN. EVERYTHING ELSE IS BULLSHIT, TO MAKE SOME FEEL INFERIOR OR SUPERIOR. ITS JUST THAT SIMPLE, NOW STOP BEING A DUMBASS AND WORK TO BE A BETTER HUMAN.

TO BE ANTI-RACIST YOU MUST UNDERSTAND THE THERE IS ONLY ONE RACE, HUMAN. EVERYTHING ELSE IS BULLSHIT, TO MAKE SOME FEEL INFERIOR OR SUPERIOR. ITS JUST THAT SIMPLE, NOW STOP BEING A DUMBASS AND WORK TO BE A BETTER HUMAN.

TO BE ANTI-RACIST YOU MUST UNDERSTAND THE THERE IS ONLY ONE RACE, HUMAN. EVERYTHING ELSE IS BULLSHIT, TO MAKE SOME FEEL INFERIOR OR SUPERIOR. ITS JUST THAT SIMPLE, NOW STOP BEING A DUMBASS AND WORK TO BE A BETTER HUMAN.

TO BE ANTI-RACIST YOU MUST UNDERSTAND THE THERE IS ONLY ONE RACE, HUMAN. EVERYTHING ELSE IS BULLSHIT, TO MAKE SOME FEEL INFERIOR OR SUPERIOR. ITS JUST THAT SIMPLE, NOW STOP BEING A DUMBASS AND WORK TO BE A BETTER HUMAN.

TO BE ANTI-RACIST YOU MUST UNDERSTAND THE THERE IS ONLY ONE RACE, HUMAN. EVERYTHING ELSE IS BULLSHIT, TO MAKE SOME FEEL INFERIOR OR SUPERIOR. ITS JUST THAT SIMPLE, NOW STOP BEING A DUMBASS AND WORK TO BE A BETTER HUMAN.

TO BE ANTI-RACIST YOU MUST UNDERSTAND THE THERE IS ONLY ONE RACE, HUMAN. EVERYTHING ELSE IS BULLSHIT, TO MAKE SOME FEEL INFERIOR OR SUPERIOR. ITS JUST THAT SIMPLE, NOW STOP BEING A DUMBASS AND WORK TO BE A BETTER HUMAN.

TO BE ANTI-RACIST YOU MUST UNDERSTAND THE THERE IS ONLY ONE RACE, HUMAN. EVERYTHING ELSE IS BULLSHIT, TO MAKE SOME FEEL INFERIOR OR SUPERIOR. ITS JUST THAT SIMPLE, NOW STOP BEING A DUMBASS AND WORK TO BE A BETTER HUMAN.

TO BE ANTI-RACIST YOU MUST UNDERSTAND THE THERE IS ONLY ONE RACE, HUMAN. EVERYTHING ELSE IS BULLSHIT, TO MAKE SOME FEEL INFERIOR OR SUPERIOR. ITS JUST THAT SIMPLE, NOW STOP BEING A DUMBASS AND WORK TO BE A BETTER HUMAN.

TO BE ANTI-RACIST YOU MUST UNDERSTAND THE THERE IS ONLY ONE RACE, HUMAN. EVERYTHING ELSE IS BULLSHIT, TO MAKE SOME FEEL INFERIOR OR SUPERIOR. ITS JUST THAT SIMPLE, NOW STOP BEING A DUMBASS AND WORK TO BE A BETTER HUMAN

JUST THAT SIMPLE, NOW STOP BEING A DUMBASS AND WORK TO BE A BETTER
HUMAN.

TO BE ANTI-RACIST YOU MUST UNDERSTAND THE THERE IS ONLY ONE RACE, HUMAN.
EVERYTHING ELSE IS BULLSHIT, TO MAKE SOME FEEL INFERIOR OR SUPERIOR. ITS
JUST THAT SIMPLE, NOW STOP BEING A DUMBASS AND WORK TO BE A BETTER
HUMAN.

TO BE ANTI-RACIST YOU MUST UNDERSTAND THE THERE IS ONLY ONE RACE, HUMAN.
EVERYTHING ELSE IS BULLSHIT, TO MAKE SOME FEEL INFERIOR OR SUPERIOR. ITS
JUST THAT SIMPLE, NOW STOP BEING A DUMBASS AND WORK TO BE A BETTER
HUMAN.

TO BE ANTI-RACIST YOU MUST UNDERSTAND THE THERE IS ONLY ONE RACE, HUMAN.
EVERYTHING ELSE IS BULLSHIT, TO MAKE SOME FEEL INFERIOR OR SUPERIOR. ITS
JUST THAT SIMPLE, NOW STOP BEING A DUMBASS AND WORK TO BE A BETTER
HUMAN.

TO BE ANTI-RACIST YOU MUST UNDERSTAND THE THERE IS ONLY ONE RACE, HUMAN.
EVERYTHING ELSE IS BULLSHIT, TO MAKE SOME FEEL INFERIOR OR SUPERIOR. ITS
JUST THAT SIMPLE, NOW STOP BEING A DUMBASS AND WORK TO BE A BETTER
HUMAN.

TO BE ANTI-RACIST YOU MUST UNDERSTAND THE THERE IS ONLY ONE RACE, HUMAN.
EVERYTHING ELSE IS BULLSHIT, TO MAKE SOME FEEL INFERIOR OR SUPERIOR. ITS
JUST THAT SIMPLE, NOW STOP BEING A DUMBASS AND WORK TO BE A BETTER
HUMAN.

TO BE ANTI-RACIST YOU MUST UNDERSTAND THE THERE IS ONLY ONE RACE, HUMAN.
EVERYTHING ELSE IS BULLSHIT, TO MAKE SOME FEEL INFERIOR OR SUPERIOR. ITS
JUST THAT SIMPLE, NOW STOP BEING A DUMBASS AND WORK TO BE A BETTER
HUMAN.

TO BE ANTI-RACIST YOU MUST UNDERSTAND THE THERE IS ONLY ONE RACE, HUMAN.
EVERYTHING ELSE IS BULLSHIT, TO MAKE SOME FEEL INFERIOR OR SUPERIOR. ITS
JUST THAT SIMPLE, NOW STOP BEING A DUMBASS AND WORK TO BE A BETTER
HUMAN.

TO BE ANTI-RACIST YOU MUST UNDERSTAND THE THERE IS ONLY ONE RACE, HUMAN.
EVERYTHING ELSE IS BULLSHIT, TO MAKE SOME FEEL INFERIOR OR SUPERIOR. ITS
JUST THAT SIMPLE, NOW STOP BEING A DUMBASS AND WORK TO BE A BETTER
HUMAN.

TO BE ANTI-RACIST YOU MUST UNDERSTAND THE THERE IS ONLY ONE RACE, HUMAN.
EVERYTHING ELSE IS BULLSHIT, TO MAKE SOME FEEL INFERIOR OR SUPERIOR. ITS
JUST THAT SIMPLE, NOW STOP BEING A DUMBASS AND WORK TO BE A BETTER
HUMAN.

TO BE ANTI-RACIST YOU MUST UNDERSTAND THE THERE IS ONLY ONE RACE, HUMAN.
EVERYTHING ELSE IS BULLSHIT, TO MAKE SOME FEEL INFERIOR OR SUPERIOR. ITS

TO BE ANTI-RACIST YOU MUST UNDERSTAND THE THERE IS ONLY ONE RACE, HUMAN. EVERYTHING ELSE IS BULLSHIT, TO MAKE SOME FEEL INFERIOR OR SUPERIOR. ITS JUST THAT SIMPLE, NOW STOP BEING A DUMBASS AND WORK TO BE A BETTER HUMAN.

TO BE ANTI-RACIST YOU MUST UNDERSTAND THE THERE IS ONLY ONE RACE, HUMAN. EVERYTHING ELSE IS BULLSHIT, TO MAKE SOME FEEL INFERIOR OR SUPERIOR. ITS JUST THAT SIMPLE, NOW STOP BEING A DUMBASS AND WORK TO BE A BETTER HUMAN.

TO BE ANTI-RACIST YOU MUST UNDERSTAND THE THERE IS ONLY ONE RACE, HUMAN. EVERYTHING ELSE IS BULLSHIT, TO MAKE SOME FEEL INFERIOR OR SUPERIOR. ITS JUST THAT SIMPLE, NOW STOP BEING A DUMBASS AND WORK TO BE A BETTER HUMAN.

TO BE ANTI-RACIST YOU MUST UNDERSTAND THE THERE IS ONLY ONE RACE, HUMAN. EVERYTHING ELSE IS BULLSHIT, TO MAKE SOME FEEL INFERIOR OR SUPERIOR. ITS JUST THAT SIMPLE, NOW STOP BEING A DUMBASS AND WORK TO BE A BETTER HUMAN.

TO BE ANTI-RACIST YOU MUST UNDERSTAND THE THERE IS ONLY ONE RACE, HUMAN. EVERYTHING ELSE IS BULLSHIT, TO MAKE SOME FEEL INFERIOR OR SUPERIOR. ITS JUST THAT SIMPLE, NOW STOP BEING A DUMBASS AND WORK TO BE A BETTER HUMAN.

TO BE ANTI-RACIST YOU MUST UNDERSTAND THE THERE IS ONLY ONE RACE, HUMAN. EVERYTHING ELSE IS BULLSHIT, TO MAKE SOME FEEL INFERIOR OR SUPERIOR. ITS JUST THAT SIMPLE, NOW STOP BEING A DUMBASS AND WORK TO BE A BETTER HUMAN.

TO BE ANTI-RACIST YOU MUST UNDERSTAND THE THERE IS ONLY ONE RACE, HUMAN. EVERYTHING ELSE IS BULLSHIT, TO MAKE SOME FEEL INFERIOR OR SUPERIOR. ITS JUST THAT SIMPLE, NOW STOP BEING A DUMBASS AND WORK TO BE A BETTER HUMAN.

TO BE ANTI-RACIST YOU MUST UNDERSTAND THE THERE IS ONLY ONE RACE, HUMAN. EVERYTHING ELSE IS BULLSHIT, TO MAKE SOME FEEL INFERIOR OR SUPERIOR. ITS JUST THAT SIMPLE, NOW STOP BEING A DUMBASS AND WORK TO BE A BETTER HUMAN.

TO BE ANTI-RACIST YOU MUST UNDERSTAND THE THERE IS ONLY ONE RACE, HUMAN. EVERYTHING ELSE IS BULLSHIT, TO MAKE SOME FEEL INFERIOR OR SUPERIOR. ITS JUST THAT SIMPLE, NOW STOP BEING A DUMBASS AND WORK TO BE A BETTER HUMAN.

TO BE ANTI-RACIST YOU MUST UNDERSTAND THE THERE IS ONLY ONE RACE, HUMAN. EVERYTHING ELSE IS BULLSHIT, TO MAKE SOME FEEL INFERIOR OR SUPERIOR. ITS JUST THAT SIMPLE, NOW STOP BEING A DUMBASS AND WORK TO BE A BETTER HUMAN.

TO BE ANTI-RACIST YOU MUST UNDERSTAND THE THERE IS ONLY ONE RACE, HUMAN. EVERYTHING ELSE IS BULLSHIT, TO MAKE SOME FEEL INFERIOR OR SUPERIOR. ITS JUST THAT SIMPLE, NOW STOP BEING A DUMBASS AND WORK TO BE A BETTER HUMAN.

JUST THAT SIMPLE, NOW STOP BEING A DUMBASS AND WORK TO BE A BETTER HUMAN.

TO BE ANTI-RACIST YOU MUST UNDERSTAND THE THERE IS ONLY ONE RACE, HUMAN. EVERYTHING ELSE IS BULLSHIT, TO MAKE SOME FEEL INFERIOR OR SUPERIOR. ITS JUST THAT SIMPLE, NOW STOP BEING A DUMBASS AND WORK TO BE A BETTER HUMAN.

TO BE ANTI-RACIST YOU MUST UNDERSTAND THE THERE IS ONLY ONE RACE, HUMAN. EVERYTHING ELSE IS BULLSHIT, TO MAKE SOME FEEL INFERIOR OR SUPERIOR. ITS JUST THAT SIMPLE, NOW STOP BEING A DUMBASS AND WORK TO BE A BETTER HUMAN.

TO BE ANTI-RACIST YOU MUST UNDERSTAND THE THERE IS ONLY ONE RACE, HUMAN. EVERYTHING ELSE IS BULLSHIT, TO MAKE SOME FEEL INFERIOR OR SUPERIOR. ITS JUST THAT SIMPLE, NOW STOP BEING A DUMBASS AND WORK TO BE A BETTER HUMAN.

TO BE ANTI-RACIST YOU MUST UNDERSTAND THE THERE IS ONLY ONE RACE, HUMAN. EVERYTHING ELSE IS BULLSHIT, TO MAKE SOME FEEL INFERIOR OR SUPERIOR. ITS JUST THAT SIMPLE, NOW STOP BEING A DUMBASS AND WORK TO BE A BETTER HUMAN.

TO BE ANTI-RACIST YOU MUST UNDERSTAND THE THERE IS ONLY ONE RACE, HUMAN. EVERYTHING ELSE IS BULLSHIT, TO MAKE SOME FEEL INFERIOR OR SUPERIOR. ITS JUST THAT SIMPLE, NOW STOP BEING A DUMBASS AND WORK TO BE A BETTER HUMAN.

TO BE ANTI-RACIST YOU MUST UNDERSTAND THE THERE IS ONLY ONE RACE, HUMAN. EVERYTHING ELSE IS BULLSHIT, TO MAKE SOME FEEL INFERIOR OR SUPERIOR. ITS JUST THAT SIMPLE, NOW STOP BEING A DUMBASS AND WORK TO BE A BETTER HUMAN.

TO BE ANTI-RACIST YOU MUST UNDERSTAND THE THERE IS ONLY ONE RACE, HUMAN. EVERYTHING ELSE IS BULLSHIT, TO MAKE SOME FEEL INFERIOR OR SUPERIOR. ITS JUST THAT SIMPLE, NOW STOP BEING A DUMBASS AND WORK TO BE A BETTER HUMAN.

TO BE ANTI-RACIST YOU MUST UNDERSTAND THE THERE IS ONLY ONE RACE, HUMAN. EVERYTHING ELSE IS BULLSHIT, TO MAKE SOME FEEL INFERIOR OR SUPERIOR. ITS JUST THAT SIMPLE, NOW STOP BEING A DUMBASS AND WORK TO BE A BETTER HUMAN.

TO BE ANTI-RACIST YOU MUST UNDERSTAND THE THERE IS ONLY ONE RACE, HUMAN. EVERYTHING ELSE IS BULLSHIT, TO MAKE SOME FEEL INFERIOR OR SUPERIOR. ITS JUST THAT SIMPLE, NOW STOP BEING A DUMBASS AND WORK TO BE A BETTER HUMAN.

TO BE ANTI-RACIST YOU MUST UNDERSTAND THE THERE IS ONLY ONE RACE, HUMAN. EVERYTHING ELSE IS BULLSHIT, TO MAKE SOME FEEL INFERIOR OR SUPERIOR, ITS

TO BE ANTI-RACIST YOU MUST UNDERSTAND THE THERE IS ONLY ONE RACE, HUMAN. EVERYTHING ELSE IS BULLSHIT, TO MAKE SOME FEEL INFERIOR OR SUPERIOR. ITS JUST THAT SIMPLE, NOW STOP BEING A DUMBASS AND WORK TO BE A BETTER HUMAN.

TO BE ANTI-RACIST YOU MUST UNDERSTAND THE THERE IS ONLY ONE RACE, HUMAN. EVERYTHING ELSE IS BULLSHIT, TO MAKE SOME FEEL INFERIOR OR SUPERIOR. ITS JUST THAT SIMPLE, NOW STOP BEING A DUMBASS AND WORK TO BE A BETTER HUMAN.

TO BE ANTI-RACIST YOU MUST UNDERSTAND THE THERE IS ONLY ONE RACE, HUMAN. EVERYTHING ELSE IS BULLSHIT, TO MAKE SOME FEEL INFERIOR OR SUPERIOR. ITS JUST THAT SIMPLE, NOW STOP BEING A DUMBASS AND WORK TO BE A BETTER HUMAN.

TO BE ANTI-RACIST YOU MUST UNDERSTAND THE THERE IS ONLY ONE RACE, HUMAN. EVERYTHING ELSE IS BULLSHIT, TO MAKE SOME FEEL INFERIOR OR SUPERIOR. ITS JUST THAT SIMPLE, NOW STOP BEING A DUMBASS AND WORK TO BE A BETTER HUMAN.

TO BE ANTI-RACIST YOU MUST UNDERSTAND THE THERE IS ONLY ONE RACE, HUMAN. EVERYTHING ELSE IS BULLSHIT, TO MAKE SOME FEEL INFERIOR OR SUPERIOR. ITS JUST THAT SIMPLE, NOW STOP BEING A DUMBASS AND WORK TO BE A BETTER HUMAN.

TO BE ANTI-RACIST YOU MUST UNDERSTAND THE THERE IS ONLY ONE RACE, HUMAN. EVERYTHING ELSE IS BULLSHIT, TO MAKE SOME FEEL INFERIOR OR SUPERIOR. ITS JUST THAT SIMPLE, NOW STOP BEING A DUMBASS AND WORK TO BE A BETTER HUMAN.

TO BE ANTI-RACIST YOU MUST UNDERSTAND THE THERE IS ONLY ONE RACE, HUMAN. EVERYTHING ELSE IS BULLSHIT, TO MAKE SOME FEEL INFERIOR OR SUPERIOR. ITS JUST THAT SIMPLE, NOW STOP BEING A DUMBASS AND WORK TO BE A BETTER HUMAN.

TO BE ANTI-RACIST YOU MUST UNDERSTAND THE THERE IS ONLY ONE RACE, HUMAN. EVERYTHING ELSE IS BULLSHIT, TO MAKE SOME FEEL INFERIOR OR SUPERIOR. ITS JUST THAT SIMPLE, NOW STOP BEING A DUMBASS AND WORK TO BE A BETTER HUMAN.

TO BE ANTI-RACIST YOU MUST UNDERSTAND THE THERE IS ONLY ONE RACE, HUMAN. EVERYTHING ELSE IS BULLSHIT, TO MAKE SOME FEEL INFERIOR OR SUPERIOR. ITS JUST THAT SIMPLE, NOW STOP BEING A DUMBASS AND WORK TO BE A BETTER HUMAN.

TO BE ANTI-RACIST YOU MUST UNDERSTAND THE THERE IS ONLY ONE RACE, HUMAN. EVERYTHING ELSE IS BULLSHIT, TO MAKE SOME FEEL INFERIOR OR SUPERIOR. ITS JUST THAT SIMPLE, NOW STOP BEING A DUMBASS AND WORK TO BE A BETTER HUMAN.

TO BE ANTI-RACIST YOU MUST UNDERSTAND THE THERE IS ONLY ONE RACE, HUMAN. EVERYTHING ELSE IS BULLSHIT, TO MAKE SOME FEEL INFERIOR OR SUPERIOR. ITS JUST THAT SIMPLE, NOW STOP BEING A DUMBASS AND WORK TO BE A BETTER HUMAN.

JUST THAT SIMPLE, NOW STOP BEING A DUMBASS AND WORK TO BE A BETTER
HUMAN.

TO BE ANTI-RACIST YOU MUST UNDERSTAND THE THERE IS ONLY ONE RACE, HUMAN.
EVERYTHING ELSE IS BULLSHIT, TO MAKE SOME FEEL INFERIOR OR SUPERIOR. ITS
JUST THAT SIMPLE, NOW STOP BEING A DUMBASS AND WORK TO BE A BETTER
HUMAN.

TO BE ANTI-RACIST YOU MUST UNDERSTAND THE THERE IS ONLY ONE RACE, HUMAN.
EVERYTHING ELSE IS BULLSHIT, TO MAKE SOME FEEL INFERIOR OR SUPERIOR. ITS
JUST THAT SIMPLE, NOW STOP BEING A DUMBASS AND WORK TO BE A BETTER
HUMAN.

TO BE ANTI-RACIST YOU MUST UNDERSTAND THE THERE IS ONLY ONE RACE, HUMAN.
EVERYTHING ELSE IS BULLSHIT, TO MAKE SOME FEEL INFERIOR OR SUPERIOR. ITS
JUST THAT SIMPLE, NOW STOP BEING A DUMBASS AND WORK TO BE A BETTER
HUMAN.

TO BE ANTI-RACIST YOU MUST UNDERSTAND THE THERE IS ONLY ONE RACE, HUMAN.
EVERYTHING ELSE IS BULLSHIT, TO MAKE SOME FEEL INFERIOR OR SUPERIOR. ITS
JUST THAT SIMPLE, NOW STOP BEING A DUMBASS AND WORK TO BE A BETTER
HUMAN.

TO BE ANTI-RACIST YOU MUST UNDERSTAND THE THERE IS ONLY ONE RACE, HUMAN.
EVERYTHING ELSE IS BULLSHIT, TO MAKE SOME FEEL INFERIOR OR SUPERIOR. ITS
JUST THAT SIMPLE, NOW STOP BEING A DUMBASS AND WORK TO BE A BETTER
HUMAN.

TO BE ANTI-RACIST YOU MUST UNDERSTAND THE THERE IS ONLY ONE RACE, HUMAN.
EVERYTHING ELSE IS BULLSHIT, TO MAKE SOME FEEL INFERIOR OR SUPERIOR. ITS
JUST THAT SIMPLE, NOW STOP BEING A DUMBASS AND WORK TO BE A BETTER
HUMAN.

TO BE ANTI-RACIST YOU MUST UNDERSTAND THE THERE IS ONLY ONE RACE, HUMAN.
EVERYTHING ELSE IS BULLSHIT, TO MAKE SOME FEEL INFERIOR OR SUPERIOR. ITS
JUST THAT SIMPLE, NOW STOP BEING A DUMBASS AND WORK TO BE A BETTER
HUMAN.

TO BE ANTI-RACIST YOU MUST UNDERSTAND THE THERE IS ONLY ONE RACE, HUMAN.
EVERYTHING ELSE IS BULLSHIT, TO MAKE SOME FEEL INFERIOR OR SUPERIOR. ITS
JUST THAT SIMPLE, NOW STOP BEING A DUMBASS AND WORK TO BE A BETTER
HUMAN.

TO BE ANTI-RACIST YOU MUST UNDERSTAND THE THERE IS ONLY ONE RACE, HUMAN.
EVERYTHING ELSE IS BULLSHIT, TO MAKE SOME FEEL INFERIOR OR SUPERIOR. ITS
JUST THAT SIMPLE, NOW STOP BEING A DUMBASS AND WORK TO BE A BETTER
HUMAN.

TO BE ANTI-RACIST YOU MUST UNDERSTAND THE THERE IS ONLY ONE RACE, HUMAN.
EVERYTHING ELSE IS BULLSHIT, TO MAKE SOME FEEL INFERIOR OR SUPERIOR. ITS

TO BE ANTI-RACIST YOU MUST UNDERSTAND THE THERE IS ONLY ONE RACE, HUMAN. EVERYTHING ELSE IS BULLSHIT, TO MAKE SOME FEEL INFERIOR OR SUPERIOR. ITS JUST THAT SIMPLE, NOW STOP BEING A DUMBASS AND WORK TO BE A BETTER HUMAN.

TO BE ANTI-RACIST YOU MUST UNDERSTAND THE THERE IS ONLY ONE RACE, HUMAN. EVERYTHING ELSE IS BULLSHIT, TO MAKE SOME FEEL INFERIOR OR SUPERIOR. ITS JUST THAT SIMPLE, NOW STOP BEING A DUMBASS AND WORK TO BE A BETTER HUMAN.

TO BE ANTI-RACIST YOU MUST UNDERSTAND THE THERE IS ONLY ONE RACE, HUMAN. EVERYTHING ELSE IS BULLSHIT, TO MAKE SOME FEEL INFERIOR OR SUPERIOR. ITS JUST THAT SIMPLE, NOW STOP BEING A DUMBASS AND WORK TO BE A BETTER HUMAN.

TO BE ANTI-RACIST YOU MUST UNDERSTAND THE THERE IS ONLY ONE RACE, HUMAN. EVERYTHING ELSE IS BULLSHIT, TO MAKE SOME FEEL INFERIOR OR SUPERIOR. ITS JUST THAT SIMPLE, NOW STOP BEING A DUMBASS AND WORK TO BE A BETTER HUMAN.

TO BE ANTI-RACIST YOU MUST UNDERSTAND THE THERE IS ONLY ONE RACE, HUMAN. EVERYTHING ELSE IS BULLSHIT, TO MAKE SOME FEEL INFERIOR OR SUPERIOR. ITS JUST THAT SIMPLE, NOW STOP BEING A DUMBASS AND WORK TO BE A BETTER HUMAN.

TO BE ANTI-RACIST YOU MUST UNDERSTAND THE THERE IS ONLY ONE RACE, HUMAN. EVERYTHING ELSE IS BULLSHIT, TO MAKE SOME FEEL INFERIOR OR SUPERIOR. ITS JUST THAT SIMPLE, NOW STOP BEING A DUMBASS AND WORK TO BE A BETTER HUMAN.

TO BE ANTI-RACIST YOU MUST UNDERSTAND THE THERE IS ONLY ONE RACE, HUMAN. EVERYTHING ELSE IS BULLSHIT, TO MAKE SOME FEEL INFERIOR OR SUPERIOR. ITS JUST THAT SIMPLE, NOW STOP BEING A DUMBASS AND WORK TO BE A BETTER HUMAN.

TO BE ANTI-RACIST YOU MUST UNDERSTAND THE THERE IS ONLY ONE RACE, HUMAN. EVERYTHING ELSE IS BULLSHIT, TO MAKE SOME FEEL INFERIOR OR SUPERIOR. ITS JUST THAT SIMPLE, NOW STOP BEING A DUMBASS AND WORK TO BE A BETTER HUMAN.

TO BE ANTI-RACIST YOU MUST UNDERSTAND THE THERE IS ONLY ONE RACE, HUMAN. EVERYTHING ELSE IS BULLSHIT, TO MAKE SOME FEEL INFERIOR OR SUPERIOR. ITS JUST THAT SIMPLE, NOW STOP BEING A DUMBASS AND WORK TO BE A BETTER HUMAN.

TO BE ANTI-RACIST YOU MUST UNDERSTAND THE THERE IS ONLY ONE RACE, HUMAN. EVERYTHING ELSE IS BULLSHIT, TO MAKE SOME FEEL INFERIOR OR SUPERIOR. ITS JUST THAT SIMPLE, NOW STOP BEING A DUMBASS AND WORK TO BE A BETTER HUMAN.

TO BE ANTI-RACIST YOU MUST UNDERSTAND THE THERE IS ONLY ONE RACE, HUMAN. EVERYTHING ELSE IS BULLSHIT, TO MAKE SOME FEEL INFERIOR OR SUPERIOR. ITS JUST THAT SIMPLE, NOW STOP BEING A DUMBASS AND WORK TO BE A BETTER HUMAN.

JUST THAT SIMPLE, NOW STOP BEING A DUMBASS AND WORK TO BE A BETTER HUMAN.

TO BE ANTI-RACIST YOU MUST UNDERSTAND THE THERE IS ONLY ONE RACE, HUMAN. EVERYTHING ELSE IS BULLSHIT, TO MAKE SOME FEEL INFERIOR OR SUPERIOR. ITS JUST THAT SIMPLE, NOW STOP BEING A DUMBASS AND WORK TO BE A BETTER HUMAN.

TO BE ANTI-RACIST YOU MUST UNDERSTAND THE THERE IS ONLY ONE RACE, HUMAN. EVERYTHING ELSE IS BULLSHIT, TO MAKE SOME FEEL INFERIOR OR SUPERIOR. ITS JUST THAT SIMPLE, NOW STOP BEING A DUMBASS AND WORK TO BE A BETTER HUMAN.

TO BE ANTI-RACIST YOU MUST UNDERSTAND THE THERE IS ONLY ONE RACE, HUMAN. EVERYTHING ELSE IS BULLSHIT, TO MAKE SOME FEEL INFERIOR OR SUPERIOR. ITS JUST THAT SIMPLE, NOW STOP BEING A DUMBASS AND WORK TO BE A BETTER HUMAN.

TO BE ANTI-RACIST YOU MUST UNDERSTAND THE THERE IS ONLY ONE RACE, HUMAN. EVERYTHING ELSE IS BULLSHIT, TO MAKE SOME FEEL INFERIOR OR SUPERIOR. ITS JUST THAT SIMPLE, NOW STOP BEING A DUMBASS AND WORK TO BE A BETTER HUMAN.

TO BE ANTI-RACIST YOU MUST UNDERSTAND THE THERE IS ONLY ONE RACE, HUMAN. EVERYTHING ELSE IS BULLSHIT, TO MAKE SOME FEEL INFERIOR OR SUPERIOR. ITS JUST THAT SIMPLE, NOW STOP BEING A DUMBASS AND WORK TO BE A BETTER HUMAN.

TO BE ANTI-RACIST YOU MUST UNDERSTAND THE THERE IS ONLY ONE RACE, HUMAN. EVERYTHING ELSE IS BULLSHIT, TO MAKE SOME FEEL INFERIOR OR SUPERIOR. ITS JUST THAT SIMPLE, NOW STOP BEING A DUMBASS AND WORK TO BE A BETTER HUMAN.

TO BE ANTI-RACIST YOU MUST UNDERSTAND THE THERE IS ONLY ONE RACE, HUMAN. EVERYTHING ELSE IS BULLSHIT, TO MAKE SOME FEEL INFERIOR OR SUPERIOR. ITS JUST THAT SIMPLE, NOW STOP BEING A DUMBASS AND WORK TO BE A BETTER HUMAN.

TO BE ANTI-RACIST YOU MUST UNDERSTAND THE THERE IS ONLY ONE RACE, HUMAN. EVERYTHING ELSE IS BULLSHIT, TO MAKE SOME FEEL INFERIOR OR SUPERIOR. ITS JUST THAT SIMPLE, NOW STOP BEING A DUMBASS AND WORK TO BE A BETTER HUMAN.

TO BE ANTI-RACIST YOU MUST UNDERSTAND THE THERE IS ONLY ONE RACE, HUMAN. EVERYTHING ELSE IS BULLSHIT, TO MAKE SOME FEEL INFERIOR OR SUPERIOR. ITS JUST THAT SIMPLE, NOW STOP BEING A DUMBASS AND WORK TO BE A BETTER HUMAN.

TO BE ANTI-RACIST YOU MUST UNDERSTAND THE THERE IS ONLY ONE RACE, HUMAN. EVERYTHING ELSE IS BULLSHIT, TO MAKE SOME FEEL INFERIOR OR SUPERIOR. ITS JUST THAT SIMPLE, NOW STOP BEING A DUMBASS AND WORK TO BE A BETTER HUMAN.

TO BE ANTI-RACIST YOU MUST UNDERSTAND THE THERE IS ONLY ONE RACE, HUMAN. EVERYTHING ELSE IS BULLSHIT, TO MAKE SOME FEEL INFERIOR OR SUPERIOR, ITS

TO BE ANTI-RACIST YOU MUST UNDERSTAND THE THERE IS ONLY ONE RACE, HUMAN. EVERYTHING ELSE IS BULLSHIT, TO MAKE SOME FEEL INFERIOR OR SUPERIOR. ITS JUST THAT SIMPLE, NOW STOP BEING A DUMBASS AND WORK TO BE A BETTER HUMAN.

TO BE ANTI-RACIST YOU MUST UNDERSTAND THE THERE IS ONLY ONE RACE, HUMAN. EVERYTHING ELSE IS BULLSHIT, TO MAKE SOME FEEL INFERIOR OR SUPERIOR. ITS JUST THAT SIMPLE, NOW STOP BEING A DUMBASS AND WORK TO BE A BETTER HUMAN.

TO BE ANTI-RACIST YOU MUST UNDERSTAND THE THERE IS ONLY ONE RACE, HUMAN. EVERYTHING ELSE IS BULLSHIT, TO MAKE SOME FEEL INFERIOR OR SUPERIOR. ITS JUST THAT SIMPLE, NOW STOP BEING A DUMBASS AND WORK TO BE A BETTER HUMAN.

TO BE ANTI-RACIST YOU MUST UNDERSTAND THE THERE IS ONLY ONE RACE, HUMAN. EVERYTHING ELSE IS BULLSHIT, TO MAKE SOME FEEL INFERIOR OR SUPERIOR. ITS JUST THAT SIMPLE, NOW STOP BEING A DUMBASS AND WORK TO BE A BETTER HUMAN.

TO BE ANTI-RACIST YOU MUST UNDERSTAND THE THERE IS ONLY ONE RACE, HUMAN. EVERYTHING ELSE IS BULLSHIT, TO MAKE SOME FEEL INFERIOR OR SUPERIOR. ITS JUST THAT SIMPLE, NOW STOP BEING A DUMBASS AND WORK TO BE A BETTER HUMAN.

TO BE ANTI-RACIST YOU MUST UNDERSTAND THE THERE IS ONLY ONE RACE, HUMAN. EVERYTHING ELSE IS BULLSHIT, TO MAKE SOME FEEL INFERIOR OR SUPERIOR. ITS JUST THAT SIMPLE, NOW STOP BEING A DUMBASS AND WORK TO BE A BETTER HUMAN.

TO BE ANTI-RACIST YOU MUST UNDERSTAND THE THERE IS ONLY ONE RACE, HUMAN. EVERYTHING ELSE IS BULLSHIT, TO MAKE SOME FEEL INFERIOR OR SUPERIOR. ITS JUST THAT SIMPLE, NOW STOP BEING A DUMBASS AND WORK TO BE A BETTER HUMAN.

TO BE ANTI-RACIST YOU MUST UNDERSTAND THE THERE IS ONLY ONE RACE, HUMAN. EVERYTHING ELSE IS BULLSHIT, TO MAKE SOME FEEL INFERIOR OR SUPERIOR. ITS JUST THAT SIMPLE, NOW STOP BEING A DUMBASS AND WORK TO BE A BETTER HUMAN.

TO BE ANTI-RACIST YOU MUST UNDERSTAND THE THERE IS ONLY ONE RACE, HUMAN. EVERYTHING ELSE IS BULLSHIT, TO MAKE SOME FEEL INFERIOR OR SUPERIOR. ITS JUST THAT SIMPLE, NOW STOP BEING A DUMBASS AND WORK TO BE A BETTER HUMAN.

TO BE ANTI-RACIST YOU MUST UNDERSTAND THE THERE IS ONLY ONE RACE, HUMAN. EVERYTHING ELSE IS BULLSHIT, TO MAKE SOME FEEL INFERIOR OR SUPERIOR. ITS JUST THAT SIMPLE, NOW STOP BEING A DUMBASS AND WORK TO BE A BETTER HUMAN.

TO BE ANTI-RACIST YOU MUST UNDERSTAND THE THERE IS ONLY ONE RACE, HUMAN. EVERYTHING ELSE IS BULLSHIT, TO MAKE SOME FEEL INFERIOR OR SUPERIOR. ITS JUST THAT SIMPLE, NOW STOP BEING A DUMBASS AND WORK TO BE A BETTER HUMAN

JUST THAT SIMPLE, NOW STOP BEING A DUMBASS AND WORK TO BE A BETTER HUMAN.

TO BE ANTI-RACIST YOU MUST UNDERSTAND THE THERE IS ONLY ONE RACE, HUMAN. EVERYTHING ELSE IS BULLSHIT, TO MAKE SOME FEEL INFERIOR OR SUPERIOR. ITS JUST THAT SIMPLE, NOW STOP BEING A DUMBASS AND WORK TO BE A BETTER HUMAN.

TO BE ANTI-RACIST YOU MUST UNDERSTAND THE THERE IS ONLY ONE RACE, HUMAN. EVERYTHING ELSE IS BULLSHIT, TO MAKE SOME FEEL INFERIOR OR SUPERIOR. ITS JUST THAT SIMPLE, NOW STOP BEING A DUMBASS AND WORK TO BE A BETTER HUMAN.

TO BE ANTI-RACIST YOU MUST UNDERSTAND THE THERE IS ONLY ONE RACE, HUMAN. EVERYTHING ELSE IS BULLSHIT, TO MAKE SOME FEEL INFERIOR OR SUPERIOR. ITS JUST THAT SIMPLE, NOW STOP BEING A DUMBASS AND WORK TO BE A BETTER HUMAN.

TO BE ANTI-RACIST YOU MUST UNDERSTAND THE THERE IS ONLY ONE RACE, HUMAN. EVERYTHING ELSE IS BULLSHIT, TO MAKE SOME FEEL INFERIOR OR SUPERIOR. ITS JUST THAT SIMPLE, NOW STOP BEING A DUMBASS AND WORK TO BE A BETTER HUMAN.

TO BE ANTI-RACIST YOU MUST UNDERSTAND THE THERE IS ONLY ONE RACE, HUMAN. EVERYTHING ELSE IS BULLSHIT, TO MAKE SOME FEEL INFERIOR OR SUPERIOR. ITS JUST THAT SIMPLE, NOW STOP BEING A DUMBASS AND WORK TO BE A BETTER HUMAN.

TO BE ANTI-RACIST YOU MUST UNDERSTAND THE THERE IS ONLY ONE RACE, HUMAN. EVERYTHING ELSE IS BULLSHIT, TO MAKE SOME FEEL INFERIOR OR SUPERIOR. ITS JUST THAT SIMPLE, NOW STOP BEING A DUMBASS AND WORK TO BE A BETTER HUMAN.

TO BE ANTI-RACIST YOU MUST UNDERSTAND THE THERE IS ONLY ONE RACE, HUMAN. EVERYTHING ELSE IS BULLSHIT, TO MAKE SOME FEEL INFERIOR OR SUPERIOR. ITS JUST THAT SIMPLE, NOW STOP BEING A DUMBASS AND WORK TO BE A BETTER HUMAN.

TO BE ANTI-RACIST YOU MUST UNDERSTAND THE THERE IS ONLY ONE RACE, HUMAN. EVERYTHING ELSE IS BULLSHIT, TO MAKE SOME FEEL INFERIOR OR SUPERIOR. ITS JUST THAT SIMPLE, NOW STOP BEING A DUMBASS AND WORK TO BE A BETTER HUMAN.

TO BE ANTI-RACIST YOU MUST UNDERSTAND THE THERE IS ONLY ONE RACE, HUMAN. EVERYTHING ELSE IS BULLSHIT, TO MAKE SOME FEEL INFERIOR OR SUPERIOR. ITS JUST THAT SIMPLE, NOW STOP BEING A DUMBASS AND WORK TO BE A BETTER HUMAN.

TO BE ANTI-RACIST YOU MUST UNDERSTAND THE THERE IS ONLY ONE RACE, HUMAN. EVERYTHING ELSE IS BULLSHIT, TO MAKE SOME FEEL INFERIOR OR SUPERIOR. ITS

TO BE ANTI-RACIST YOU MUST UNDERSTAND THE THERE IS ONLY ONE RACE, HUMAN. EVERYTHING ELSE IS BULLSHIT, TO MAKE SOME FEEL INFERIOR OR SUPERIOR. ITS JUST THAT SIMPLE, NOW STOP BEING A DUMBASS AND WORK TO BE A BETTER HUMAN.

TO BE ANTI-RACIST YOU MUST UNDERSTAND THE THERE IS ONLY ONE RACE, HUMAN. EVERYTHING ELSE IS BULLSHIT, TO MAKE SOME FEEL INFERIOR OR SUPERIOR. ITS JUST THAT SIMPLE, NOW STOP BEING A DUMBASS AND WORK TO BE A BETTER HUMAN.

TO BE ANTI-RACIST YOU MUST UNDERSTAND THE THERE IS ONLY ONE RACE, HUMAN. EVERYTHING ELSE IS BULLSHIT, TO MAKE SOME FEEL INFERIOR OR SUPERIOR. ITS JUST THAT SIMPLE, NOW STOP BEING A DUMBASS AND WORK TO BE A BETTER HUMAN.

TO BE ANTI-RACIST YOU MUST UNDERSTAND THE THERE IS ONLY ONE RACE, HUMAN. EVERYTHING ELSE IS BULLSHIT, TO MAKE SOME FEEL INFERIOR OR SUPERIOR. ITS JUST THAT SIMPLE, NOW STOP BEING A DUMBASS AND WORK TO BE A BETTER HUMAN.

TO BE ANTI-RACIST YOU MUST UNDERSTAND THE THERE IS ONLY ONE RACE, HUMAN. EVERYTHING ELSE IS BULLSHIT, TO MAKE SOME FEEL INFERIOR OR SUPERIOR. ITS JUST THAT SIMPLE, NOW STOP BEING A DUMBASS AND WORK TO BE A BETTER HUMAN.

TO BE ANTI-RACIST YOU MUST UNDERSTAND THE THERE IS ONLY ONE RACE, HUMAN. EVERYTHING ELSE IS BULLSHIT, TO MAKE SOME FEEL INFERIOR OR SUPERIOR. ITS JUST THAT SIMPLE, NOW STOP BEING A DUMBASS AND WORK TO BE A BETTER HUMAN.

TO BE ANTI-RACIST YOU MUST UNDERSTAND THE THERE IS ONLY ONE RACE, HUMAN. EVERYTHING ELSE IS BULLSHIT, TO MAKE SOME FEEL INFERIOR OR SUPERIOR. ITS JUST THAT SIMPLE, NOW STOP BEING A DUMBASS AND WORK TO BE A BETTER HUMAN.

TO BE ANTI-RACIST YOU MUST UNDERSTAND THE THERE IS ONLY ONE RACE, HUMAN. EVERYTHING ELSE IS BULLSHIT, TO MAKE SOME FEEL INFERIOR OR SUPERIOR. ITS JUST THAT SIMPLE, NOW STOP BEING A DUMBASS AND WORK TO BE A BETTER HUMAN.

TO BE ANTI-RACIST YOU MUST UNDERSTAND THE THERE IS ONLY ONE RACE, HUMAN. EVERYTHING ELSE IS BULLSHIT, TO MAKE SOME FEEL INFERIOR OR SUPERIOR. ITS JUST THAT SIMPLE, NOW STOP BEING A DUMBASS AND WORK TO BE A BETTER HUMAN.

TO BE ANTI-RACIST YOU MUST UNDERSTAND THE THERE IS ONLY ONE RACE, HUMAN. EVERYTHING ELSE IS BULLSHIT, TO MAKE SOME FEEL INFERIOR OR SUPERIOR. ITS JUST THAT SIMPLE, NOW STOP BEING A DUMBASS AND WORK TO BE A BETTER HUMAN.

TO BE ANTI-RACIST YOU MUST UNDERSTAND THE THERE IS ONLY ONE RACE, HUMAN. EVERYTHING ELSE IS BULLSHIT, TO MAKE SOME FEEL INFERIOR OR SUPERIOR. ITS JUST THAT SIMPLE, NOW STOP BEING A DUMBASS AND WORK TO BE A BETTER HUMAN

JUST THAT SIMPLE, NOW STOP BEING A DUMBASS AND WORK TO BE A BETTER
HUMAN.

TO BE ANTI-RACIST YOU MUST UNDERSTAND THE THERE IS ONLY ONE RACE, HUMAN.
EVERYTHING ELSE IS BULLSHIT, TO MAKE SOME FEEL INFERIOR OR SUPERIOR. ITS
JUST THAT SIMPLE, NOW STOP BEING A DUMBASS AND WORK TO BE A BETTER
HUMAN.

TO BE ANTI-RACIST YOU MUST UNDERSTAND THE THERE IS ONLY ONE RACE, HUMAN.
EVERYTHING ELSE IS BULLSHIT, TO MAKE SOME FEEL INFERIOR OR SUPERIOR. ITS
JUST THAT SIMPLE, NOW STOP BEING A DUMBASS AND WORK TO BE A BETTER
HUMAN.

TO BE ANTI-RACIST YOU MUST UNDERSTAND THE THERE IS ONLY ONE RACE, HUMAN.
EVERYTHING ELSE IS BULLSHIT, TO MAKE SOME FEEL INFERIOR OR SUPERIOR. ITS
JUST THAT SIMPLE, NOW STOP BEING A DUMBASS AND WORK TO BE A BETTER
HUMAN.

TO BE ANTI-RACIST YOU MUST UNDERSTAND THE THERE IS ONLY ONE RACE, HUMAN.
EVERYTHING ELSE IS BULLSHIT, TO MAKE SOME FEEL INFERIOR OR SUPERIOR. ITS
JUST THAT SIMPLE, NOW STOP BEING A DUMBASS AND WORK TO BE A BETTER
HUMAN.

TO BE ANTI-RACIST YOU MUST UNDERSTAND THE THERE IS ONLY ONE RACE, HUMAN.
EVERYTHING ELSE IS BULLSHIT, TO MAKE SOME FEEL INFERIOR OR SUPERIOR. ITS
JUST THAT SIMPLE, NOW STOP BEING A DUMBASS AND WORK TO BE A BETTER
HUMAN.

TO BE ANTI-RACIST YOU MUST UNDERSTAND THE THERE IS ONLY ONE RACE, HUMAN.
EVERYTHING ELSE IS BULLSHIT, TO MAKE SOME FEEL INFERIOR OR SUPERIOR. ITS
JUST THAT SIMPLE, NOW STOP BEING A DUMBASS AND WORK TO BE A BETTER
HUMAN.

TO BE ANTI-RACIST YOU MUST UNDERSTAND THE THERE IS ONLY ONE RACE, HUMAN.
EVERYTHING ELSE IS BULLSHIT, TO MAKE SOME FEEL INFERIOR OR SUPERIOR. ITS
JUST THAT SIMPLE, NOW STOP BEING A DUMBASS AND WORK TO BE A BETTER
HUMAN.

TO BE ANTI-RACIST YOU MUST UNDERSTAND THE THERE IS ONLY ONE RACE, HUMAN.
EVERYTHING ELSE IS BULLSHIT, TO MAKE SOME FEEL INFERIOR OR SUPERIOR. ITS
JUST THAT SIMPLE, NOW STOP BEING A DUMBASS AND WORK TO BE A BETTER
HUMAN.

TO BE ANTI-RACIST YOU MUST UNDERSTAND THE THERE IS ONLY ONE RACE, HUMAN.
EVERYTHING ELSE IS BULLSHIT, TO MAKE SOME FEEL INFERIOR OR SUPERIOR. ITS
JUST THAT SIMPLE, NOW STOP BEING A DUMBASS AND WORK TO BE A BETTER
HUMAN.

TO BE ANTI-RACIST YOU MUST UNDERSTAND THE THERE IS ONLY ONE RACE, HUMAN.
EVERYTHING ELSE IS BULLSHIT, TO MAKE SOME FEEL INFERIOR OR SUPERIOR. ITS

TO BE ANTI-RACIST YOU MUST UNDERSTAND THE THERE IS ONLY ONE RACE, HUMAN. EVERYTHING ELSE IS BULLSHIT, TO MAKE SOME FEEL INFERIOR OR SUPERIOR. ITS JUST THAT SIMPLE, NOW STOP BEING A DUMBASS AND WORK TO BE A BETTER HUMAN.

TO BE ANTI-RACIST YOU MUST UNDERSTAND THE THERE IS ONLY ONE RACE, HUMAN. EVERYTHING ELSE IS BULLSHIT, TO MAKE SOME FEEL INFERIOR OR SUPERIOR. ITS JUST THAT SIMPLE, NOW STOP BEING A DUMBASS AND WORK TO BE A BETTER HUMAN.

TO BE ANTI-RACIST YOU MUST UNDERSTAND THE THERE IS ONLY ONE RACE, HUMAN. EVERYTHING ELSE IS BULLSHIT, TO MAKE SOME FEEL INFERIOR OR SUPERIOR. ITS JUST THAT SIMPLE, NOW STOP BEING A DUMBASS AND WORK TO BE A BETTER HUMAN.

TO BE ANTI-RACIST YOU MUST UNDERSTAND THE THERE IS ONLY ONE RACE, HUMAN. EVERYTHING ELSE IS BULLSHIT, TO MAKE SOME FEEL INFERIOR OR SUPERIOR. ITS JUST THAT SIMPLE, NOW STOP BEING A DUMBASS AND WORK TO BE A BETTER HUMAN.

TO BE ANTI-RACIST YOU MUST UNDERSTAND THE THERE IS ONLY ONE RACE, HUMAN. EVERYTHING ELSE IS BULLSHIT, TO MAKE SOME FEEL INFERIOR OR SUPERIOR. ITS JUST THAT SIMPLE, NOW STOP BEING A DUMBASS AND WORK TO BE A BETTER HUMAN.

TO BE ANTI-RACIST YOU MUST UNDERSTAND THE THERE IS ONLY ONE RACE, HUMAN. EVERYTHING ELSE IS BULLSHIT, TO MAKE SOME FEEL INFERIOR OR SUPERIOR. ITS JUST THAT SIMPLE, NOW STOP BEING A DUMBASS AND WORK TO BE A BETTER HUMAN.

TO BE ANTI-RACIST YOU MUST UNDERSTAND THE THERE IS ONLY ONE RACE, HUMAN. EVERYTHING ELSE IS BULLSHIT, TO MAKE SOME FEEL INFERIOR OR SUPERIOR. ITS JUST THAT SIMPLE, NOW STOP BEING A DUMBASS AND WORK TO BE A BETTER HUMAN.

TO BE ANTI-RACIST YOU MUST UNDERSTAND THE THERE IS ONLY ONE RACE, HUMAN. EVERYTHING ELSE IS BULLSHIT, TO MAKE SOME FEEL INFERIOR OR SUPERIOR. ITS JUST THAT SIMPLE, NOW STOP BEING A DUMBASS AND WORK TO BE A BETTER HUMAN.

TO BE ANTI-RACIST YOU MUST UNDERSTAND THE THERE IS ONLY ONE RACE, HUMAN. EVERYTHING ELSE IS BULLSHIT, TO MAKE SOME FEEL INFERIOR OR SUPERIOR. ITS JUST THAT SIMPLE, NOW STOP BEING A DUMBASS AND WORK TO BE A BETTER HUMAN.

TO BE ANTI-RACIST YOU MUST UNDERSTAND THE THERE IS ONLY ONE RACE, HUMAN. EVERYTHING ELSE IS BULLSHIT, TO MAKE SOME FEEL INFERIOR OR SUPERIOR. ITS JUST THAT SIMPLE, NOW STOP BEING A DUMBASS AND WORK TO BE A BETTER HUMAN.

TO BE ANTI-RACIST YOU MUST UNDERSTAND THE THERE IS ONLY ONE RACE, HUMAN. EVERYTHING ELSE IS BULLSHIT, TO MAKE SOME FEEL INFERIOR OR SUPERIOR. ITS JUST THAT SIMPLE, NOW STOP BEING A DUMBASS AND WORK TO BE A BETTER HUMAN

JUST THAT SIMPLE, NOW STOP BEING A DUMBASS AND WORK TO BE A BETTER HUMAN.

TO BE ANTI-RACIST YOU MUST UNDERSTAND THE THERE IS ONLY ONE RACE, HUMAN. EVERYTHING ELSE IS BULLSHIT, TO MAKE SOME FEEL INFERIOR OR SUPERIOR. ITS JUST THAT SIMPLE, NOW STOP BEING A DUMBASS AND WORK TO BE A BETTER HUMAN.

TO BE ANTI-RACIST YOU MUST UNDERSTAND THE THERE IS ONLY ONE RACE, HUMAN. EVERYTHING ELSE IS BULLSHIT, TO MAKE SOME FEEL INFERIOR OR SUPERIOR. ITS JUST THAT SIMPLE, NOW STOP BEING A DUMBASS AND WORK TO BE A BETTER HUMAN.

TO BE ANTI-RACIST YOU MUST UNDERSTAND THE THERE IS ONLY ONE RACE, HUMAN. EVERYTHING ELSE IS BULLSHIT, TO MAKE SOME FEEL INFERIOR OR SUPERIOR. ITS JUST THAT SIMPLE, NOW STOP BEING A DUMBASS AND WORK TO BE A BETTER HUMAN.

TO BE ANTI-RACIST YOU MUST UNDERSTAND THE THERE IS ONLY ONE RACE, HUMAN. EVERYTHING ELSE IS BULLSHIT, TO MAKE SOME FEEL INFERIOR OR SUPERIOR. ITS JUST THAT SIMPLE, NOW STOP BEING A DUMBASS AND WORK TO BE A BETTER HUMAN.

TO BE ANTI-RACIST YOU MUST UNDERSTAND THE THERE IS ONLY ONE RACE, HUMAN. EVERYTHING ELSE IS BULLSHIT, TO MAKE SOME FEEL INFERIOR OR SUPERIOR. ITS JUST THAT SIMPLE, NOW STOP BEING A DUMBASS AND WORK TO BE A BETTER HUMAN.

TO BE ANTI-RACIST YOU MUST UNDERSTAND THE THERE IS ONLY ONE RACE, HUMAN. EVERYTHING ELSE IS BULLSHIT, TO MAKE SOME FEEL INFERIOR OR SUPERIOR. ITS JUST THAT SIMPLE, NOW STOP BEING A DUMBASS AND WORK TO BE A BETTER HUMAN.

TO BE ANTI-RACIST YOU MUST UNDERSTAND THE THERE IS ONLY ONE RACE, HUMAN. EVERYTHING ELSE IS BULLSHIT, TO MAKE SOME FEEL INFERIOR OR SUPERIOR. ITS JUST THAT SIMPLE, NOW STOP BEING A DUMBASS AND WORK TO BE A BETTER HUMAN.

TO BE ANTI-RACIST YOU MUST UNDERSTAND THE THERE IS ONLY ONE RACE, HUMAN. EVERYTHING ELSE IS BULLSHIT, TO MAKE SOME FEEL INFERIOR OR SUPERIOR. ITS JUST THAT SIMPLE, NOW STOP BEING A DUMBASS AND WORK TO BE A BETTER HUMAN.

TO BE ANTI-RACIST YOU MUST UNDERSTAND THE THERE IS ONLY ONE RACE, HUMAN. EVERYTHING ELSE IS BULLSHIT, TO MAKE SOME FEEL INFERIOR OR SUPERIOR. ITS JUST THAT SIMPLE, NOW STOP BEING A DUMBASS AND WORK TO BE A BETTER HUMAN.

TO BE ANTI-RACIST YOU MUST UNDERSTAND THE THERE IS ONLY ONE RACE, HUMAN. EVERYTHING ELSE IS BULLSHIT, TO MAKE SOME FEEL INFERIOR OR SUPERIOR. ITS

TO BE ANTI-RACIST YOU MUST UNDERSTAND THE THERE IS ONLY ONE RACE, HUMAN. EVERYTHING ELSE IS BULLSHIT, TO MAKE SOME FEEL INFERIOR OR SUPERIOR. ITS JUST THAT SIMPLE, NOW STOP BEING A DUMBASS AND WORK TO BE A BETTER HUMAN.

TO BE ANTI-RACIST YOU MUST UNDERSTAND THE THERE IS ONLY ONE RACE, HUMAN. EVERYTHING ELSE IS BULLSHIT, TO MAKE SOME FEEL INFERIOR OR SUPERIOR. ITS JUST THAT SIMPLE, NOW STOP BEING A DUMBASS AND WORK TO BE A BETTER HUMAN.

TO BE ANTI-RACIST YOU MUST UNDERSTAND THE THERE IS ONLY ONE RACE, HUMAN. EVERYTHING ELSE IS BULLSHIT, TO MAKE SOME FEEL INFERIOR OR SUPERIOR. ITS JUST THAT SIMPLE, NOW STOP BEING A DUMBASS AND WORK TO BE A BETTER HUMAN.

TO BE ANTI-RACIST YOU MUST UNDERSTAND THE THERE IS ONLY ONE RACE, HUMAN. EVERYTHING ELSE IS BULLSHIT, TO MAKE SOME FEEL INFERIOR OR SUPERIOR. ITS JUST THAT SIMPLE, NOW STOP BEING A DUMBASS AND WORK TO BE A BETTER HUMAN.

TO BE ANTI-RACIST YOU MUST UNDERSTAND THE THERE IS ONLY ONE RACE, HUMAN. EVERYTHING ELSE IS BULLSHIT, TO MAKE SOME FEEL INFERIOR OR SUPERIOR. ITS JUST THAT SIMPLE, NOW STOP BEING A DUMBASS AND WORK TO BE A BETTER HUMAN.

TO BE ANTI-RACIST YOU MUST UNDERSTAND THE THERE IS ONLY ONE RACE, HUMAN. EVERYTHING ELSE IS BULLSHIT, TO MAKE SOME FEEL INFERIOR OR SUPERIOR. ITS JUST THAT SIMPLE, NOW STOP BEING A DUMBASS AND WORK TO BE A BETTER HUMAN.

TO BE ANTI-RACIST YOU MUST UNDERSTAND THE THERE IS ONLY ONE RACE, HUMAN. EVERYTHING ELSE IS BULLSHIT, TO MAKE SOME FEEL INFERIOR OR SUPERIOR. ITS JUST THAT SIMPLE, NOW STOP BEING A DUMBASS AND WORK TO BE A BETTER HUMAN.

TO BE ANTI-RACIST YOU MUST UNDERSTAND THE THERE IS ONLY ONE RACE, HUMAN. EVERYTHING ELSE IS BULLSHIT, TO MAKE SOME FEEL INFERIOR OR SUPERIOR. ITS JUST THAT SIMPLE, NOW STOP BEING A DUMBASS AND WORK TO BE A BETTER HUMAN.

TO BE ANTI-RACIST YOU MUST UNDERSTAND THE THERE IS ONLY ONE RACE, HUMAN. EVERYTHING ELSE IS BULLSHIT, TO MAKE SOME FEEL INFERIOR OR SUPERIOR. ITS JUST THAT SIMPLE, NOW STOP BEING A DUMBASS AND WORK TO BE A BETTER HUMAN.

TO BE ANTI-RACIST YOU MUST UNDERSTAND THE THERE IS ONLY ONE RACE, HUMAN. EVERYTHING ELSE IS BULLSHIT, TO MAKE SOME FEEL INFERIOR OR SUPERIOR. ITS JUST THAT SIMPLE, NOW STOP BEING A DUMBASS AND WORK TO BE A BETTER HUMAN.

TO BE ANTI-RACIST YOU MUST UNDERSTAND THE THERE IS ONLY ONE RACE, HUMAN. EVERYTHING ELSE IS BULLSHIT, TO MAKE SOME FEEL INFERIOR OR SUPERIOR. ITS JUST THAT SIMPLE, NOW STOP BEING A DUMBASS AND WORK TO BE A BETTER HUMAN.

JUST THAT SIMPLE, NOW STOP BEING A DUMBASS AND WORK TO BE A BETTER HUMAN.

TO BE ANTI-RACIST YOU MUST UNDERSTAND THE THERE IS ONLY ONE RACE, HUMAN. EVERYTHING ELSE IS BULLSHIT, TO MAKE SOME FEEL INFERIOR OR SUPERIOR. ITS JUST THAT SIMPLE, NOW STOP BEING A DUMBASS AND WORK TO BE A BETTER HUMAN.

TO BE ANTI-RACIST YOU MUST UNDERSTAND THE THERE IS ONLY ONE RACE, HUMAN. EVERYTHING ELSE IS BULLSHIT, TO MAKE SOME FEEL INFERIOR OR SUPERIOR. ITS JUST THAT SIMPLE, NOW STOP BEING A DUMBASS AND WORK TO BE A BETTER HUMAN.

TO BE ANTI-RACIST YOU MUST UNDERSTAND THE THERE IS ONLY ONE RACE, HUMAN. EVERYTHING ELSE IS BULLSHIT, TO MAKE SOME FEEL INFERIOR OR SUPERIOR. ITS JUST THAT SIMPLE, NOW STOP BEING A DUMBASS AND WORK TO BE A BETTER HUMAN.

TO BE ANTI-RACIST YOU MUST UNDERSTAND THE THERE IS ONLY ONE RACE, HUMAN. EVERYTHING ELSE IS BULLSHIT, TO MAKE SOME FEEL INFERIOR OR SUPERIOR. ITS JUST THAT SIMPLE, NOW STOP BEING A DUMBASS AND WORK TO BE A BETTER HUMAN.

TO BE ANTI-RACIST YOU MUST UNDERSTAND THE THERE IS ONLY ONE RACE, HUMAN. EVERYTHING ELSE IS BULLSHIT, TO MAKE SOME FEEL INFERIOR OR SUPERIOR. ITS JUST THAT SIMPLE, NOW STOP BEING A DUMBASS AND WORK TO BE A BETTER HUMAN.

TO BE ANTI-RACIST YOU MUST UNDERSTAND THE THERE IS ONLY ONE RACE, HUMAN. EVERYTHING ELSE IS BULLSHIT, TO MAKE SOME FEEL INFERIOR OR SUPERIOR. ITS JUST THAT SIMPLE, NOW STOP BEING A DUMBASS AND WORK TO BE A BETTER HUMAN.

TO BE ANTI-RACIST YOU MUST UNDERSTAND THE THERE IS ONLY ONE RACE, HUMAN. EVERYTHING ELSE IS BULLSHIT, TO MAKE SOME FEEL INFERIOR OR SUPERIOR. ITS JUST THAT SIMPLE, NOW STOP BEING A DUMBASS AND WORK TO BE A BETTER HUMAN.

TO BE ANTI-RACIST YOU MUST UNDERSTAND THE THERE IS ONLY ONE RACE, HUMAN. EVERYTHING ELSE IS BULLSHIT, TO MAKE SOME FEEL INFERIOR OR SUPERIOR. ITS JUST THAT SIMPLE, NOW STOP BEING A DUMBASS AND WORK TO BE A BETTER HUMAN.

TO BE ANTI-RACIST YOU MUST UNDERSTAND THE THERE IS ONLY ONE RACE, HUMAN. EVERYTHING ELSE IS BULLSHIT, TO MAKE SOME FEEL INFERIOR OR SUPERIOR. ITS JUST THAT SIMPLE, NOW STOP BEING A DUMBASS AND WORK TO BE A BETTER HUMAN.

TO BE ANTI-RACIST YOU MUST UNDERSTAND THE THERE IS ONLY ONE RACE, HUMAN. EVERYTHING ELSE IS BULLSHIT, TO MAKE SOME FEEL INFERIOR OR SUPERIOR. ITS

TO BE ANTI-RACIST YOU MUST UNDERSTAND THE THERE IS ONLY ONE RACE, HUMAN. EVERYTHING ELSE IS BULLSHIT, TO MAKE SOME FEEL INFERIOR OR SUPERIOR. ITS JUST THAT SIMPLE, NOW STOP BEING A DUMBASS AND WORK TO BE A BETTER HUMAN.

TO BE ANTI-RACIST YOU MUST UNDERSTAND THE THERE IS ONLY ONE RACE, HUMAN. EVERYTHING ELSE IS BULLSHIT, TO MAKE SOME FEEL INFERIOR OR SUPERIOR. ITS JUST THAT SIMPLE, NOW STOP BEING A DUMBASS AND WORK TO BE A BETTER HUMAN.

TO BE ANTI-RACIST YOU MUST UNDERSTAND THE THERE IS ONLY ONE RACE, HUMAN. EVERYTHING ELSE IS BULLSHIT, TO MAKE SOME FEEL INFERIOR OR SUPERIOR. ITS JUST THAT SIMPLE, NOW STOP BEING A DUMBASS AND WORK TO BE A BETTER HUMAN.

TO BE ANTI-RACIST YOU MUST UNDERSTAND THE THERE IS ONLY ONE RACE, HUMAN. EVERYTHING ELSE IS BULLSHIT, TO MAKE SOME FEEL INFERIOR OR SUPERIOR. ITS JUST THAT SIMPLE, NOW STOP BEING A DUMBASS AND WORK TO BE A BETTER HUMAN.

TO BE ANTI-RACIST YOU MUST UNDERSTAND THE THERE IS ONLY ONE RACE, HUMAN. EVERYTHING ELSE IS BULLSHIT, TO MAKE SOME FEEL INFERIOR OR SUPERIOR. ITS JUST THAT SIMPLE, NOW STOP BEING A DUMBASS AND WORK TO BE A BETTER HUMAN.

TO BE ANTI-RACIST YOU MUST UNDERSTAND THE THERE IS ONLY ONE RACE, HUMAN. EVERYTHING ELSE IS BULLSHIT, TO MAKE SOME FEEL INFERIOR OR SUPERIOR. ITS JUST THAT SIMPLE, NOW STOP BEING A DUMBASS AND WORK TO BE A BETTER HUMAN.

TO BE ANTI-RACIST YOU MUST UNDERSTAND THE THERE IS ONLY ONE RACE, HUMAN. EVERYTHING ELSE IS BULLSHIT, TO MAKE SOME FEEL INFERIOR OR SUPERIOR. ITS JUST THAT SIMPLE, NOW STOP BEING A DUMBASS AND WORK TO BE A BETTER HUMAN.

TO BE ANTI-RACIST YOU MUST UNDERSTAND THE THERE IS ONLY ONE RACE, HUMAN. EVERYTHING ELSE IS BULLSHIT, TO MAKE SOME FEEL INFERIOR OR SUPERIOR. ITS JUST THAT SIMPLE, NOW STOP BEING A DUMBASS AND WORK TO BE A BETTER HUMAN.

TO BE ANTI-RACIST YOU MUST UNDERSTAND THE THERE IS ONLY ONE RACE, HUMAN. EVERYTHING ELSE IS BULLSHIT, TO MAKE SOME FEEL INFERIOR OR SUPERIOR. ITS JUST THAT SIMPLE, NOW STOP BEING A DUMBASS AND WORK TO BE A BETTER HUMAN.

TO BE ANTI-RACIST YOU MUST UNDERSTAND THE THERE IS ONLY ONE RACE, HUMAN. EVERYTHING ELSE IS BULLSHIT, TO MAKE SOME FEEL INFERIOR OR SUPERIOR. ITS JUST THAT SIMPLE, NOW STOP BEING A DUMBASS AND WORK TO BE A BETTER HUMAN.

JUST THAT SIMPLE, NOW STOP BEING A DUMBASS AND WORK TO BE A BETTER HUMAN.

TO BE ANTI-RACIST YOU MUST UNDERSTAND THE THERE IS ONLY ONE RACE, HUMAN. EVERYTHING ELSE IS BULLSHIT, TO MAKE SOME FEEL INFERIOR OR SUPERIOR. ITS JUST THAT SIMPLE, NOW STOP BEING A DUMBASS AND WORK TO BE A BETTER HUMAN.

TO BE ANTI-RACIST YOU MUST UNDERSTAND THE THERE IS ONLY ONE RACE, HUMAN. EVERYTHING ELSE IS BULLSHIT, TO MAKE SOME FEEL INFERIOR OR SUPERIOR. ITS JUST THAT SIMPLE, NOW STOP BEING A DUMBASS AND WORK TO BE A BETTER HUMAN.

TO BE ANTI-RACIST YOU MUST UNDERSTAND THE THERE IS ONLY ONE RACE, HUMAN. EVERYTHING ELSE IS BULLSHIT, TO MAKE SOME FEEL INFERIOR OR SUPERIOR. ITS JUST THAT SIMPLE, NOW STOP BEING A DUMBASS AND WORK TO BE A BETTER HUMAN.

TO BE ANTI-RACIST YOU MUST UNDERSTAND THE THERE IS ONLY ONE RACE, HUMAN. EVERYTHING ELSE IS BULLSHIT, TO MAKE SOME FEEL INFERIOR OR SUPERIOR. ITS JUST THAT SIMPLE, NOW STOP BEING A DUMBASS AND WORK TO BE A BETTER HUMAN.

TO BE ANTI-RACIST YOU MUST UNDERSTAND THE THERE IS ONLY ONE RACE, HUMAN. EVERYTHING ELSE IS BULLSHIT, TO MAKE SOME FEEL INFERIOR OR SUPERIOR. ITS JUST THAT SIMPLE, NOW STOP BEING A DUMBASS AND WORK TO BE A BETTER HUMAN.

TO BE ANTI-RACIST YOU MUST UNDERSTAND THE THERE IS ONLY ONE RACE, HUMAN. EVERYTHING ELSE IS BULLSHIT, TO MAKE SOME FEEL INFERIOR OR SUPERIOR. ITS JUST THAT SIMPLE, NOW STOP BEING A DUMBASS AND WORK TO BE A BETTER HUMAN.

TO BE ANTI-RACIST YOU MUST UNDERSTAND THE THERE IS ONLY ONE RACE, HUMAN. EVERYTHING ELSE IS BULLSHIT, TO MAKE SOME FEEL INFERIOR OR SUPERIOR. ITS JUST THAT SIMPLE, NOW STOP BEING A DUMBASS AND WORK TO BE A BETTER HUMAN.

TO BE ANTI-RACIST YOU MUST UNDERSTAND THE THERE IS ONLY ONE RACE, HUMAN. EVERYTHING ELSE IS BULLSHIT, TO MAKE SOME FEEL INFERIOR OR SUPERIOR. ITS JUST THAT SIMPLE, NOW STOP BEING A DUMBASS AND WORK TO BE A BETTER HUMAN.

TO BE ANTI-RACIST YOU MUST UNDERSTAND THE THERE IS ONLY ONE RACE, HUMAN. EVERYTHING ELSE IS BULLSHIT, TO MAKE SOME FEEL INFERIOR OR SUPERIOR. ITS JUST THAT SIMPLE, NOW STOP BEING A DUMBASS AND WORK TO BE A BETTER HUMAN.

TO BE ANTI-RACIST YOU MUST UNDERSTAND THE THERE IS ONLY ONE RACE, HUMAN. EVERYTHING ELSE IS BULLSHIT, TO MAKE SOME FEEL INFERIOR OR SUPERIOR. ITS

TO BE ANTI-RACIST YOU MUST UNDERSTAND THE THERE IS ONLY ONE RACE, HUMAN. EVERYTHING ELSE IS BULLSHIT, TO MAKE SOME FEEL INFERIOR OR SUPERIOR. ITS JUST THAT SIMPLE, NOW STOP BEING A DUMBASS AND WORK TO BE A BETTER HUMAN.

TO BE ANTI-RACIST YOU MUST UNDERSTAND THE THERE IS ONLY ONE RACE, HUMAN. EVERYTHING ELSE IS BULLSHIT, TO MAKE SOME FEEL INFERIOR OR SUPERIOR. ITS JUST THAT SIMPLE, NOW STOP BEING A DUMBASS AND WORK TO BE A BETTER HUMAN.

TO BE ANTI-RACIST YOU MUST UNDERSTAND THE THERE IS ONLY ONE RACE, HUMAN. EVERYTHING ELSE IS BULLSHIT, TO MAKE SOME FEEL INFERIOR OR SUPERIOR. ITS JUST THAT SIMPLE, NOW STOP BEING A DUMBASS AND WORK TO BE A BETTER HUMAN.

TO BE ANTI-RACIST YOU MUST UNDERSTAND THE THERE IS ONLY ONE RACE, HUMAN. EVERYTHING ELSE IS BULLSHIT, TO MAKE SOME FEEL INFERIOR OR SUPERIOR. ITS JUST THAT SIMPLE, NOW STOP BEING A DUMBASS AND WORK TO BE A BETTER HUMAN.

TO BE ANTI-RACIST YOU MUST UNDERSTAND THE THERE IS ONLY ONE RACE, HUMAN. EVERYTHING ELSE IS BULLSHIT, TO MAKE SOME FEEL INFERIOR OR SUPERIOR. ITS JUST THAT SIMPLE, NOW STOP BEING A DUMBASS AND WORK TO BE A BETTER HUMAN.

TO BE ANTI-RACIST YOU MUST UNDERSTAND THE THERE IS ONLY ONE RACE, HUMAN. EVERYTHING ELSE IS BULLSHIT, TO MAKE SOME FEEL INFERIOR OR SUPERIOR. ITS JUST THAT SIMPLE, NOW STOP BEING A DUMBASS AND WORK TO BE A BETTER HUMAN.

TO BE ANTI-RACIST YOU MUST UNDERSTAND THE THERE IS ONLY ONE RACE, HUMAN. EVERYTHING ELSE IS BULLSHIT, TO MAKE SOME FEEL INFERIOR OR SUPERIOR. ITS JUST THAT SIMPLE, NOW STOP BEING A DUMBASS AND WORK TO BE A BETTER HUMAN.

TO BE ANTI-RACIST YOU MUST UNDERSTAND THE THERE IS ONLY ONE RACE, HUMAN. EVERYTHING ELSE IS BULLSHIT, TO MAKE SOME FEEL INFERIOR OR SUPERIOR. ITS JUST THAT SIMPLE, NOW STOP BEING A DUMBASS AND WORK TO BE A BETTER HUMAN.

TO BE ANTI-RACIST YOU MUST UNDERSTAND THE THERE IS ONLY ONE RACE, HUMAN. EVERYTHING ELSE IS BULLSHIT, TO MAKE SOME FEEL INFERIOR OR SUPERIOR. ITS JUST THAT SIMPLE, NOW STOP BEING A DUMBASS AND WORK TO BE A BETTER HUMAN.

TO BE ANTI-RACIST YOU MUST UNDERSTAND THE THERE IS ONLY ONE RACE, HUMAN. EVERYTHING ELSE IS BULLSHIT, TO MAKE SOME FEEL INFERIOR OR SUPERIOR. ITS JUST THAT SIMPLE, NOW STOP BEING A DUMBASS AND WORK TO BE A BETTER HUMAN.

TO BE ANTI-RACIST YOU MUST UNDERSTAND THE THERE IS ONLY ONE RACE, HUMAN. EVERYTHING ELSE IS BULLSHIT, TO MAKE SOME FEEL INFERIOR OR SUPERIOR. ITS JUST THAT SIMPLE, NOW STOP BEING A DUMBASS AND WORK TO BE A BETTER HUMAN.

JUST THAT SIMPLE, NOW STOP BEING A DUMBASS AND WORK TO BE A BETTER
HUMAN.

TO BE ANTI-RACIST YOU MUST UNDERSTAND THE THERE IS ONLY ONE RACE, HUMAN.
EVERYTHING ELSE IS BULLSHIT, TO MAKE SOME FEEL INFERIOR OR SUPERIOR. ITS
JUST THAT SIMPLE, NOW STOP BEING A DUMBASS AND WORK TO BE A BETTER
HUMAN.

TO BE ANTI-RACIST YOU MUST UNDERSTAND THE THERE IS ONLY ONE RACE, HUMAN.
EVERYTHING ELSE IS BULLSHIT, TO MAKE SOME FEEL INFERIOR OR SUPERIOR. ITS
JUST THAT SIMPLE, NOW STOP BEING A DUMBASS AND WORK TO BE A BETTER
HUMAN.

TO BE ANTI-RACIST YOU MUST UNDERSTAND THE THERE IS ONLY ONE RACE, HUMAN.
EVERYTHING ELSE IS BULLSHIT, TO MAKE SOME FEEL INFERIOR OR SUPERIOR. ITS
JUST THAT SIMPLE, NOW STOP BEING A DUMBASS AND WORK TO BE A BETTER
HUMAN.

TO BE ANTI-RACIST YOU MUST UNDERSTAND THE THERE IS ONLY ONE RACE, HUMAN.
EVERYTHING ELSE IS BULLSHIT, TO MAKE SOME FEEL INFERIOR OR SUPERIOR. ITS
JUST THAT SIMPLE, NOW STOP BEING A DUMBASS AND WORK TO BE A BETTER
HUMAN.

TO BE ANTI-RACIST YOU MUST UNDERSTAND THE THERE IS ONLY ONE RACE, HUMAN.
EVERYTHING ELSE IS BULLSHIT, TO MAKE SOME FEEL INFERIOR OR SUPERIOR. ITS
JUST THAT SIMPLE, NOW STOP BEING A DUMBASS AND WORK TO BE A BETTER
HUMAN.

TO BE ANTI-RACIST YOU MUST UNDERSTAND THE THERE IS ONLY ONE RACE, HUMAN.
EVERYTHING ELSE IS BULLSHIT, TO MAKE SOME FEEL INFERIOR OR SUPERIOR. ITS
JUST THAT SIMPLE, NOW STOP BEING A DUMBASS AND WORK TO BE A BETTER
HUMAN.

TO BE ANTI-RACIST YOU MUST UNDERSTAND THE THERE IS ONLY ONE RACE, HUMAN.
EVERYTHING ELSE IS BULLSHIT, TO MAKE SOME FEEL INFERIOR OR SUPERIOR. ITS
JUST THAT SIMPLE, NOW STOP BEING A DUMBASS AND WORK TO BE A BETTER
HUMAN.

TO BE ANTI-RACIST YOU MUST UNDERSTAND THE THERE IS ONLY ONE RACE, HUMAN.
EVERYTHING ELSE IS BULLSHIT, TO MAKE SOME FEEL INFERIOR OR SUPERIOR. ITS
JUST THAT SIMPLE, NOW STOP BEING A DUMBASS AND WORK TO BE A BETTER
HUMAN.

TO BE ANTI-RACIST YOU MUST UNDERSTAND THE THERE IS ONLY ONE RACE, HUMAN.
EVERYTHING ELSE IS BULLSHIT, TO MAKE SOME FEEL INFERIOR OR SUPERIOR. ITS
JUST THAT SIMPLE, NOW STOP BEING A DUMBASS AND WORK TO BE A BETTER
HUMAN.

TO BE ANTI-RACIST YOU MUST UNDERSTAND THE THERE IS ONLY ONE RACE, HUMAN.
EVERYTHING ELSE IS BULLSHIT, TO MAKE SOME FEEL INFERIOR OR SUPERIOR. ITS

TO BE ANTI-RACIST YOU MUST UNDERSTAND THE THERE IS ONLY ONE RACE, HUMAN. EVERYTHING ELSE IS BULLSHIT, TO MAKE SOME FEEL INFERIOR OR SUPERIOR. ITS JUST THAT SIMPLE, NOW STOP BEING A DUMBASS AND WORK TO BE A BETTER HUMAN.

TO BE ANTI-RACIST YOU MUST UNDERSTAND THE THERE IS ONLY ONE RACE, HUMAN. EVERYTHING ELSE IS BULLSHIT, TO MAKE SOME FEEL INFERIOR OR SUPERIOR. ITS JUST THAT SIMPLE, NOW STOP BEING A DUMBASS AND WORK TO BE A BETTER HUMAN.

TO BE ANTI-RACIST YOU MUST UNDERSTAND THE THERE IS ONLY ONE RACE, HUMAN. EVERYTHING ELSE IS BULLSHIT, TO MAKE SOME FEEL INFERIOR OR SUPERIOR. ITS JUST THAT SIMPLE, NOW STOP BEING A DUMBASS AND WORK TO BE A BETTER HUMAN.

TO BE ANTI-RACIST YOU MUST UNDERSTAND THE THERE IS ONLY ONE RACE, HUMAN. EVERYTHING ELSE IS BULLSHIT, TO MAKE SOME FEEL INFERIOR OR SUPERIOR. ITS JUST THAT SIMPLE, NOW STOP BEING A DUMBASS AND WORK TO BE A BETTER HUMAN.

TO BE ANTI-RACIST YOU MUST UNDERSTAND THE THERE IS ONLY ONE RACE, HUMAN. EVERYTHING ELSE IS BULLSHIT, TO MAKE SOME FEEL INFERIOR OR SUPERIOR. ITS JUST THAT SIMPLE, NOW STOP BEING A DUMBASS AND WORK TO BE A BETTER HUMAN.

TO BE ANTI-RACIST YOU MUST UNDERSTAND THE THERE IS ONLY ONE RACE, HUMAN. EVERYTHING ELSE IS BULLSHIT, TO MAKE SOME FEEL INFERIOR OR SUPERIOR. ITS JUST THAT SIMPLE, NOW STOP BEING A DUMBASS AND WORK TO BE A BETTER HUMAN.

TO BE ANTI-RACIST YOU MUST UNDERSTAND THE THERE IS ONLY ONE RACE, HUMAN. EVERYTHING ELSE IS BULLSHIT, TO MAKE SOME FEEL INFERIOR OR SUPERIOR. ITS JUST THAT SIMPLE, NOW STOP BEING A DUMBASS AND WORK TO BE A BETTER HUMAN.

TO BE ANTI-RACIST YOU MUST UNDERSTAND THE THERE IS ONLY ONE RACE, HUMAN. EVERYTHING ELSE IS BULLSHIT, TO MAKE SOME FEEL INFERIOR OR SUPERIOR. ITS JUST THAT SIMPLE, NOW STOP BEING A DUMBASS AND WORK TO BE A BETTER HUMAN.

TO BE ANTI-RACIST YOU MUST UNDERSTAND THE THERE IS ONLY ONE RACE, HUMAN. EVERYTHING ELSE IS BULLSHIT, TO MAKE SOME FEEL INFERIOR OR SUPERIOR. ITS JUST THAT SIMPLE, NOW STOP BEING A DUMBASS AND WORK TO BE A BETTER HUMAN.

TO BE ANTI-RACIST YOU MUST UNDERSTAND THE THERE IS ONLY ONE RACE, HUMAN. EVERYTHING ELSE IS BULLSHIT, TO MAKE SOME FEEL INFERIOR OR SUPERIOR. ITS JUST THAT SIMPLE, NOW STOP BEING A DUMBASS AND WORK TO BE A BETTER HUMAN.

TO BE ANTI-RACIST YOU MUST UNDERSTAND THE THERE IS ONLY ONE RACE, HUMAN. EVERYTHING ELSE IS BULLSHIT, TO MAKE SOME FEEL INFERIOR OR SUPERIOR. ITS JUST THAT SIMPLE, NOW STOP BEING A DUMBASS AND WORK TO BE A BETTER HUMAN.

JUST THAT SIMPLE, NOW STOP BEING A DUMBASS AND WORK TO BE A BETTER
HUMAN.
TO BE ANTI-RACIST YOU MUST UNDERSTAND THE THERE IS ONLY ONE RACE, HUMAN.
EVERYTHING ELSE IS BULLSHIT, TO MAKE SOME FEEL INFERIOR OR SUPERIOR. ITS
JUST THAT SIMPLE, NOW STOP BEING A DUMBASS AND WORK TO BE A BETTER
HUMAN.
TO BE ANTI-RACIST YOU MUST UNDERSTAND THE THERE IS ONLY ONE RACE, HUMAN.
EVERYTHING ELSE IS BULLSHIT, TO MAKE SOME FEEL INFERIOR OR SUPERIOR. ITS
JUST THAT SIMPLE, NOW STOP BEING A DUMBASS AND WORK TO BE A BETTER
HUMAN.
TO BE ANTI-RACIST YOU MUST UNDERSTAND THE THERE IS ONLY ONE RACE, HUMAN.
EVERYTHING ELSE IS BULLSHIT, TO MAKE SOME FEEL INFERIOR OR SUPERIOR. ITS
JUST THAT SIMPLE, NOW STOP BEING A DUMBASS AND WORK TO BE A BETTER
HUMAN.
TO BE ANTI-RACIST YOU MUST UNDERSTAND THE THERE IS ONLY ONE RACE, HUMAN.
EVERYTHING ELSE IS BULLSHIT, TO MAKE SOME FEEL INFERIOR OR SUPERIOR. ITS
JUST THAT SIMPLE, NOW STOP BEING A DUMBASS AND WORK TO BE A BETTER
HUMAN.
TO BE ANTI-RACIST YOU MUST UNDERSTAND THE THERE IS ONLY ONE RACE, HUMAN.
EVERYTHING ELSE IS BULLSHIT, TO MAKE SOME FEEL INFERIOR OR SUPERIOR. ITS
JUST THAT SIMPLE, NOW STOP BEING A DUMBASS AND WORK TO BE A BETTER
HUMAN.
TO BE ANTI-RACIST YOU MUST UNDERSTAND THE THERE IS ONLY ONE RACE, HUMAN.
EVERYTHING ELSE IS BULLSHIT, TO MAKE SOME FEEL INFERIOR OR SUPERIOR. ITS
JUST THAT SIMPLE, NOW STOP BEING A DUMBASS AND WORK TO BE A BETTER
HUMAN.
TO BE ANTI-RACIST YOU MUST UNDERSTAND THE THERE IS ONLY ONE RACE, HUMAN.
EVERYTHING ELSE IS BULLSHIT, TO MAKE SOME FEEL INFERIOR OR SUPERIOR. ITS
JUST THAT SIMPLE, NOW STOP BEING A DUMBASS AND WORK TO BE A BETTER
HUMAN.
TO BE ANTI-RACIST YOU MUST UNDERSTAND THE THERE IS ONLY ONE RACE, HUMAN.
EVERYTHING ELSE IS BULLSHIT, TO MAKE SOME FEEL INFERIOR OR SUPERIOR. ITS
JUST THAT SIMPLE, NOW STOP BEING A DUMBASS AND WORK TO BE A BETTER
HUMAN.
TO BE ANTI-RACIST YOU MUST UNDERSTAND THE THERE IS ONLY ONE RACE, HUMAN.
EVERYTHING ELSE IS BULLSHIT, TO MAKE SOME FEEL INFERIOR OR SUPERIOR. ITS
JUST THAT SIMPLE, NOW STOP BEING A DUMBASS AND WORK TO BE A BETTER
HUMAN.
TO BE ANTI-RACIST YOU MUST UNDERSTAND THE THERE IS ONLY ONE RACE, HUMAN.
EVERYTHING ELSE IS BULLSHIT, TO MAKE SOME FEEL INFERIOR OR SUPERIOR. ITS

TO BE ANTI-RACIST YOU MUST UNDERSTAND THE THERE IS ONLY ONE RACE, HUMAN. EVERYTHING ELSE IS BULLSHIT, TO MAKE SOME FEEL INFERIOR OR SUPERIOR. ITS JUST THAT SIMPLE, NOW STOP BEING A DUMBASS AND WORK TO BE A BETTER HUMAN.

TO BE ANTI-RACIST YOU MUST UNDERSTAND THE THERE IS ONLY ONE RACE, HUMAN. EVERYTHING ELSE IS BULLSHIT, TO MAKE SOME FEEL INFERIOR OR SUPERIOR. ITS JUST THAT SIMPLE, NOW STOP BEING A DUMBASS AND WORK TO BE A BETTER HUMAN.

TO BE ANTI-RACIST YOU MUST UNDERSTAND THE THERE IS ONLY ONE RACE, HUMAN. EVERYTHING ELSE IS BULLSHIT, TO MAKE SOME FEEL INFERIOR OR SUPERIOR. ITS JUST THAT SIMPLE, NOW STOP BEING A DUMBASS AND WORK TO BE A BETTER HUMAN.

TO BE ANTI-RACIST YOU MUST UNDERSTAND THE THERE IS ONLY ONE RACE, HUMAN. EVERYTHING ELSE IS BULLSHIT, TO MAKE SOME FEEL INFERIOR OR SUPERIOR. ITS JUST THAT SIMPLE, NOW STOP BEING A DUMBASS AND WORK TO BE A BETTER HUMAN.

TO BE ANTI-RACIST YOU MUST UNDERSTAND THE THERE IS ONLY ONE RACE, HUMAN. EVERYTHING ELSE IS BULLSHIT, TO MAKE SOME FEEL INFERIOR OR SUPERIOR. ITS JUST THAT SIMPLE, NOW STOP BEING A DUMBASS AND WORK TO BE A BETTER HUMAN.

TO BE ANTI-RACIST YOU MUST UNDERSTAND THE THERE IS ONLY ONE RACE, HUMAN. EVERYTHING ELSE IS BULLSHIT, TO MAKE SOME FEEL INFERIOR OR SUPERIOR. ITS JUST THAT SIMPLE, NOW STOP BEING A DUMBASS AND WORK TO BE A BETTER HUMAN.

TO BE ANTI-RACIST YOU MUST UNDERSTAND THE THERE IS ONLY ONE RACE, HUMAN. EVERYTHING ELSE IS BULLSHIT, TO MAKE SOME FEEL INFERIOR OR SUPERIOR. ITS JUST THAT SIMPLE, NOW STOP BEING A DUMBASS AND WORK TO BE A BETTER HUMAN.

TO BE ANTI-RACIST YOU MUST UNDERSTAND THE THERE IS ONLY ONE RACE, HUMAN. EVERYTHING ELSE IS BULLSHIT, TO MAKE SOME FEEL INFERIOR OR SUPERIOR. ITS JUST THAT SIMPLE, NOW STOP BEING A DUMBASS AND WORK TO BE A BETTER HUMAN.

TO BE ANTI-RACIST YOU MUST UNDERSTAND THE THERE IS ONLY ONE RACE, HUMAN. EVERYTHING ELSE IS BULLSHIT, TO MAKE SOME FEEL INFERIOR OR SUPERIOR. ITS JUST THAT SIMPLE, NOW STOP BEING A DUMBASS AND WORK TO BE A BETTER HUMAN.

TO BE ANTI-RACIST YOU MUST UNDERSTAND THE THERE IS ONLY ONE RACE, HUMAN. EVERYTHING ELSE IS BULLSHIT, TO MAKE SOME FEEL INFERIOR OR SUPERIOR. ITS JUST THAT SIMPLE, NOW STOP BEING A DUMBASS AND WORK TO BE A BETTER HUMAN.

TO BE ANTI-RACIST YOU MUST UNDERSTAND THE THERE IS ONLY ONE RACE, HUMAN. EVERYTHING ELSE IS BULLSHIT, TO MAKE SOME FEEL INFERIOR OR SUPERIOR. ITS JUST THAT SIMPLE, NOW STOP BEING A DUMBASS AND WORK TO BE A BETTER HUMAN.

JUST THAT SIMPLE, NOW STOP BEING A DUMBASS AND WORK TO BE A BETTER HUMAN.

TO BE ANTI-RACIST YOU MUST UNDERSTAND THE THERE IS ONLY ONE RACE, HUMAN. EVERYTHING ELSE IS BULLSHIT, TO MAKE SOME FEEL INFERIOR OR SUPERIOR. ITS JUST THAT SIMPLE, NOW STOP BEING A DUMBASS AND WORK TO BE A BETTER HUMAN.

TO BE ANTI-RACIST YOU MUST UNDERSTAND THE THERE IS ONLY ONE RACE, HUMAN. EVERYTHING ELSE IS BULLSHIT, TO MAKE SOME FEEL INFERIOR OR SUPERIOR. ITS JUST THAT SIMPLE, NOW STOP BEING A DUMBASS AND WORK TO BE A BETTER HUMAN.

TO BE ANTI-RACIST YOU MUST UNDERSTAND THE THERE IS ONLY ONE RACE, HUMAN. EVERYTHING ELSE IS BULLSHIT, TO MAKE SOME FEEL INFERIOR OR SUPERIOR. ITS JUST THAT SIMPLE, NOW STOP BEING A DUMBASS AND WORK TO BE A BETTER HUMAN.

TO BE ANTI-RACIST YOU MUST UNDERSTAND THE THERE IS ONLY ONE RACE, HUMAN. EVERYTHING ELSE IS BULLSHIT, TO MAKE SOME FEEL INFERIOR OR SUPERIOR. ITS JUST THAT SIMPLE, NOW STOP BEING A DUMBASS AND WORK TO BE A BETTER HUMAN.

TO BE ANTI-RACIST YOU MUST UNDERSTAND THE THERE IS ONLY ONE RACE, HUMAN. EVERYTHING ELSE IS BULLSHIT, TO MAKE SOME FEEL INFERIOR OR SUPERIOR. ITS JUST THAT SIMPLE, NOW STOP BEING A DUMBASS AND WORK TO BE A BETTER HUMAN.

TO BE ANTI-RACIST YOU MUST UNDERSTAND THE THERE IS ONLY ONE RACE, HUMAN. EVERYTHING ELSE IS BULLSHIT, TO MAKE SOME FEEL INFERIOR OR SUPERIOR. ITS JUST THAT SIMPLE, NOW STOP BEING A DUMBASS AND WORK TO BE A BETTER HUMAN.

TO BE ANTI-RACIST YOU MUST UNDERSTAND THE THERE IS ONLY ONE RACE, HUMAN. EVERYTHING ELSE IS BULLSHIT, TO MAKE SOME FEEL INFERIOR OR SUPERIOR. ITS JUST THAT SIMPLE, NOW STOP BEING A DUMBASS AND WORK TO BE A BETTER HUMAN.

TO BE ANTI-RACIST YOU MUST UNDERSTAND THE THERE IS ONLY ONE RACE, HUMAN. EVERYTHING ELSE IS BULLSHIT, TO MAKE SOME FEEL INFERIOR OR SUPERIOR. ITS JUST THAT SIMPLE, NOW STOP BEING A DUMBASS AND WORK TO BE A BETTER HUMAN.

TO BE ANTI-RACIST YOU MUST UNDERSTAND THE THERE IS ONLY ONE RACE, HUMAN. EVERYTHING ELSE IS BULLSHIT, TO MAKE SOME FEEL INFERIOR OR SUPERIOR. ITS JUST THAT SIMPLE, NOW STOP BEING A DUMBASS AND WORK TO BE A BETTER HUMAN.

TO BE ANTI-RACIST YOU MUST UNDERSTAND THE THERE IS ONLY ONE RACE, HUMAN. EVERYTHING ELSE IS BULLSHIT, TO MAKE SOME FEEL INFERIOR OR SUPERIOR. ITS

TO BE ANTI-RACIST YOU MUST UNDERSTAND THE THERE IS ONLY ONE RACE, HUMAN. EVERYTHING ELSE IS BULLSHIT, TO MAKE SOME FEEL INFERIOR OR SUPERIOR. ITS JUST THAT SIMPLE, NOW STOP BEING A DUMBASS AND WORK TO BE A BETTER HUMAN.

TO BE ANTI-RACIST YOU MUST UNDERSTAND THE THERE IS ONLY ONE RACE, HUMAN. EVERYTHING ELSE IS BULLSHIT, TO MAKE SOME FEEL INFERIOR OR SUPERIOR. ITS JUST THAT SIMPLE, NOW STOP BEING A DUMBASS AND WORK TO BE A BETTER HUMAN.

TO BE ANTI-RACIST YOU MUST UNDERSTAND THE THERE IS ONLY ONE RACE, HUMAN. EVERYTHING ELSE IS BULLSHIT, TO MAKE SOME FEEL INFERIOR OR SUPERIOR. ITS JUST THAT SIMPLE, NOW STOP BEING A DUMBASS AND WORK TO BE A BETTER HUMAN.

TO BE ANTI-RACIST YOU MUST UNDERSTAND THE THERE IS ONLY ONE RACE, HUMAN. EVERYTHING ELSE IS BULLSHIT, TO MAKE SOME FEEL INFERIOR OR SUPERIOR. ITS JUST THAT SIMPLE, NOW STOP BEING A DUMBASS AND WORK TO BE A BETTER HUMAN.

TO BE ANTI-RACIST YOU MUST UNDERSTAND THE THERE IS ONLY ONE RACE, HUMAN. EVERYTHING ELSE IS BULLSHIT, TO MAKE SOME FEEL INFERIOR OR SUPERIOR. ITS JUST THAT SIMPLE, NOW STOP BEING A DUMBASS AND WORK TO BE A BETTER HUMAN.

TO BE ANTI-RACIST YOU MUST UNDERSTAND THE THERE IS ONLY ONE RACE, HUMAN. EVERYTHING ELSE IS BULLSHIT, TO MAKE SOME FEEL INFERIOR OR SUPERIOR. ITS JUST THAT SIMPLE, NOW STOP BEING A DUMBASS AND WORK TO BE A BETTER HUMAN.

TO BE ANTI-RACIST YOU MUST UNDERSTAND THE THERE IS ONLY ONE RACE, HUMAN. EVERYTHING ELSE IS BULLSHIT, TO MAKE SOME FEEL INFERIOR OR SUPERIOR. ITS JUST THAT SIMPLE, NOW STOP BEING A DUMBASS AND WORK TO BE A BETTER HUMAN.

TO BE ANTI-RACIST YOU MUST UNDERSTAND THE THERE IS ONLY ONE RACE, HUMAN. EVERYTHING ELSE IS BULLSHIT, TO MAKE SOME FEEL INFERIOR OR SUPERIOR. ITS JUST THAT SIMPLE, NOW STOP BEING A DUMBASS AND WORK TO BE A BETTER HUMAN.

TO BE ANTI-RACIST YOU MUST UNDERSTAND THE THERE IS ONLY ONE RACE, HUMAN. EVERYTHING ELSE IS BULLSHIT, TO MAKE SOME FEEL INFERIOR OR SUPERIOR. ITS JUST THAT SIMPLE, NOW STOP BEING A DUMBASS AND WORK TO BE A BETTER HUMAN.

TO BE ANTI-RACIST YOU MUST UNDERSTAND THE THERE IS ONLY ONE RACE, HUMAN. EVERYTHING ELSE IS BULLSHIT, TO MAKE SOME FEEL INFERIOR OR SUPERIOR. ITS JUST THAT SIMPLE, NOW STOP BEING A DUMBASS AND WORK TO BE A BETTER HUMAN.

TO BE ANTI-RACIST YOU MUST UNDERSTAND THE THERE IS ONLY ONE RACE, HUMAN. EVERYTHING ELSE IS BULLSHIT, TO MAKE SOME FEEL INFERIOR OR SUPERIOR. ITS JUST THAT SIMPLE, NOW STOP BEING A DUMBASS AND WORK TO BE A BETTER HUMAN.

JUST THAT SIMPLE, NOW STOP BEING A DUMBASS AND WORK TO BE A BETTER HUMAN.

TO BE ANTI-RACIST YOU MUST UNDERSTAND THE THERE IS ONLY ONE RACE, HUMAN. EVERYTHING ELSE IS BULLSHIT, TO MAKE SOME FEEL INFERIOR OR SUPERIOR. ITS JUST THAT SIMPLE, NOW STOP BEING A DUMBASS AND WORK TO BE A BETTER HUMAN.

TO BE ANTI-RACIST YOU MUST UNDERSTAND THE THERE IS ONLY ONE RACE, HUMAN. EVERYTHING ELSE IS BULLSHIT, TO MAKE SOME FEEL INFERIOR OR SUPERIOR. ITS JUST THAT SIMPLE, NOW STOP BEING A DUMBASS AND WORK TO BE A BETTER HUMAN.

TO BE ANTI-RACIST YOU MUST UNDERSTAND THE THERE IS ONLY ONE RACE, HUMAN. EVERYTHING ELSE IS BULLSHIT, TO MAKE SOME FEEL INFERIOR OR SUPERIOR. ITS JUST THAT SIMPLE, NOW STOP BEING A DUMBASS AND WORK TO BE A BETTER HUMAN.

TO BE ANTI-RACIST YOU MUST UNDERSTAND THE THERE IS ONLY ONE RACE, HUMAN. EVERYTHING ELSE IS BULLSHIT, TO MAKE SOME FEEL INFERIOR OR SUPERIOR. ITS JUST THAT SIMPLE, NOW STOP BEING A DUMBASS AND WORK TO BE A BETTER HUMAN.

TO BE ANTI-RACIST YOU MUST UNDERSTAND THE THERE IS ONLY ONE RACE, HUMAN. EVERYTHING ELSE IS BULLSHIT, TO MAKE SOME FEEL INFERIOR OR SUPERIOR. ITS JUST THAT SIMPLE, NOW STOP BEING A DUMBASS AND WORK TO BE A BETTER HUMAN.

TO BE ANTI-RACIST YOU MUST UNDERSTAND THE THERE IS ONLY ONE RACE, HUMAN. EVERYTHING ELSE IS BULLSHIT, TO MAKE SOME FEEL INFERIOR OR SUPERIOR. ITS JUST THAT SIMPLE, NOW STOP BEING A DUMBASS AND WORK TO BE A BETTER HUMAN.

TO BE ANTI-RACIST YOU MUST UNDERSTAND THE THERE IS ONLY ONE RACE, HUMAN. EVERYTHING ELSE IS BULLSHIT, TO MAKE SOME FEEL INFERIOR OR SUPERIOR. ITS JUST THAT SIMPLE, NOW STOP BEING A DUMBASS AND WORK TO BE A BETTER HUMAN.

TO BE ANTI-RACIST YOU MUST UNDERSTAND THE THERE IS ONLY ONE RACE, HUMAN. EVERYTHING ELSE IS BULLSHIT, TO MAKE SOME FEEL INFERIOR OR SUPERIOR. ITS JUST THAT SIMPLE, NOW STOP BEING A DUMBASS AND WORK TO BE A BETTER HUMAN.

TO BE ANTI-RACIST YOU MUST UNDERSTAND THE THERE IS ONLY ONE RACE, HUMAN. EVERYTHING ELSE IS BULLSHIT, TO MAKE SOME FEEL INFERIOR OR SUPERIOR. ITS JUST THAT SIMPLE, NOW STOP BEING A DUMBASS AND WORK TO BE A BETTER HUMAN.

TO BE ANTI-RACIST YOU MUST UNDERSTAND THE THERE IS ONLY ONE RACE, HUMAN. EVERYTHING ELSE IS BULLSHIT, TO MAKE SOME FEEL INFERIOR OR SUPERIOR, ITS

TO BE ANTI-RACIST YOU MUST UNDERSTAND THE THERE IS ONLY ONE RACE, HUMAN. EVERYTHING ELSE IS BULLSHIT, TO MAKE SOME FEEL INFERIOR OR SUPERIOR. ITS JUST THAT SIMPLE, NOW STOP BEING A DUMBASS AND WORK TO BE A BETTER HUMAN.

TO BE ANTI-RACIST YOU MUST UNDERSTAND THE THERE IS ONLY ONE RACE, HUMAN. EVERYTHING ELSE IS BULLSHIT, TO MAKE SOME FEEL INFERIOR OR SUPERIOR. ITS JUST THAT SIMPLE, NOW STOP BEING A DUMBASS AND WORK TO BE A BETTER HUMAN.

TO BE ANTI-RACIST YOU MUST UNDERSTAND THE THERE IS ONLY ONE RACE, HUMAN. EVERYTHING ELSE IS BULLSHIT, TO MAKE SOME FEEL INFERIOR OR SUPERIOR. ITS JUST THAT SIMPLE, NOW STOP BEING A DUMBASS AND WORK TO BE A BETTER HUMAN.

TO BE ANTI-RACIST YOU MUST UNDERSTAND THE THERE IS ONLY ONE RACE, HUMAN. EVERYTHING ELSE IS BULLSHIT, TO MAKE SOME FEEL INFERIOR OR SUPERIOR. ITS JUST THAT SIMPLE, NOW STOP BEING A DUMBASS AND WORK TO BE A BETTER HUMAN.

TO BE ANTI-RACIST YOU MUST UNDERSTAND THE THERE IS ONLY ONE RACE, HUMAN. EVERYTHING ELSE IS BULLSHIT, TO MAKE SOME FEEL INFERIOR OR SUPERIOR. ITS JUST THAT SIMPLE, NOW STOP BEING A DUMBASS AND WORK TO BE A BETTER HUMAN.

TO BE ANTI-RACIST YOU MUST UNDERSTAND THE THERE IS ONLY ONE RACE, HUMAN. EVERYTHING ELSE IS BULLSHIT, TO MAKE SOME FEEL INFERIOR OR SUPERIOR. ITS JUST THAT SIMPLE, NOW STOP BEING A DUMBASS AND WORK TO BE A BETTER HUMAN.

TO BE ANTI-RACIST YOU MUST UNDERSTAND THE THERE IS ONLY ONE RACE, HUMAN. EVERYTHING ELSE IS BULLSHIT, TO MAKE SOME FEEL INFERIOR OR SUPERIOR. ITS JUST THAT SIMPLE, NOW STOP BEING A DUMBASS AND WORK TO BE A BETTER HUMAN.

TO BE ANTI-RACIST YOU MUST UNDERSTAND THE THERE IS ONLY ONE RACE, HUMAN. EVERYTHING ELSE IS BULLSHIT, TO MAKE SOME FEEL INFERIOR OR SUPERIOR. ITS JUST THAT SIMPLE, NOW STOP BEING A DUMBASS AND WORK TO BE A BETTER HUMAN.

TO BE ANTI-RACIST YOU MUST UNDERSTAND THE THERE IS ONLY ONE RACE, HUMAN. EVERYTHING ELSE IS BULLSHIT, TO MAKE SOME FEEL INFERIOR OR SUPERIOR. ITS JUST THAT SIMPLE, NOW STOP BEING A DUMBASS AND WORK TO BE A BETTER HUMAN.

TO BE ANTI-RACIST YOU MUST UNDERSTAND THE THERE IS ONLY ONE RACE, HUMAN. EVERYTHING ELSE IS BULLSHIT, TO MAKE SOME FEEL INFERIOR OR SUPERIOR. ITS JUST THAT SIMPLE, NOW STOP BEING A DUMBASS AND WORK TO BE A BETTER HUMAN.

JUST THAT SIMPLE, NOW STOP BEING A DUMBASS AND WORK TO BE A BETTER HUMAN.

TO BE ANTI-RACIST YOU MUST UNDERSTAND THE THERE IS ONLY ONE RACE, HUMAN. EVERYTHING ELSE IS BULLSHIT, TO MAKE SOME FEEL INFERIOR OR SUPERIOR. ITS JUST THAT SIMPLE, NOW STOP BEING A DUMBASS AND WORK TO BE A BETTER HUMAN.

TO BE ANTI-RACIST YOU MUST UNDERSTAND THE THERE IS ONLY ONE RACE, HUMAN. EVERYTHING ELSE IS BULLSHIT, TO MAKE SOME FEEL INFERIOR OR SUPERIOR. ITS JUST THAT SIMPLE, NOW STOP BEING A DUMBASS AND WORK TO BE A BETTER HUMAN.

TO BE ANTI-RACIST YOU MUST UNDERSTAND THE THERE IS ONLY ONE RACE, HUMAN. EVERYTHING ELSE IS BULLSHIT, TO MAKE SOME FEEL INFERIOR OR SUPERIOR. ITS JUST THAT SIMPLE, NOW STOP BEING A DUMBASS AND WORK TO BE A BETTER HUMAN.

TO BE ANTI-RACIST YOU MUST UNDERSTAND THE THERE IS ONLY ONE RACE, HUMAN. EVERYTHING ELSE IS BULLSHIT, TO MAKE SOME FEEL INFERIOR OR SUPERIOR. ITS JUST THAT SIMPLE, NOW STOP BEING A DUMBASS AND WORK TO BE A BETTER HUMAN.

TO BE ANTI-RACIST YOU MUST UNDERSTAND THE THERE IS ONLY ONE RACE, HUMAN. EVERYTHING ELSE IS BULLSHIT, TO MAKE SOME FEEL INFERIOR OR SUPERIOR. ITS JUST THAT SIMPLE, NOW STOP BEING A DUMBASS AND WORK TO BE A BETTER HUMAN.

TO BE ANTI-RACIST YOU MUST UNDERSTAND THE THERE IS ONLY ONE RACE, HUMAN. EVERYTHING ELSE IS BULLSHIT, TO MAKE SOME FEEL INFERIOR OR SUPERIOR. ITS JUST THAT SIMPLE, NOW STOP BEING A DUMBASS AND WORK TO BE A BETTER HUMAN.

TO BE ANTI-RACIST YOU MUST UNDERSTAND THE THERE IS ONLY ONE RACE, HUMAN. EVERYTHING ELSE IS BULLSHIT, TO MAKE SOME FEEL INFERIOR OR SUPERIOR. ITS JUST THAT SIMPLE, NOW STOP BEING A DUMBASS AND WORK TO BE A BETTER HUMAN.

TO BE ANTI-RACIST YOU MUST UNDERSTAND THE THERE IS ONLY ONE RACE, HUMAN. EVERYTHING ELSE IS BULLSHIT, TO MAKE SOME FEEL INFERIOR OR SUPERIOR. ITS JUST THAT SIMPLE, NOW STOP BEING A DUMBASS AND WORK TO BE A BETTER HUMAN.

TO BE ANTI-RACIST YOU MUST UNDERSTAND THE THERE IS ONLY ONE RACE, HUMAN. EVERYTHING ELSE IS BULLSHIT, TO MAKE SOME FEEL INFERIOR OR SUPERIOR. ITS JUST THAT SIMPLE, NOW STOP BEING A DUMBASS AND WORK TO BE A BETTER HUMAN.

TO BE ANTI-RACIST YOU MUST UNDERSTAND THE THERE IS ONLY ONE RACE, HUMAN. EVERYTHING ELSE IS BULLSHIT, TO MAKE SOME FEEL INFERIOR OR SUPERIOR. ITS

TO BE ANTI-RACIST YOU MUST UNDERSTAND THE THERE IS ONLY ONE RACE, HUMAN. EVERYTHING ELSE IS BULLSHIT, TO MAKE SOME FEEL INFERIOR OR SUPERIOR. ITS JUST THAT SIMPLE, NOW STOP BEING A DUMBASS AND WORK TO BE A BETTER HUMAN.

TO BE ANTI-RACIST YOU MUST UNDERSTAND THE THERE IS ONLY ONE RACE, HUMAN. EVERYTHING ELSE IS BULLSHIT, TO MAKE SOME FEEL INFERIOR OR SUPERIOR. ITS JUST THAT SIMPLE, NOW STOP BEING A DUMBASS AND WORK TO BE A BETTER HUMAN.

TO BE ANTI-RACIST YOU MUST UNDERSTAND THE THERE IS ONLY ONE RACE, HUMAN. EVERYTHING ELSE IS BULLSHIT, TO MAKE SOME FEEL INFERIOR OR SUPERIOR. ITS JUST THAT SIMPLE, NOW STOP BEING A DUMBASS AND WORK TO BE A BETTER HUMAN.

TO BE ANTI-RACIST YOU MUST UNDERSTAND THE THERE IS ONLY ONE RACE, HUMAN. EVERYTHING ELSE IS BULLSHIT, TO MAKE SOME FEEL INFERIOR OR SUPERIOR. ITS JUST THAT SIMPLE, NOW STOP BEING A DUMBASS AND WORK TO BE A BETTER HUMAN.

TO BE ANTI-RACIST YOU MUST UNDERSTAND THE THERE IS ONLY ONE RACE, HUMAN. EVERYTHING ELSE IS BULLSHIT, TO MAKE SOME FEEL INFERIOR OR SUPERIOR. ITS JUST THAT SIMPLE, NOW STOP BEING A DUMBASS AND WORK TO BE A BETTER HUMAN.

TO BE ANTI-RACIST YOU MUST UNDERSTAND THE THERE IS ONLY ONE RACE, HUMAN. EVERYTHING ELSE IS BULLSHIT, TO MAKE SOME FEEL INFERIOR OR SUPERIOR. ITS JUST THAT SIMPLE, NOW STOP BEING A DUMBASS AND WORK TO BE A BETTER HUMAN.

TO BE ANTI-RACIST YOU MUST UNDERSTAND THE THERE IS ONLY ONE RACE, HUMAN. EVERYTHING ELSE IS BULLSHIT, TO MAKE SOME FEEL INFERIOR OR SUPERIOR. ITS JUST THAT SIMPLE, NOW STOP BEING A DUMBASS AND WORK TO BE A BETTER HUMAN.

TO BE ANTI-RACIST YOU MUST UNDERSTAND THE THERE IS ONLY ONE RACE, HUMAN. EVERYTHING ELSE IS BULLSHIT, TO MAKE SOME FEEL INFERIOR OR SUPERIOR. ITS JUST THAT SIMPLE, NOW STOP BEING A DUMBASS AND WORK TO BE A BETTER HUMAN.

TO BE ANTI-RACIST YOU MUST UNDERSTAND THE THERE IS ONLY ONE RACE, HUMAN. EVERYTHING ELSE IS BULLSHIT, TO MAKE SOME FEEL INFERIOR OR SUPERIOR. ITS JUST THAT SIMPLE, NOW STOP BEING A DUMBASS AND WORK TO BE A BETTER HUMAN.

TO BE ANTI-RACIST YOU MUST UNDERSTAND THE THERE IS ONLY ONE RACE, HUMAN. EVERYTHING ELSE IS BULLSHIT, TO MAKE SOME FEEL INFERIOR OR SUPERIOR. ITS JUST THAT SIMPLE, NOW STOP BEING A DUMBASS AND WORK TO BE A BETTER HUMAN.

JUST THAT SIMPLE, NOW STOP BEING A DUMBASS AND WORK TO BE A BETTER
HUMAN.
TO BE ANTI-RACIST YOU MUST UNDERSTAND THE THERE IS ONLY ONE RACE, HUMAN.
EVERYTHING ELSE IS BULLSHIT, TO MAKE SOME FEEL INFERIOR OR SUPERIOR. ITS
JUST THAT SIMPLE, NOW STOP BEING A DUMBASS AND WORK TO BE A BETTER
HUMAN.
TO BE ANTI-RACIST YOU MUST UNDERSTAND THE THERE IS ONLY ONE RACE, HUMAN.
EVERYTHING ELSE IS BULLSHIT, TO MAKE SOME FEEL INFERIOR OR SUPERIOR. ITS
JUST THAT SIMPLE, NOW STOP BEING A DUMBASS AND WORK TO BE A BETTER
HUMAN.
TO BE ANTI-RACIST YOU MUST UNDERSTAND THE THERE IS ONLY ONE RACE, HUMAN.
EVERYTHING ELSE IS BULLSHIT, TO MAKE SOME FEEL INFERIOR OR SUPERIOR. ITS
JUST THAT SIMPLE, NOW STOP BEING A DUMBASS AND WORK TO BE A BETTER
HUMAN.
TO BE ANTI-RACIST YOU MUST UNDERSTAND THE THERE IS ONLY ONE RACE, HUMAN.
EVERYTHING ELSE IS BULLSHIT, TO MAKE SOME FEEL INFERIOR OR SUPERIOR. ITS
JUST THAT SIMPLE, NOW STOP BEING A DUMBASS AND WORK TO BE A BETTER
HUMAN.
TO BE ANTI-RACIST YOU MUST UNDERSTAND THE THERE IS ONLY ONE RACE, HUMAN.
EVERYTHING ELSE IS BULLSHIT, TO MAKE SOME FEEL INFERIOR OR SUPERIOR. ITS
JUST THAT SIMPLE, NOW STOP BEING A DUMBASS AND WORK TO BE A BETTER
HUMAN.
TO BE ANTI-RACIST YOU MUST UNDERSTAND THE THERE IS ONLY ONE RACE, HUMAN.
EVERYTHING ELSE IS BULLSHIT, TO MAKE SOME FEEL INFERIOR OR SUPERIOR. ITS
JUST THAT SIMPLE, NOW STOP BEING A DUMBASS AND WORK TO BE A BETTER
HUMAN.
TO BE ANTI-RACIST YOU MUST UNDERSTAND THE THERE IS ONLY ONE RACE, HUMAN.
EVERYTHING ELSE IS BULLSHIT, TO MAKE SOME FEEL INFERIOR OR SUPERIOR. ITS
JUST THAT SIMPLE, NOW STOP BEING A DUMBASS AND WORK TO BE A BETTER
HUMAN.
TO BE ANTI-RACIST YOU MUST UNDERSTAND THE THERE IS ONLY ONE RACE, HUMAN.
EVERYTHING ELSE IS BULLSHIT, TO MAKE SOME FEEL INFERIOR OR SUPERIOR. ITS
JUST THAT SIMPLE, NOW STOP BEING A DUMBASS AND WORK TO BE A BETTER
HUMAN.
TO BE ANTI-RACIST YOU MUST UNDERSTAND THE THERE IS ONLY ONE RACE, HUMAN.
EVERYTHING ELSE IS BULLSHIT, TO MAKE SOME FEEL INFERIOR OR SUPERIOR. ITS
JUST THAT SIMPLE, NOW STOP BEING A DUMBASS AND WORK TO BE A BETTER
HUMAN.
TO BE ANTI-RACIST YOU MUST UNDERSTAND THE THERE IS ONLY ONE RACE, HUMAN.
EVERYTHING ELSE IS BULLSHIT, TO MAKE SOME FEEL INFERIOR OR SUPERIOR. ITS

TO BE ANTI-RACIST YOU MUST UNDERSTAND THE THERE IS ONLY ONE RACE, HUMAN. EVERYTHING ELSE IS BULLSHIT, TO MAKE SOME FEEL INFERIOR OR SUPERIOR. ITS JUST THAT SIMPLE, NOW STOP BEING A DUMBASS AND WORK TO BE A BETTER HUMAN.

TO BE ANTI-RACIST YOU MUST UNDERSTAND THE THERE IS ONLY ONE RACE, HUMAN. EVERYTHING ELSE IS BULLSHIT, TO MAKE SOME FEEL INFERIOR OR SUPERIOR. ITS JUST THAT SIMPLE, NOW STOP BEING A DUMBASS AND WORK TO BE A BETTER HUMAN.

TO BE ANTI-RACIST YOU MUST UNDERSTAND THE THERE IS ONLY ONE RACE, HUMAN. EVERYTHING ELSE IS BULLSHIT, TO MAKE SOME FEEL INFERIOR OR SUPERIOR. ITS JUST THAT SIMPLE, NOW STOP BEING A DUMBASS AND WORK TO BE A BETTER HUMAN.

TO BE ANTI-RACIST YOU MUST UNDERSTAND THE THERE IS ONLY ONE RACE, HUMAN. EVERYTHING ELSE IS BULLSHIT, TO MAKE SOME FEEL INFERIOR OR SUPERIOR. ITS JUST THAT SIMPLE, NOW STOP BEING A DUMBASS AND WORK TO BE A BETTER HUMAN.

TO BE ANTI-RACIST YOU MUST UNDERSTAND THE THERE IS ONLY ONE RACE, HUMAN. EVERYTHING ELSE IS BULLSHIT, TO MAKE SOME FEEL INFERIOR OR SUPERIOR. ITS JUST THAT SIMPLE, NOW STOP BEING A DUMBASS AND WORK TO BE A BETTER HUMAN.

TO BE ANTI-RACIST YOU MUST UNDERSTAND THE THERE IS ONLY ONE RACE, HUMAN. EVERYTHING ELSE IS BULLSHIT, TO MAKE SOME FEEL INFERIOR OR SUPERIOR. ITS JUST THAT SIMPLE, NOW STOP BEING A DUMBASS AND WORK TO BE A BETTER HUMAN.

TO BE ANTI-RACIST YOU MUST UNDERSTAND THE THERE IS ONLY ONE RACE, HUMAN. EVERYTHING ELSE IS BULLSHIT, TO MAKE SOME FEEL INFERIOR OR SUPERIOR. ITS JUST THAT SIMPLE, NOW STOP BEING A DUMBASS AND WORK TO BE A BETTER HUMAN.

TO BE ANTI-RACIST YOU MUST UNDERSTAND THE THERE IS ONLY ONE RACE, HUMAN. EVERYTHING ELSE IS BULLSHIT, TO MAKE SOME FEEL INFERIOR OR SUPERIOR. ITS JUST THAT SIMPLE, NOW STOP BEING A DUMBASS AND WORK TO BE A BETTER HUMAN.

TO BE ANTI-RACIST YOU MUST UNDERSTAND THE THERE IS ONLY ONE RACE, HUMAN. EVERYTHING ELSE IS BULLSHIT, TO MAKE SOME FEEL INFERIOR OR SUPERIOR. ITS JUST THAT SIMPLE, NOW STOP BEING A DUMBASS AND WORK TO BE A BETTER HUMAN.

TO BE ANTI-RACIST YOU MUST UNDERSTAND THE THERE IS ONLY ONE RACE, HUMAN. EVERYTHING ELSE IS BULLSHIT, TO MAKE SOME FEEL INFERIOR OR SUPERIOR. ITS JUST THAT SIMPLE, NOW STOP BEING A DUMBASS AND WORK TO BE A BETTER HUMAN.

TO BE ANTI-RACIST YOU MUST UNDERSTAND THE THERE IS ONLY ONE RACE, HUMAN. EVERYTHING ELSE IS BULLSHIT, TO MAKE SOME FEEL INFERIOR OR SUPERIOR. ITS JUST THAT SIMPLE, NOW STOP BEING A DUMBASS AND WORK TO BE A BETTER HUMAN

JUST THAT SIMPLE, NOW STOP BEING A DUMBASS AND WORK TO BE A BETTER HUMAN.

TO BE ANTI-RACIST YOU MUST UNDERSTAND THE THERE IS ONLY ONE RACE, HUMAN. EVERYTHING ELSE IS BULLSHIT, TO MAKE SOME FEEL INFERIOR OR SUPERIOR. ITS JUST THAT SIMPLE, NOW STOP BEING A DUMBASS AND WORK TO BE A BETTER HUMAN.

TO BE ANTI-RACIST YOU MUST UNDERSTAND THE THERE IS ONLY ONE RACE, HUMAN. EVERYTHING ELSE IS BULLSHIT, TO MAKE SOME FEEL INFERIOR OR SUPERIOR. ITS JUST THAT SIMPLE, NOW STOP BEING A DUMBASS AND WORK TO BE A BETTER HUMAN.

TO BE ANTI-RACIST YOU MUST UNDERSTAND THE THERE IS ONLY ONE RACE, HUMAN. EVERYTHING ELSE IS BULLSHIT, TO MAKE SOME FEEL INFERIOR OR SUPERIOR. ITS JUST THAT SIMPLE, NOW STOP BEING A DUMBASS AND WORK TO BE A BETTER HUMAN.

TO BE ANTI-RACIST YOU MUST UNDERSTAND THE THERE IS ONLY ONE RACE, HUMAN. EVERYTHING ELSE IS BULLSHIT, TO MAKE SOME FEEL INFERIOR OR SUPERIOR. ITS JUST THAT SIMPLE, NOW STOP BEING A DUMBASS AND WORK TO BE A BETTER HUMAN.

TO BE ANTI-RACIST YOU MUST UNDERSTAND THE THERE IS ONLY ONE RACE, HUMAN. EVERYTHING ELSE IS BULLSHIT, TO MAKE SOME FEEL INFERIOR OR SUPERIOR. ITS JUST THAT SIMPLE, NOW STOP BEING A DUMBASS AND WORK TO BE A BETTER HUMAN.

TO BE ANTI-RACIST YOU MUST UNDERSTAND THE THERE IS ONLY ONE RACE, HUMAN. EVERYTHING ELSE IS BULLSHIT, TO MAKE SOME FEEL INFERIOR OR SUPERIOR. ITS JUST THAT SIMPLE, NOW STOP BEING A DUMBASS AND WORK TO BE A BETTER HUMAN.

TO BE ANTI-RACIST YOU MUST UNDERSTAND THE THERE IS ONLY ONE RACE, HUMAN. EVERYTHING ELSE IS BULLSHIT, TO MAKE SOME FEEL INFERIOR OR SUPERIOR. ITS JUST THAT SIMPLE, NOW STOP BEING A DUMBASS AND WORK TO BE A BETTER HUMAN.

TO BE ANTI-RACIST YOU MUST UNDERSTAND THE THERE IS ONLY ONE RACE, HUMAN. EVERYTHING ELSE IS BULLSHIT, TO MAKE SOME FEEL INFERIOR OR SUPERIOR. ITS JUST THAT SIMPLE, NOW STOP BEING A DUMBASS AND WORK TO BE A BETTER HUMAN.

TO BE ANTI-RACIST YOU MUST UNDERSTAND THE THERE IS ONLY ONE RACE, HUMAN. EVERYTHING ELSE IS BULLSHIT, TO MAKE SOME FEEL INFERIOR OR SUPERIOR. ITS

TO BE ANTI-RACIST YOU MUST UNDERSTAND THE THERE IS ONLY ONE RACE, HUMAN. EVERYTHING ELSE IS BULLSHIT, TO MAKE SOME FEEL INFERIOR OR SUPERIOR. ITS JUST THAT SIMPLE, NOW STOP BEING A DUMBASS AND WORK TO BE A BETTER HUMAN.

TO BE ANTI-RACIST YOU MUST UNDERSTAND THE THERE IS ONLY ONE RACE, HUMAN. EVERYTHING ELSE IS BULLSHIT, TO MAKE SOME FEEL INFERIOR OR SUPERIOR. ITS JUST THAT SIMPLE, NOW STOP BEING A DUMBASS AND WORK TO BE A BETTER HUMAN.

TO BE ANTI-RACIST YOU MUST UNDERSTAND THE THERE IS ONLY ONE RACE, HUMAN. EVERYTHING ELSE IS BULLSHIT, TO MAKE SOME FEEL INFERIOR OR SUPERIOR. ITS JUST THAT SIMPLE, NOW STOP BEING A DUMBASS AND WORK TO BE A BETTER HUMAN.

TO BE ANTI-RACIST YOU MUST UNDERSTAND THE THERE IS ONLY ONE RACE, HUMAN. EVERYTHING ELSE IS BULLSHIT, TO MAKE SOME FEEL INFERIOR OR SUPERIOR. ITS JUST THAT SIMPLE, NOW STOP BEING A DUMBASS AND WORK TO BE A BETTER HUMAN.

TO BE ANTI-RACIST YOU MUST UNDERSTAND THE THERE IS ONLY ONE RACE, HUMAN. EVERYTHING ELSE IS BULLSHIT, TO MAKE SOME FEEL INFERIOR OR SUPERIOR. ITS JUST THAT SIMPLE, NOW STOP BEING A DUMBASS AND WORK TO BE A BETTER HUMAN.

TO BE ANTI-RACIST YOU MUST UNDERSTAND THE THERE IS ONLY ONE RACE, HUMAN. EVERYTHING ELSE IS BULLSHIT, TO MAKE SOME FEEL INFERIOR OR SUPERIOR. ITS JUST THAT SIMPLE, NOW STOP BEING A DUMBASS AND WORK TO BE A BETTER HUMAN.

TO BE ANTI-RACIST YOU MUST UNDERSTAND THE THERE IS ONLY ONE RACE, HUMAN. EVERYTHING ELSE IS BULLSHIT, TO MAKE SOME FEEL INFERIOR OR SUPERIOR. ITS JUST THAT SIMPLE, NOW STOP BEING A DUMBASS AND WORK TO BE A BETTER HUMAN.

TO BE ANTI-RACIST YOU MUST UNDERSTAND THE THERE IS ONLY ONE RACE, HUMAN. EVERYTHING ELSE IS BULLSHIT, TO MAKE SOME FEEL INFERIOR OR SUPERIOR. ITS JUST THAT SIMPLE, NOW STOP BEING A DUMBASS AND WORK TO BE A BETTER HUMAN.

TO BE ANTI-RACIST YOU MUST UNDERSTAND THE THERE IS ONLY ONE RACE, HUMAN. EVERYTHING ELSE IS BULLSHIT, TO MAKE SOME FEEL INFERIOR OR SUPERIOR. ITS JUST THAT SIMPLE, NOW STOP BEING A DUMBASS AND WORK TO BE A BETTER HUMAN.

TO BE ANTI-RACIST YOU MUST UNDERSTAND THE THERE IS ONLY ONE RACE, HUMAN. EVERYTHING ELSE IS BULLSHIT, TO MAKE SOME FEEL INFERIOR OR SUPERIOR. ITS JUST THAT SIMPLE, NOW STOP BEING A DUMBASS AND WORK TO BE A BETTER HUMAN.

TO BE ANTI-RACIST YOU MUST UNDERSTAND THE THERE IS ONLY ONE RACE, HUMAN. EVERYTHING ELSE IS BULLSHIT, TO MAKE SOME FEEL INFERIOR OR SUPERIOR. ITS JUST THAT SIMPLE, NOW STOP BEING A DUMBASS AND WORK TO BE A BETTER HUMAN.

JUST THAT SIMPLE, NOW STOP BEING A DUMBASS AND WORK TO BE A BETTER HUMAN.

TO BE ANTI-RACIST YOU MUST UNDERSTAND THE THERE IS ONLY ONE RACE, HUMAN. EVERYTHING ELSE IS BULLSHIT, TO MAKE SOME FEEL INFERIOR OR SUPERIOR. ITS JUST THAT SIMPLE, NOW STOP BEING A DUMBASS AND WORK TO BE A BETTER HUMAN.

TO BE ANTI-RACIST YOU MUST UNDERSTAND THE THERE IS ONLY ONE RACE, HUMAN. EVERYTHING ELSE IS BULLSHIT, TO MAKE SOME FEEL INFERIOR OR SUPERIOR. ITS JUST THAT SIMPLE, NOW STOP BEING A DUMBASS AND WORK TO BE A BETTER HUMAN.

TO BE ANTI-RACIST YOU MUST UNDERSTAND THE THERE IS ONLY ONE RACE, HUMAN. EVERYTHING ELSE IS BULLSHIT, TO MAKE SOME FEEL INFERIOR OR SUPERIOR. ITS JUST THAT SIMPLE, NOW STOP BEING A DUMBASS AND WORK TO BE A BETTER HUMAN.

TO BE ANTI-RACIST YOU MUST UNDERSTAND THE THERE IS ONLY ONE RACE, HUMAN. EVERYTHING ELSE IS BULLSHIT, TO MAKE SOME FEEL INFERIOR OR SUPERIOR. ITS JUST THAT SIMPLE, NOW STOP BEING A DUMBASS AND WORK TO BE A BETTER HUMAN.

TO BE ANTI-RACIST YOU MUST UNDERSTAND THE THERE IS ONLY ONE RACE, HUMAN. EVERYTHING ELSE IS BULLSHIT, TO MAKE SOME FEEL INFERIOR OR SUPERIOR. ITS JUST THAT SIMPLE, NOW STOP BEING A DUMBASS AND WORK TO BE A BETTER HUMAN.

TO BE ANTI-RACIST YOU MUST UNDERSTAND THE THERE IS ONLY ONE RACE, HUMAN. EVERYTHING ELSE IS BULLSHIT, TO MAKE SOME FEEL INFERIOR OR SUPERIOR. ITS JUST THAT SIMPLE, NOW STOP BEING A DUMBASS AND WORK TO BE A BETTER HUMAN.

TO BE ANTI-RACIST YOU MUST UNDERSTAND THE THERE IS ONLY ONE RACE, HUMAN. EVERYTHING ELSE IS BULLSHIT, TO MAKE SOME FEEL INFERIOR OR SUPERIOR. ITS JUST THAT SIMPLE, NOW STOP BEING A DUMBASS AND WORK TO BE A BETTER HUMAN.

TO BE ANTI-RACIST YOU MUST UNDERSTAND THE THERE IS ONLY ONE RACE, HUMAN. EVERYTHING ELSE IS BULLSHIT, TO MAKE SOME FEEL INFERIOR OR SUPERIOR. ITS JUST THAT SIMPLE, NOW STOP BEING A DUMBASS AND WORK TO BE A BETTER HUMAN.

TO BE ANTI-RACIST YOU MUST UNDERSTAND THE THERE IS ONLY ONE RACE, HUMAN. EVERYTHING ELSE IS BULLSHIT, TO MAKE SOME FEEL INFERIOR OR SUPERIOR. ITS

TO BE ANTI-RACIST YOU MUST UNDERSTAND THE THERE IS ONLY ONE RACE, HUMAN. EVERYTHING ELSE IS BULLSHIT, TO MAKE SOME FEEL INFERIOR OR SUPERIOR. ITS JUST THAT SIMPLE, NOW STOP BEING A DUMBASS AND WORK TO BE A BETTER HUMAN.

TO BE ANTI-RACIST YOU MUST UNDERSTAND THE THERE IS ONLY ONE RACE, HUMAN. EVERYTHING ELSE IS BULLSHIT, TO MAKE SOME FEEL INFERIOR OR SUPERIOR. ITS JUST THAT SIMPLE, NOW STOP BEING A DUMBASS AND WORK TO BE A BETTER HUMAN.

TO BE ANTI-RACIST YOU MUST UNDERSTAND THE THERE IS ONLY ONE RACE, HUMAN. EVERYTHING ELSE IS BULLSHIT, TO MAKE SOME FEEL INFERIOR OR SUPERIOR. ITS JUST THAT SIMPLE, NOW STOP BEING A DUMBASS AND WORK TO BE A BETTER HUMAN.

TO BE ANTI-RACIST YOU MUST UNDERSTAND THE THERE IS ONLY ONE RACE, HUMAN. EVERYTHING ELSE IS BULLSHIT, TO MAKE SOME FEEL INFERIOR OR SUPERIOR. ITS JUST THAT SIMPLE, NOW STOP BEING A DUMBASS AND WORK TO BE A BETTER HUMAN.

TO BE ANTI-RACIST YOU MUST UNDERSTAND THE THERE IS ONLY ONE RACE, HUMAN. EVERYTHING ELSE IS BULLSHIT, TO MAKE SOME FEEL INFERIOR OR SUPERIOR. ITS JUST THAT SIMPLE, NOW STOP BEING A DUMBASS AND WORK TO BE A BETTER HUMAN.

TO BE ANTI-RACIST YOU MUST UNDERSTAND THE THERE IS ONLY ONE RACE, HUMAN. EVERYTHING ELSE IS BULLSHIT, TO MAKE SOME FEEL INFERIOR OR SUPERIOR. ITS JUST THAT SIMPLE, NOW STOP BEING A DUMBASS AND WORK TO BE A BETTER HUMAN.

TO BE ANTI-RACIST YOU MUST UNDERSTAND THE THERE IS ONLY ONE RACE, HUMAN. EVERYTHING ELSE IS BULLSHIT, TO MAKE SOME FEEL INFERIOR OR SUPERIOR. ITS JUST THAT SIMPLE, NOW STOP BEING A DUMBASS AND WORK TO BE A BETTER HUMAN.

TO BE ANTI-RACIST YOU MUST UNDERSTAND THE THERE IS ONLY ONE RACE, HUMAN. EVERYTHING ELSE IS BULLSHIT, TO MAKE SOME FEEL INFERIOR OR SUPERIOR. ITS JUST THAT SIMPLE, NOW STOP BEING A DUMBASS AND WORK TO BE A BETTER HUMAN.

TO BE ANTI-RACIST YOU MUST UNDERSTAND THE THERE IS ONLY ONE RACE, HUMAN. EVERYTHING ELSE IS BULLSHIT, TO MAKE SOME FEEL INFERIOR OR SUPERIOR. ITS JUST THAT SIMPLE, NOW STOP BEING A DUMBASS AND WORK TO BE A BETTER HUMAN.

TO BE ANTI-RACIST YOU MUST UNDERSTAND THE THERE IS ONLY ONE RACE, HUMAN. EVERYTHING ELSE IS BULLSHIT, TO MAKE SOME FEEL INFERIOR OR SUPERIOR. ITS JUST THAT SIMPLE, NOW STOP BEING A DUMBASS AND WORK TO BE A BETTER HUMAN.

TO BE ANTI-RACIST YOU MUST UNDERSTAND THE THERE IS ONLY ONE RACE, HUMAN. EVERYTHING ELSE IS BULLSHIT, TO MAKE SOME FEEL INFERIOR OR SUPERIOR. ITS JUST THAT SIMPLE, NOW STOP BEING A DUMBASS AND WORK TO BE A BETTER HUMAN

JUST THAT SIMPLE, NOW STOP BEING A DUMBASS AND WORK TO BE A BETTER HUMAN.

TO BE ANTI-RACIST YOU MUST UNDERSTAND THE THERE IS ONLY ONE RACE, HUMAN. EVERYTHING ELSE IS BULLSHIT, TO MAKE SOME FEEL INFERIOR OR SUPERIOR. ITS JUST THAT SIMPLE, NOW STOP BEING A DUMBASS AND WORK TO BE A BETTER HUMAN.

TO BE ANTI-RACIST YOU MUST UNDERSTAND THE THERE IS ONLY ONE RACE, HUMAN. EVERYTHING ELSE IS BULLSHIT, TO MAKE SOME FEEL INFERIOR OR SUPERIOR. ITS JUST THAT SIMPLE, NOW STOP BEING A DUMBASS AND WORK TO BE A BETTER HUMAN.

TO BE ANTI-RACIST YOU MUST UNDERSTAND THE THERE IS ONLY ONE RACE, HUMAN. EVERYTHING ELSE IS BULLSHIT, TO MAKE SOME FEEL INFERIOR OR SUPERIOR. ITS JUST THAT SIMPLE, NOW STOP BEING A DUMBASS AND WORK TO BE A BETTER HUMAN.

TO BE ANTI-RACIST YOU MUST UNDERSTAND THE THERE IS ONLY ONE RACE, HUMAN. EVERYTHING ELSE IS BULLSHIT, TO MAKE SOME FEEL INFERIOR OR SUPERIOR. ITS JUST THAT SIMPLE, NOW STOP BEING A DUMBASS AND WORK TO BE A BETTER HUMAN.

TO BE ANTI-RACIST YOU MUST UNDERSTAND THE THERE IS ONLY ONE RACE, HUMAN. EVERYTHING ELSE IS BULLSHIT, TO MAKE SOME FEEL INFERIOR OR SUPERIOR. ITS JUST THAT SIMPLE, NOW STOP BEING A DUMBASS AND WORK TO BE A BETTER HUMAN.

TO BE ANTI-RACIST YOU MUST UNDERSTAND THE THERE IS ONLY ONE RACE, HUMAN. EVERYTHING ELSE IS BULLSHIT, TO MAKE SOME FEEL INFERIOR OR SUPERIOR. ITS JUST THAT SIMPLE, NOW STOP BEING A DUMBASS AND WORK TO BE A BETTER HUMAN.

TO BE ANTI-RACIST YOU MUST UNDERSTAND THE THERE IS ONLY ONE RACE, HUMAN. EVERYTHING ELSE IS BULLSHIT, TO MAKE SOME FEEL INFERIOR OR SUPERIOR. ITS JUST THAT SIMPLE, NOW STOP BEING A DUMBASS AND WORK TO BE A BETTER HUMAN.

TO BE ANTI-RACIST YOU MUST UNDERSTAND THE THERE IS ONLY ONE RACE, HUMAN. EVERYTHING ELSE IS BULLSHIT, TO MAKE SOME FEEL INFERIOR OR SUPERIOR. ITS JUST THAT SIMPLE, NOW STOP BEING A DUMBASS AND WORK TO BE A BETTER HUMAN.

TO BE ANTI-RACIST YOU MUST UNDERSTAND THE THERE IS ONLY ONE RACE, HUMAN. EVERYTHING ELSE IS BULLSHIT, TO MAKE SOME FEEL INFERIOR OR SUPERIOR. ITS JUST THAT SIMPLE, NOW STOP BEING A DUMBASS AND WORK TO BE A BETTER HUMAN.

TO BE ANTI-RACIST YOU MUST UNDERSTAND THE THERE IS ONLY ONE RACE, HUMAN. EVERYTHING ELSE IS BULLSHIT, TO MAKE SOME FEEL INFERIOR OR SUPERIOR. ITS

TO BE ANTI-RACIST YOU MUST UNDERSTAND THE THERE IS ONLY ONE RACE, HUMAN. EVERYTHING ELSE IS BULLSHIT, TO MAKE SOME FEEL INFERIOR OR SUPERIOR. ITS JUST THAT SIMPLE, NOW STOP BEING A DUMBASS AND WORK TO BE A BETTER HUMAN.

TO BE ANTI-RACIST YOU MUST UNDERSTAND THE THERE IS ONLY ONE RACE, HUMAN. EVERYTHING ELSE IS BULLSHIT, TO MAKE SOME FEEL INFERIOR OR SUPERIOR. ITS JUST THAT SIMPLE, NOW STOP BEING A DUMBASS AND WORK TO BE A BETTER HUMAN.

TO BE ANTI-RACIST YOU MUST UNDERSTAND THE THERE IS ONLY ONE RACE, HUMAN. EVERYTHING ELSE IS BULLSHIT, TO MAKE SOME FEEL INFERIOR OR SUPERIOR. ITS JUST THAT SIMPLE, NOW STOP BEING A DUMBASS AND WORK TO BE A BETTER HUMAN.

TO BE ANTI-RACIST YOU MUST UNDERSTAND THE THERE IS ONLY ONE RACE, HUMAN. EVERYTHING ELSE IS BULLSHIT, TO MAKE SOME FEEL INFERIOR OR SUPERIOR. ITS JUST THAT SIMPLE, NOW STOP BEING A DUMBASS AND WORK TO BE A BETTER HUMAN.

TO BE ANTI-RACIST YOU MUST UNDERSTAND THE THERE IS ONLY ONE RACE, HUMAN. EVERYTHING ELSE IS BULLSHIT, TO MAKE SOME FEEL INFERIOR OR SUPERIOR. ITS JUST THAT SIMPLE, NOW STOP BEING A DUMBASS AND WORK TO BE A BETTER HUMAN.

TO BE ANTI-RACIST YOU MUST UNDERSTAND THE THERE IS ONLY ONE RACE, HUMAN. EVERYTHING ELSE IS BULLSHIT, TO MAKE SOME FEEL INFERIOR OR SUPERIOR. ITS JUST THAT SIMPLE, NOW STOP BEING A DUMBASS AND WORK TO BE A BETTER HUMAN.

TO BE ANTI-RACIST YOU MUST UNDERSTAND THE THERE IS ONLY ONE RACE, HUMAN. EVERYTHING ELSE IS BULLSHIT, TO MAKE SOME FEEL INFERIOR OR SUPERIOR. ITS JUST THAT SIMPLE, NOW STOP BEING A DUMBASS AND WORK TO BE A BETTER HUMAN.

TO BE ANTI-RACIST YOU MUST UNDERSTAND THE THERE IS ONLY ONE RACE, HUMAN. EVERYTHING ELSE IS BULLSHIT, TO MAKE SOME FEEL INFERIOR OR SUPERIOR. ITS JUST THAT SIMPLE, NOW STOP BEING A DUMBASS AND WORK TO BE A BETTER HUMAN.

TO BE ANTI-RACIST YOU MUST UNDERSTAND THE THERE IS ONLY ONE RACE, HUMAN. EVERYTHING ELSE IS BULLSHIT, TO MAKE SOME FEEL INFERIOR OR SUPERIOR. ITS JUST THAT SIMPLE, NOW STOP BEING A DUMBASS AND WORK TO BE A BETTER HUMAN.

TO BE ANTI-RACIST YOU MUST UNDERSTAND THE THERE IS ONLY ONE RACE, HUMAN. EVERYTHING ELSE IS BULLSHIT, TO MAKE SOME FEEL INFERIOR OR SUPERIOR. ITS JUST THAT SIMPLE, NOW STOP BEING A DUMBASS AND WORK TO BE A BETTER HUMAN.

TO BE ANTI-RACIST YOU MUST UNDERSTAND THE THERE IS ONLY ONE RACE, HUMAN. EVERYTHING ELSE IS BULLSHIT, TO MAKE SOME FEEL INFERIOR OR SUPERIOR. ITS JUST THAT SIMPLE, NOW STOP BEING A DUMBASS AND WORK TO BE A BETTER HUMAN.

JUST THAT SIMPLE, NOW STOP BEING A DUMBASS AND WORK TO BE A BETTER
HUMAN.
TO BE ANTI-RACIST YOU MUST UNDERSTAND THE THERE IS ONLY ONE RACE, HUMAN.
EVERYTHING ELSE IS BULLSHIT, TO MAKE SOME FEEL INFERIOR OR SUPERIOR. ITS
JUST THAT SIMPLE, NOW STOP BEING A DUMBASS AND WORK TO BE A BETTER
HUMAN.
TO BE ANTI-RACIST YOU MUST UNDERSTAND THE THERE IS ONLY ONE RACE, HUMAN.
EVERYTHING ELSE IS BULLSHIT, TO MAKE SOME FEEL INFERIOR OR SUPERIOR. ITS
JUST THAT SIMPLE, NOW STOP BEING A DUMBASS AND WORK TO BE A BETTER
HUMAN.
TO BE ANTI-RACIST YOU MUST UNDERSTAND THE THERE IS ONLY ONE RACE, HUMAN.
EVERYTHING ELSE IS BULLSHIT, TO MAKE SOME FEEL INFERIOR OR SUPERIOR. ITS
JUST THAT SIMPLE, NOW STOP BEING A DUMBASS AND WORK TO BE A BETTER
HUMAN.
TO BE ANTI-RACIST YOU MUST UNDERSTAND THE THERE IS ONLY ONE RACE, HUMAN.
EVERYTHING ELSE IS BULLSHIT, TO MAKE SOME FEEL INFERIOR OR SUPERIOR. ITS
JUST THAT SIMPLE, NOW STOP BEING A DUMBASS AND WORK TO BE A BETTER
HUMAN.
TO BE ANTI-RACIST YOU MUST UNDERSTAND THE THERE IS ONLY ONE RACE, HUMAN.
EVERYTHING ELSE IS BULLSHIT, TO MAKE SOME FEEL INFERIOR OR SUPERIOR. ITS
JUST THAT SIMPLE, NOW STOP BEING A DUMBASS AND WORK TO BE A BETTER
HUMAN.
TO BE ANTI-RACIST YOU MUST UNDERSTAND THE THERE IS ONLY ONE RACE, HUMAN.
EVERYTHING ELSE IS BULLSHIT, TO MAKE SOME FEEL INFERIOR OR SUPERIOR. ITS
JUST THAT SIMPLE, NOW STOP BEING A DUMBASS AND WORK TO BE A BETTER
HUMAN.
TO BE ANTI-RACIST YOU MUST UNDERSTAND THE THERE IS ONLY ONE RACE, HUMAN.
EVERYTHING ELSE IS BULLSHIT, TO MAKE SOME FEEL INFERIOR OR SUPERIOR. ITS
JUST THAT SIMPLE, NOW STOP BEING A DUMBASS AND WORK TO BE A BETTER
HUMAN.
TO BE ANTI-RACIST YOU MUST UNDERSTAND THE THERE IS ONLY ONE RACE, HUMAN.
EVERYTHING ELSE IS BULLSHIT, TO MAKE SOME FEEL INFERIOR OR SUPERIOR. ITS
JUST THAT SIMPLE, NOW STOP BEING A DUMBASS AND WORK TO BE A BETTER
HUMAN.
TO BE ANTI-RACIST YOU MUST UNDERSTAND THE THERE IS ONLY ONE RACE, HUMAN.
EVERYTHING ELSE IS BULLSHIT, TO MAKE SOME FEEL INFERIOR OR SUPERIOR. ITS
JUST THAT SIMPLE, NOW STOP BEING A DUMBASS AND WORK TO BE A BETTER
HUMAN.
TO BE ANTI-RACIST YOU MUST UNDERSTAND THE THERE IS ONLY ONE RACE, HUMAN.
EVERYTHING ELSE IS BULLSHIT, TO MAKE SOME FEEL INFERIOR OR SUPERIOR. ITS

TO BE ANTI-RACIST YOU MUST UNDERSTAND THE THERE IS ONLY ONE RACE, HUMAN. EVERYTHING ELSE IS BULLSHIT, TO MAKE SOME FEEL INFERIOR OR SUPERIOR. ITS JUST THAT SIMPLE, NOW STOP BEING A DUMBASS AND WORK TO BE A BETTER HUMAN.

TO BE ANTI-RACIST YOU MUST UNDERSTAND THE THERE IS ONLY ONE RACE, HUMAN. EVERYTHING ELSE IS BULLSHIT, TO MAKE SOME FEEL INFERIOR OR SUPERIOR. ITS JUST THAT SIMPLE, NOW STOP BEING A DUMBASS AND WORK TO BE A BETTER HUMAN.

TO BE ANTI-RACIST YOU MUST UNDERSTAND THE THERE IS ONLY ONE RACE, HUMAN. EVERYTHING ELSE IS BULLSHIT, TO MAKE SOME FEEL INFERIOR OR SUPERIOR. ITS JUST THAT SIMPLE, NOW STOP BEING A DUMBASS AND WORK TO BE A BETTER HUMAN.

TO BE ANTI-RACIST YOU MUST UNDERSTAND THE THERE IS ONLY ONE RACE, HUMAN. EVERYTHING ELSE IS BULLSHIT, TO MAKE SOME FEEL INFERIOR OR SUPERIOR. ITS JUST THAT SIMPLE, NOW STOP BEING A DUMBASS AND WORK TO BE A BETTER HUMAN.

TO BE ANTI-RACIST YOU MUST UNDERSTAND THE THERE IS ONLY ONE RACE, HUMAN. EVERYTHING ELSE IS BULLSHIT, TO MAKE SOME FEEL INFERIOR OR SUPERIOR. ITS JUST THAT SIMPLE, NOW STOP BEING A DUMBASS AND WORK TO BE A BETTER HUMAN.

TO BE ANTI-RACIST YOU MUST UNDERSTAND THE THERE IS ONLY ONE RACE, HUMAN. EVERYTHING ELSE IS BULLSHIT, TO MAKE SOME FEEL INFERIOR OR SUPERIOR. ITS JUST THAT SIMPLE, NOW STOP BEING A DUMBASS AND WORK TO BE A BETTER HUMAN.

TO BE ANTI-RACIST YOU MUST UNDERSTAND THE THERE IS ONLY ONE RACE, HUMAN. EVERYTHING ELSE IS BULLSHIT, TO MAKE SOME FEEL INFERIOR OR SUPERIOR. ITS JUST THAT SIMPLE, NOW STOP BEING A DUMBASS AND WORK TO BE A BETTER HUMAN.

TO BE ANTI-RACIST YOU MUST UNDERSTAND THE THERE IS ONLY ONE RACE, HUMAN. EVERYTHING ELSE IS BULLSHIT, TO MAKE SOME FEEL INFERIOR OR SUPERIOR. ITS JUST THAT SIMPLE, NOW STOP BEING A DUMBASS AND WORK TO BE A BETTER HUMAN.

TO BE ANTI-RACIST YOU MUST UNDERSTAND THE THERE IS ONLY ONE RACE, HUMAN. EVERYTHING ELSE IS BULLSHIT, TO MAKE SOME FEEL INFERIOR OR SUPERIOR. ITS JUST THAT SIMPLE, NOW STOP BEING A DUMBASS AND WORK TO BE A BETTER HUMAN.

TO BE ANTI-RACIST YOU MUST UNDERSTAND THE THERE IS ONLY ONE RACE, HUMAN. EVERYTHING ELSE IS BULLSHIT, TO MAKE SOME FEEL INFERIOR OR SUPERIOR. ITS JUST THAT SIMPLE, NOW STOP BEING A DUMBASS AND WORK TO BE A BETTER HUMAN.

TO BE ANTI-RACIST YOU MUST UNDERSTAND THE THERE IS ONLY ONE RACE, HUMAN. EVERYTHING ELSE IS BULLSHIT, TO MAKE SOME FEEL INFERIOR OR SUPERIOR. ITS JUST THAT SIMPLE, NOW STOP BEING A DUMBASS AND WORK TO BE A BETTER HUMAN

JUST THAT SIMPLE, NOW STOP BEING A DUMBASS AND WORK TO BE A BETTER HUMAN.

TO BE ANTI-RACIST YOU MUST UNDERSTAND THE THERE IS ONLY ONE RACE, HUMAN. EVERYTHING ELSE IS BULLSHIT, TO MAKE SOME FEEL INFERIOR OR SUPERIOR. ITS JUST THAT SIMPLE, NOW STOP BEING A DUMBASS AND WORK TO BE A BETTER HUMAN.

TO BE ANTI-RACIST YOU MUST UNDERSTAND THE THERE IS ONLY ONE RACE, HUMAN. EVERYTHING ELSE IS BULLSHIT, TO MAKE SOME FEEL INFERIOR OR SUPERIOR. ITS JUST THAT SIMPLE, NOW STOP BEING A DUMBASS AND WORK TO BE A BETTER HUMAN.

TO BE ANTI-RACIST YOU MUST UNDERSTAND THE THERE IS ONLY ONE RACE, HUMAN. EVERYTHING ELSE IS BULLSHIT, TO MAKE SOME FEEL INFERIOR OR SUPERIOR. ITS JUST THAT SIMPLE, NOW STOP BEING A DUMBASS AND WORK TO BE A BETTER HUMAN.

TO BE ANTI-RACIST YOU MUST UNDERSTAND THE THERE IS ONLY ONE RACE, HUMAN. EVERYTHING ELSE IS BULLSHIT, TO MAKE SOME FEEL INFERIOR OR SUPERIOR. ITS JUST THAT SIMPLE, NOW STOP BEING A DUMBASS AND WORK TO BE A BETTER HUMAN.

TO BE ANTI-RACIST YOU MUST UNDERSTAND THE THERE IS ONLY ONE RACE, HUMAN. EVERYTHING ELSE IS BULLSHIT, TO MAKE SOME FEEL INFERIOR OR SUPERIOR. ITS JUST THAT SIMPLE, NOW STOP BEING A DUMBASS AND WORK TO BE A BETTER HUMAN.

TO BE ANTI-RACIST YOU MUST UNDERSTAND THE THERE IS ONLY ONE RACE, HUMAN. EVERYTHING ELSE IS BULLSHIT, TO MAKE SOME FEEL INFERIOR OR SUPERIOR. ITS JUST THAT SIMPLE, NOW STOP BEING A DUMBASS AND WORK TO BE A BETTER HUMAN.

TO BE ANTI-RACIST YOU MUST UNDERSTAND THE THERE IS ONLY ONE RACE, HUMAN. EVERYTHING ELSE IS BULLSHIT, TO MAKE SOME FEEL INFERIOR OR SUPERIOR. ITS JUST THAT SIMPLE, NOW STOP BEING A DUMBASS AND WORK TO BE A BETTER HUMAN.

TO BE ANTI-RACIST YOU MUST UNDERSTAND THE THERE IS ONLY ONE RACE, HUMAN. EVERYTHING ELSE IS BULLSHIT, TO MAKE SOME FEEL INFERIOR OR SUPERIOR. ITS JUST THAT SIMPLE, NOW STOP BEING A DUMBASS AND WORK TO BE A BETTER HUMAN.

TO BE ANTI-RACIST YOU MUST UNDERSTAND THE THERE IS ONLY ONE RACE, HUMAN. EVERYTHING ELSE IS BULLSHIT, TO MAKE SOME FEEL INFERIOR OR SUPERIOR. ITS

TO BE ANTI-RACIST YOU MUST UNDERSTAND THE THERE IS ONLY ONE RACE, HUMAN. EVERYTHING ELSE IS BULLSHIT, TO MAKE SOME FEEL INFERIOR OR SUPERIOR. ITS JUST THAT SIMPLE, NOW STOP BEING A DUMBASS AND WORK TO BE A BETTER HUMAN.

TO BE ANTI-RACIST YOU MUST UNDERSTAND THE THERE IS ONLY ONE RACE, HUMAN. EVERYTHING ELSE IS BULLSHIT, TO MAKE SOME FEEL INFERIOR OR SUPERIOR. ITS JUST THAT SIMPLE, NOW STOP BEING A DUMBASS AND WORK TO BE A BETTER HUMAN.

TO BE ANTI-RACIST YOU MUST UNDERSTAND THE THERE IS ONLY ONE RACE, HUMAN. EVERYTHING ELSE IS BULLSHIT, TO MAKE SOME FEEL INFERIOR OR SUPERIOR. ITS JUST THAT SIMPLE, NOW STOP BEING A DUMBASS AND WORK TO BE A BETTER HUMAN.

TO BE ANTI-RACIST YOU MUST UNDERSTAND THE THERE IS ONLY ONE RACE, HUMAN. EVERYTHING ELSE IS BULLSHIT, TO MAKE SOME FEEL INFERIOR OR SUPERIOR. ITS JUST THAT SIMPLE, NOW STOP BEING A DUMBASS AND WORK TO BE A BETTER HUMAN.

TO BE ANTI-RACIST YOU MUST UNDERSTAND THE THERE IS ONLY ONE RACE, HUMAN. EVERYTHING ELSE IS BULLSHIT, TO MAKE SOME FEEL INFERIOR OR SUPERIOR. ITS JUST THAT SIMPLE, NOW STOP BEING A DUMBASS AND WORK TO BE A BETTER HUMAN.

TO BE ANTI-RACIST YOU MUST UNDERSTAND THE THERE IS ONLY ONE RACE, HUMAN. EVERYTHING ELSE IS BULLSHIT, TO MAKE SOME FEEL INFERIOR OR SUPERIOR. ITS JUST THAT SIMPLE, NOW STOP BEING A DUMBASS AND WORK TO BE A BETTER HUMAN.

TO BE ANTI-RACIST YOU MUST UNDERSTAND THE THERE IS ONLY ONE RACE, HUMAN. EVERYTHING ELSE IS BULLSHIT, TO MAKE SOME FEEL INFERIOR OR SUPERIOR. ITS JUST THAT SIMPLE, NOW STOP BEING A DUMBASS AND WORK TO BE A BETTER HUMAN.

TO BE ANTI-RACIST YOU MUST UNDERSTAND THE THERE IS ONLY ONE RACE, HUMAN. EVERYTHING ELSE IS BULLSHIT, TO MAKE SOME FEEL INFERIOR OR SUPERIOR. ITS JUST THAT SIMPLE, NOW STOP BEING A DUMBASS AND WORK TO BE A BETTER HUMAN.

TO BE ANTI-RACIST YOU MUST UNDERSTAND THE THERE IS ONLY ONE RACE, HUMAN. EVERYTHING ELSE IS BULLSHIT, TO MAKE SOME FEEL INFERIOR OR SUPERIOR. ITS JUST THAT SIMPLE, NOW STOP BEING A DUMBASS AND WORK TO BE A BETTER HUMAN.

TO BE ANTI-RACIST YOU MUST UNDERSTAND THE THERE IS ONLY ONE RACE, HUMAN. EVERYTHING ELSE IS BULLSHIT, TO MAKE SOME FEEL INFERIOR OR SUPERIOR. ITS JUST THAT SIMPLE, NOW STOP BEING A DUMBASS AND WORK TO BE A BETTER HUMAN.

JUST THAT SIMPLE, NOW STOP BEING A DUMBASS AND WORK TO BE A BETTER HUMAN.
TO BE ANTI-RACIST YOU MUST UNDERSTAND THE THERE IS ONLY ONE RACE, HUMAN. EVERYTHING ELSE IS BULLSHIT, TO MAKE SOME FEEL INFERIOR OR SUPERIOR. ITS JUST THAT SIMPLE, NOW STOP BEING A DUMBASS AND WORK TO BE A BETTER HUMAN.
TO BE ANTI-RACIST YOU MUST UNDERSTAND THE THERE IS ONLY ONE RACE, HUMAN. EVERYTHING ELSE IS BULLSHIT, TO MAKE SOME FEEL INFERIOR OR SUPERIOR. ITS JUST THAT SIMPLE, NOW STOP BEING A DUMBASS AND WORK TO BE A BETTER HUMAN.
TO BE ANTI-RACIST YOU MUST UNDERSTAND THE THERE IS ONLY ONE RACE, HUMAN. EVERYTHING ELSE IS BULLSHIT, TO MAKE SOME FEEL INFERIOR OR SUPERIOR. ITS JUST THAT SIMPLE, NOW STOP BEING A DUMBASS AND WORK TO BE A BETTER HUMAN.
TO BE ANTI-RACIST YOU MUST UNDERSTAND THE THERE IS ONLY ONE RACE, HUMAN. EVERYTHING ELSE IS BULLSHIT, TO MAKE SOME FEEL INFERIOR OR SUPERIOR. ITS JUST THAT SIMPLE, NOW STOP BEING A DUMBASS AND WORK TO BE A BETTER HUMAN.
TO BE ANTI-RACIST YOU MUST UNDERSTAND THE THERE IS ONLY ONE RACE, HUMAN. EVERYTHING ELSE IS BULLSHIT, TO MAKE SOME FEEL INFERIOR OR SUPERIOR. ITS JUST THAT SIMPLE, NOW STOP BEING A DUMBASS AND WORK TO BE A BETTER HUMAN.
TO BE ANTI-RACIST YOU MUST UNDERSTAND THE THERE IS ONLY ONE RACE, HUMAN. EVERYTHING ELSE IS BULLSHIT, TO MAKE SOME FEEL INFERIOR OR SUPERIOR. ITS JUST THAT SIMPLE, NOW STOP BEING A DUMBASS AND WORK TO BE A BETTER HUMAN.
TO BE ANTI-RACIST YOU MUST UNDERSTAND THE THERE IS ONLY ONE RACE, HUMAN. EVERYTHING ELSE IS BULLSHIT, TO MAKE SOME FEEL INFERIOR OR SUPERIOR. ITS JUST THAT SIMPLE, NOW STOP BEING A DUMBASS AND WORK TO BE A BETTER HUMAN.
TO BE ANTI-RACIST YOU MUST UNDERSTAND THE THERE IS ONLY ONE RACE, HUMAN. EVERYTHING ELSE IS BULLSHIT, TO MAKE SOME FEEL INFERIOR OR SUPERIOR. ITS JUST THAT SIMPLE, NOW STOP BEING A DUMBASS AND WORK TO BE A BETTER HUMAN.
TO BE ANTI-RACIST YOU MUST UNDERSTAND THE THERE IS ONLY ONE RACE, HUMAN. EVERYTHING ELSE IS BULLSHIT, TO MAKE SOME FEEL INFERIOR OR SUPERIOR. ITS JUST THAT SIMPLE, NOW STOP BEING A DUMBASS AND WORK TO BE A BETTER HUMAN.
TO BE ANTI-RACIST YOU MUST UNDERSTAND THE THERE IS ONLY ONE RACE, HUMAN. EVERYTHING ELSE IS BULLSHIT, TO MAKE SOME FEEL INFERIOR OR SUPERIOR. ITS JUST THAT SIMPLE, NOW STOP BEING A DUMBASS AND WORK TO BE A BETTER HUMAN.
TO BE ANTI-RACIST YOU MUST UNDERSTAND THE THERE IS ONLY ONE RACE, HUMAN. EVERYTHING ELSE IS BULLSHIT, TO MAKE SOME FEEL INFERIOR OR SUPERIOR. ITS

TO BE ANTI-RACIST YOU MUST UNDERSTAND THE THERE IS ONLY ONE RACE, HUMAN. EVERYTHING ELSE IS BULLSHIT, TO MAKE SOME FEEL INFERIOR OR SUPERIOR. ITS JUST THAT SIMPLE, NOW STOP BEING A DUMBASS AND WORK TO BE A BETTER HUMAN.

TO BE ANTI-RACIST YOU MUST UNDERSTAND THE THERE IS ONLY ONE RACE, HUMAN. EVERYTHING ELSE IS BULLSHIT, TO MAKE SOME FEEL INFERIOR OR SUPERIOR. ITS JUST THAT SIMPLE, NOW STOP BEING A DUMBASS AND WORK TO BE A BETTER HUMAN.

TO BE ANTI-RACIST YOU MUST UNDERSTAND THE THERE IS ONLY ONE RACE, HUMAN. EVERYTHING ELSE IS BULLSHIT, TO MAKE SOME FEEL INFERIOR OR SUPERIOR. ITS JUST THAT SIMPLE, NOW STOP BEING A DUMBASS AND WORK TO BE A BETTER HUMAN.

TO BE ANTI-RACIST YOU MUST UNDERSTAND THE THERE IS ONLY ONE RACE, HUMAN. EVERYTHING ELSE IS BULLSHIT, TO MAKE SOME FEEL INFERIOR OR SUPERIOR. ITS JUST THAT SIMPLE, NOW STOP BEING A DUMBASS AND WORK TO BE A BETTER HUMAN.

TO BE ANTI-RACIST YOU MUST UNDERSTAND THE THERE IS ONLY ONE RACE, HUMAN. EVERYTHING ELSE IS BULLSHIT, TO MAKE SOME FEEL INFERIOR OR SUPERIOR. ITS JUST THAT SIMPLE, NOW STOP BEING A DUMBASS AND WORK TO BE A BETTER HUMAN.

TO BE ANTI-RACIST YOU MUST UNDERSTAND THE THERE IS ONLY ONE RACE, HUMAN. EVERYTHING ELSE IS BULLSHIT, TO MAKE SOME FEEL INFERIOR OR SUPERIOR. ITS JUST THAT SIMPLE, NOW STOP BEING A DUMBASS AND WORK TO BE A BETTER HUMAN.

TO BE ANTI-RACIST YOU MUST UNDERSTAND THE THERE IS ONLY ONE RACE, HUMAN. EVERYTHING ELSE IS BULLSHIT, TO MAKE SOME FEEL INFERIOR OR SUPERIOR. ITS JUST THAT SIMPLE, NOW STOP BEING A DUMBASS AND WORK TO BE A BETTER HUMAN.

TO BE ANTI-RACIST YOU MUST UNDERSTAND THE THERE IS ONLY ONE RACE, HUMAN. EVERYTHING ELSE IS BULLSHIT, TO MAKE SOME FEEL INFERIOR OR SUPERIOR. ITS JUST THAT SIMPLE, NOW STOP BEING A DUMBASS AND WORK TO BE A BETTER HUMAN.

TO BE ANTI-RACIST YOU MUST UNDERSTAND THE THERE IS ONLY ONE RACE, HUMAN. EVERYTHING ELSE IS BULLSHIT, TO MAKE SOME FEEL INFERIOR OR SUPERIOR. ITS JUST THAT SIMPLE, NOW STOP BEING A DUMBASS AND WORK TO BE A BETTER HUMAN.

TO BE ANTI-RACIST YOU MUST UNDERSTAND THE THERE IS ONLY ONE RACE, HUMAN. EVERYTHING ELSE IS BULLSHIT, TO MAKE SOME FEEL INFERIOR OR SUPERIOR. ITS JUST THAT SIMPLE, NOW STOP BEING A DUMBASS AND WORK TO BE A BETTER HUMAN.

TO BE ANTI-RACIST YOU MUST UNDERSTAND THE THERE IS ONLY ONE RACE, HUMAN. EVERYTHING ELSE IS BULLSHIT, TO MAKE SOME FEEL INFERIOR OR SUPERIOR. ITS JUST THAT SIMPLE, NOW STOP BEING A DUMBASS AND WORK TO BE A BETTER HUMAN.

JUST THAT SIMPLE, NOW STOP BEING A DUMBASS AND WORK TO BE A BETTER
HUMAN.

TO BE ANTI-RACIST YOU MUST UNDERSTAND THE THERE IS ONLY ONE RACE, HUMAN.
EVERYTHING ELSE IS BULLSHIT, TO MAKE SOME FEEL INFERIOR OR SUPERIOR. ITS
JUST THAT SIMPLE, NOW STOP BEING A DUMBASS AND WORK TO BE A BETTER
HUMAN.

TO BE ANTI-RACIST YOU MUST UNDERSTAND THE THERE IS ONLY ONE RACE, HUMAN.
EVERYTHING ELSE IS BULLSHIT, TO MAKE SOME FEEL INFERIOR OR SUPERIOR. ITS
JUST THAT SIMPLE, NOW STOP BEING A DUMBASS AND WORK TO BE A BETTER
HUMAN.

TO BE ANTI-RACIST YOU MUST UNDERSTAND THE THERE IS ONLY ONE RACE, HUMAN.
EVERYTHING ELSE IS BULLSHIT, TO MAKE SOME FEEL INFERIOR OR SUPERIOR. ITS
JUST THAT SIMPLE, NOW STOP BEING A DUMBASS AND WORK TO BE A BETTER
HUMAN.

TO BE ANTI-RACIST YOU MUST UNDERSTAND THE THERE IS ONLY ONE RACE, HUMAN.
EVERYTHING ELSE IS BULLSHIT, TO MAKE SOME FEEL INFERIOR OR SUPERIOR. ITS
JUST THAT SIMPLE, NOW STOP BEING A DUMBASS AND WORK TO BE A BETTER
HUMAN.

TO BE ANTI-RACIST YOU MUST UNDERSTAND THE THERE IS ONLY ONE RACE, HUMAN.
EVERYTHING ELSE IS BULLSHIT, TO MAKE SOME FEEL INFERIOR OR SUPERIOR. ITS
JUST THAT SIMPLE, NOW STOP BEING A DUMBASS AND WORK TO BE A BETTER
HUMAN.

TO BE ANTI-RACIST YOU MUST UNDERSTAND THE THERE IS ONLY ONE RACE, HUMAN.
EVERYTHING ELSE IS BULLSHIT, TO MAKE SOME FEEL INFERIOR OR SUPERIOR. ITS
JUST THAT SIMPLE, NOW STOP BEING A DUMBASS AND WORK TO BE A BETTER
HUMAN.

TO BE ANTI-RACIST YOU MUST UNDERSTAND THE THERE IS ONLY ONE RACE, HUMAN.
EVERYTHING ELSE IS BULLSHIT, TO MAKE SOME FEEL INFERIOR OR SUPERIOR. ITS
JUST THAT SIMPLE, NOW STOP BEING A DUMBASS AND WORK TO BE A BETTER
HUMAN.

TO BE ANTI-RACIST YOU MUST UNDERSTAND THE THERE IS ONLY ONE RACE, HUMAN.
EVERYTHING ELSE IS BULLSHIT, TO MAKE SOME FEEL INFERIOR OR SUPERIOR. ITS
JUST THAT SIMPLE, NOW STOP BEING A DUMBASS AND WORK TO BE A BETTER
HUMAN.

TO BE ANTI-RACIST YOU MUST UNDERSTAND THE THERE IS ONLY ONE RACE, HUMAN.
EVERYTHING ELSE IS BULLSHIT, TO MAKE SOME FEEL INFERIOR OR SUPERIOR. ITS
JUST THAT SIMPLE, NOW STOP BEING A DUMBASS AND WORK TO BE A BETTER
HUMAN.

TO BE ANTI-RACIST YOU MUST UNDERSTAND THE THERE IS ONLY ONE RACE, HUMAN.
EVERYTHING ELSE IS BULLSHIT, TO MAKE SOME FEEL INFERIOR OR SUPERIOR. ITS

TO BE ANTI-RACIST YOU MUST UNDERSTAND THE THERE IS ONLY ONE RACE, HUMAN. EVERYTHING ELSE IS BULLSHIT, TO MAKE SOME FEEL INFERIOR OR SUPERIOR. ITS JUST THAT SIMPLE, NOW STOP BEING A DUMBASS AND WORK TO BE A BETTER HUMAN.

TO BE ANTI-RACIST YOU MUST UNDERSTAND THE THERE IS ONLY ONE RACE, HUMAN. EVERYTHING ELSE IS BULLSHIT, TO MAKE SOME FEEL INFERIOR OR SUPERIOR. ITS JUST THAT SIMPLE, NOW STOP BEING A DUMBASS AND WORK TO BE A BETTER HUMAN.

TO BE ANTI-RACIST YOU MUST UNDERSTAND THE THERE IS ONLY ONE RACE, HUMAN. EVERYTHING ELSE IS BULLSHIT, TO MAKE SOME FEEL INFERIOR OR SUPERIOR. ITS JUST THAT SIMPLE, NOW STOP BEING A DUMBASS AND WORK TO BE A BETTER HUMAN.

TO BE ANTI-RACIST YOU MUST UNDERSTAND THE THERE IS ONLY ONE RACE, HUMAN. EVERYTHING ELSE IS BULLSHIT, TO MAKE SOME FEEL INFERIOR OR SUPERIOR. ITS JUST THAT SIMPLE, NOW STOP BEING A DUMBASS AND WORK TO BE A BETTER HUMAN.

TO BE ANTI-RACIST YOU MUST UNDERSTAND THE THERE IS ONLY ONE RACE, HUMAN. EVERYTHING ELSE IS BULLSHIT, TO MAKE SOME FEEL INFERIOR OR SUPERIOR. ITS JUST THAT SIMPLE, NOW STOP BEING A DUMBASS AND WORK TO BE A BETTER HUMAN.

TO BE ANTI-RACIST YOU MUST UNDERSTAND THE THERE IS ONLY ONE RACE, HUMAN. EVERYTHING ELSE IS BULLSHIT, TO MAKE SOME FEEL INFERIOR OR SUPERIOR. ITS JUST THAT SIMPLE, NOW STOP BEING A DUMBASS AND WORK TO BE A BETTER HUMAN.

TO BE ANTI-RACIST YOU MUST UNDERSTAND THE THERE IS ONLY ONE RACE, HUMAN. EVERYTHING ELSE IS BULLSHIT, TO MAKE SOME FEEL INFERIOR OR SUPERIOR. ITS JUST THAT SIMPLE, NOW STOP BEING A DUMBASS AND WORK TO BE A BETTER HUMAN.

TO BE ANTI-RACIST YOU MUST UNDERSTAND THE THERE IS ONLY ONE RACE, HUMAN. EVERYTHING ELSE IS BULLSHIT, TO MAKE SOME FEEL INFERIOR OR SUPERIOR. ITS JUST THAT SIMPLE, NOW STOP BEING A DUMBASS AND WORK TO BE A BETTER HUMAN.

TO BE ANTI-RACIST YOU MUST UNDERSTAND THE THERE IS ONLY ONE RACE, HUMAN. EVERYTHING ELSE IS BULLSHIT, TO MAKE SOME FEEL INFERIOR OR SUPERIOR. ITS JUST THAT SIMPLE, NOW STOP BEING A DUMBASS AND WORK TO BE A BETTER HUMAN.

TO BE ANTI-RACIST YOU MUST UNDERSTAND THE THERE IS ONLY ONE RACE, HUMAN. EVERYTHING ELSE IS BULLSHIT, TO MAKE SOME FEEL INFERIOR OR SUPERIOR. ITS JUST THAT SIMPLE, NOW STOP BEING A DUMBASS AND WORK TO BE A BETTER HUMAN.

JUST THAT SIMPLE, NOW STOP BEING A DUMBASS AND WORK TO BE A BETTER
HUMAN.
TO BE ANTI-RACIST YOU MUST UNDERSTAND THE THERE IS ONLY ONE RACE, HUMAN.
EVERYTHING ELSE IS BULLSHIT, TO MAKE SOME FEEL INFERIOR OR SUPERIOR. ITS
JUST THAT SIMPLE, NOW STOP BEING A DUMBASS AND WORK TO BE A BETTER
HUMAN.
TO BE ANTI-RACIST YOU MUST UNDERSTAND THE THERE IS ONLY ONE RACE, HUMAN.
EVERYTHING ELSE IS BULLSHIT, TO MAKE SOME FEEL INFERIOR OR SUPERIOR. ITS
JUST THAT SIMPLE, NOW STOP BEING A DUMBASS AND WORK TO BE A BETTER
HUMAN.
TO BE ANTI-RACIST YOU MUST UNDERSTAND THE THERE IS ONLY ONE RACE, HUMAN.
EVERYTHING ELSE IS BULLSHIT, TO MAKE SOME FEEL INFERIOR OR SUPERIOR. ITS
JUST THAT SIMPLE, NOW STOP BEING A DUMBASS AND WORK TO BE A BETTER
HUMAN.
TO BE ANTI-RACIST YOU MUST UNDERSTAND THE THERE IS ONLY ONE RACE, HUMAN.
EVERYTHING ELSE IS BULLSHIT, TO MAKE SOME FEEL INFERIOR OR SUPERIOR. ITS
JUST THAT SIMPLE, NOW STOP BEING A DUMBASS AND WORK TO BE A BETTER
HUMAN.
TO BE ANTI-RACIST YOU MUST UNDERSTAND THE THERE IS ONLY ONE RACE, HUMAN.
EVERYTHING ELSE IS BULLSHIT, TO MAKE SOME FEEL INFERIOR OR SUPERIOR. ITS
JUST THAT SIMPLE, NOW STOP BEING A DUMBASS AND WORK TO BE A BETTER
HUMAN.
TO BE ANTI-RACIST YOU MUST UNDERSTAND THE THERE IS ONLY ONE RACE, HUMAN.
EVERYTHING ELSE IS BULLSHIT, TO MAKE SOME FEEL INFERIOR OR SUPERIOR. ITS
JUST THAT SIMPLE, NOW STOP BEING A DUMBASS AND WORK TO BE A BETTER
HUMAN.
TO BE ANTI-RACIST YOU MUST UNDERSTAND THE THERE IS ONLY ONE RACE, HUMAN.
EVERYTHING ELSE IS BULLSHIT, TO MAKE SOME FEEL INFERIOR OR SUPERIOR. ITS
JUST THAT SIMPLE, NOW STOP BEING A DUMBASS AND WORK TO BE A BETTER
HUMAN.
TO BE ANTI-RACIST YOU MUST UNDERSTAND THE THERE IS ONLY ONE RACE, HUMAN.
EVERYTHING ELSE IS BULLSHIT, TO MAKE SOME FEEL INFERIOR OR SUPERIOR. ITS
JUST THAT SIMPLE, NOW STOP BEING A DUMBASS AND WORK TO BE A BETTER
HUMAN.
TO BE ANTI-RACIST YOU MUST UNDERSTAND THE THERE IS ONLY ONE RACE, HUMAN.
EVERYTHING ELSE IS BULLSHIT, TO MAKE SOME FEEL INFERIOR OR SUPERIOR. ITS
JUST THAT SIMPLE, NOW STOP BEING A DUMBASS AND WORK TO BE A BETTER
HUMAN.
TO BE ANTI-RACIST YOU MUST UNDERSTAND THE THERE IS ONLY ONE RACE, HUMAN.
EVERYTHING ELSE IS BULLSHIT, TO MAKE SOME FEEL INFERIOR OR SUPERIOR. ITS

TO BE ANTI-RACIST YOU MUST UNDERSTAND THE THERE IS ONLY ONE RACE, HUMAN. EVERYTHING ELSE IS BULLSHIT, TO MAKE SOME FEEL INFERIOR OR SUPERIOR. ITS JUST THAT SIMPLE, NOW STOP BEING A DUMBASS AND WORK TO BE A BETTER HUMAN.

TO BE ANTI-RACIST YOU MUST UNDERSTAND THE THERE IS ONLY ONE RACE, HUMAN. EVERYTHING ELSE IS BULLSHIT, TO MAKE SOME FEEL INFERIOR OR SUPERIOR. ITS JUST THAT SIMPLE, NOW STOP BEING A DUMBASS AND WORK TO BE A BETTER HUMAN.

TO BE ANTI-RACIST YOU MUST UNDERSTAND THE THERE IS ONLY ONE RACE, HUMAN. EVERYTHING ELSE IS BULLSHIT, TO MAKE SOME FEEL INFERIOR OR SUPERIOR. ITS JUST THAT SIMPLE, NOW STOP BEING A DUMBASS AND WORK TO BE A BETTER HUMAN.

TO BE ANTI-RACIST YOU MUST UNDERSTAND THE THERE IS ONLY ONE RACE, HUMAN. EVERYTHING ELSE IS BULLSHIT, TO MAKE SOME FEEL INFERIOR OR SUPERIOR. ITS JUST THAT SIMPLE, NOW STOP BEING A DUMBASS AND WORK TO BE A BETTER HUMAN.

TO BE ANTI-RACIST YOU MUST UNDERSTAND THE THERE IS ONLY ONE RACE, HUMAN. EVERYTHING ELSE IS BULLSHIT, TO MAKE SOME FEEL INFERIOR OR SUPERIOR. ITS JUST THAT SIMPLE, NOW STOP BEING A DUMBASS AND WORK TO BE A BETTER HUMAN.

TO BE ANTI-RACIST YOU MUST UNDERSTAND THE THERE IS ONLY ONE RACE, HUMAN. EVERYTHING ELSE IS BULLSHIT, TO MAKE SOME FEEL INFERIOR OR SUPERIOR. ITS JUST THAT SIMPLE, NOW STOP BEING A DUMBASS AND WORK TO BE A BETTER HUMAN.

TO BE ANTI-RACIST YOU MUST UNDERSTAND THE THERE IS ONLY ONE RACE, HUMAN. EVERYTHING ELSE IS BULLSHIT, TO MAKE SOME FEEL INFERIOR OR SUPERIOR. ITS JUST THAT SIMPLE, NOW STOP BEING A DUMBASS AND WORK TO BE A BETTER HUMAN.

TO BE ANTI-RACIST YOU MUST UNDERSTAND THE THERE IS ONLY ONE RACE, HUMAN. EVERYTHING ELSE IS BULLSHIT, TO MAKE SOME FEEL INFERIOR OR SUPERIOR. ITS JUST THAT SIMPLE, NOW STOP BEING A DUMBASS AND WORK TO BE A BETTER HUMAN.

TO BE ANTI-RACIST YOU MUST UNDERSTAND THE THERE IS ONLY ONE RACE, HUMAN. EVERYTHING ELSE IS BULLSHIT, TO MAKE SOME FEEL INFERIOR OR SUPERIOR. ITS JUST THAT SIMPLE, NOW STOP BEING A DUMBASS AND WORK TO BE A BETTER HUMAN.

TO BE ANTI-RACIST YOU MUST UNDERSTAND THE THERE IS ONLY ONE RACE, HUMAN. EVERYTHING ELSE IS BULLSHIT, TO MAKE SOME FEEL INFERIOR OR SUPERIOR. ITS JUST THAT SIMPLE, NOW STOP BEING A DUMBASS AND WORK TO BE A BETTER HUMAN.

TO BE ANTI-RACIST YOU MUST UNDERSTAND THE THERE IS ONLY ONE RACE, HUMAN. EVERYTHING ELSE IS BULLSHIT, TO MAKE SOME FEEL INFERIOR OR SUPERIOR. ITS JUST THAT SIMPLE, NOW STOP BEING A DUMBASS AND WORK TO BE A BETTER HUMAN.

JUST THAT SIMPLE, NOW STOP BEING A DUMBASS AND WORK TO BE A BETTER HUMAN.

TO BE ANTI-RACIST YOU MUST UNDERSTAND THE THERE IS ONLY ONE RACE, HUMAN. EVERYTHING ELSE IS BULLSHIT, TO MAKE SOME FEEL INFERIOR OR SUPERIOR. ITS JUST THAT SIMPLE, NOW STOP BEING A DUMBASS AND WORK TO BE A BETTER HUMAN.

TO BE ANTI-RACIST YOU MUST UNDERSTAND THE THERE IS ONLY ONE RACE, HUMAN. EVERYTHING ELSE IS BULLSHIT, TO MAKE SOME FEEL INFERIOR OR SUPERIOR. ITS JUST THAT SIMPLE, NOW STOP BEING A DUMBASS AND WORK TO BE A BETTER HUMAN.

TO BE ANTI-RACIST YOU MUST UNDERSTAND THE THERE IS ONLY ONE RACE, HUMAN. EVERYTHING ELSE IS BULLSHIT, TO MAKE SOME FEEL INFERIOR OR SUPERIOR. ITS JUST THAT SIMPLE, NOW STOP BEING A DUMBASS AND WORK TO BE A BETTER HUMAN.

TO BE ANTI-RACIST YOU MUST UNDERSTAND THE THERE IS ONLY ONE RACE, HUMAN. EVERYTHING ELSE IS BULLSHIT, TO MAKE SOME FEEL INFERIOR OR SUPERIOR. ITS JUST THAT SIMPLE, NOW STOP BEING A DUMBASS AND WORK TO BE A BETTER HUMAN.

TO BE ANTI-RACIST YOU MUST UNDERSTAND THE THERE IS ONLY ONE RACE, HUMAN. EVERYTHING ELSE IS BULLSHIT, TO MAKE SOME FEEL INFERIOR OR SUPERIOR. ITS JUST THAT SIMPLE, NOW STOP BEING A DUMBASS AND WORK TO BE A BETTER HUMAN.

TO BE ANTI-RACIST YOU MUST UNDERSTAND THE THERE IS ONLY ONE RACE, HUMAN. EVERYTHING ELSE IS BULLSHIT, TO MAKE SOME FEEL INFERIOR OR SUPERIOR. ITS JUST THAT SIMPLE, NOW STOP BEING A DUMBASS AND WORK TO BE A BETTER HUMAN.

TO BE ANTI-RACIST YOU MUST UNDERSTAND THE THERE IS ONLY ONE RACE, HUMAN. EVERYTHING ELSE IS BULLSHIT, TO MAKE SOME FEEL INFERIOR OR SUPERIOR. ITS JUST THAT SIMPLE, NOW STOP BEING A DUMBASS AND WORK TO BE A BETTER HUMAN.

TO BE ANTI-RACIST YOU MUST UNDERSTAND THE THERE IS ONLY ONE RACE, HUMAN. EVERYTHING ELSE IS BULLSHIT, TO MAKE SOME FEEL INFERIOR OR SUPERIOR. ITS JUST THAT SIMPLE, NOW STOP BEING A DUMBASS AND WORK TO BE A BETTER HUMAN.

TO BE ANTI-RACIST YOU MUST UNDERSTAND THE THERE IS ONLY ONE RACE, HUMAN. EVERYTHING ELSE IS BULLSHIT, TO MAKE SOME FEEL INFERIOR OR SUPERIOR. ITS JUST THAT SIMPLE, NOW STOP BEING A DUMBASS AND WORK TO BE A BETTER HUMAN.

TO BE ANTI-RACIST YOU MUST UNDERSTAND THE THERE IS ONLY ONE RACE, HUMAN. EVERYTHING ELSE IS BULLSHIT, TO MAKE SOME FEEL INFERIOR OR SUPERIOR. ITS

TO BE ANTI-RACIST YOU MUST UNDERSTAND THE THERE IS ONLY ONE RACE, HUMAN. EVERYTHING ELSE IS BULLSHIT, TO MAKE SOME FEEL INFERIOR OR SUPERIOR. ITS JUST THAT SIMPLE, NOW STOP BEING A DUMBASS AND WORK TO BE A BETTER HUMAN.

TO BE ANTI-RACIST YOU MUST UNDERSTAND THE THERE IS ONLY ONE RACE, HUMAN. EVERYTHING ELSE IS BULLSHIT, TO MAKE SOME FEEL INFERIOR OR SUPERIOR. ITS JUST THAT SIMPLE, NOW STOP BEING A DUMBASS AND WORK TO BE A BETTER HUMAN.

TO BE ANTI-RACIST YOU MUST UNDERSTAND THE THERE IS ONLY ONE RACE, HUMAN. EVERYTHING ELSE IS BULLSHIT, TO MAKE SOME FEEL INFERIOR OR SUPERIOR. ITS JUST THAT SIMPLE, NOW STOP BEING A DUMBASS AND WORK TO BE A BETTER HUMAN.

TO BE ANTI-RACIST YOU MUST UNDERSTAND THE THERE IS ONLY ONE RACE, HUMAN. EVERYTHING ELSE IS BULLSHIT, TO MAKE SOME FEEL INFERIOR OR SUPERIOR. ITS JUST THAT SIMPLE, NOW STOP BEING A DUMBASS AND WORK TO BE A BETTER HUMAN.

TO BE ANTI-RACIST YOU MUST UNDERSTAND THE THERE IS ONLY ONE RACE, HUMAN. EVERYTHING ELSE IS BULLSHIT, TO MAKE SOME FEEL INFERIOR OR SUPERIOR. ITS JUST THAT SIMPLE, NOW STOP BEING A DUMBASS AND WORK TO BE A BETTER HUMAN.

TO BE ANTI-RACIST YOU MUST UNDERSTAND THE THERE IS ONLY ONE RACE, HUMAN. EVERYTHING ELSE IS BULLSHIT, TO MAKE SOME FEEL INFERIOR OR SUPERIOR. ITS JUST THAT SIMPLE, NOW STOP BEING A DUMBASS AND WORK TO BE A BETTER HUMAN.

TO BE ANTI-RACIST YOU MUST UNDERSTAND THE THERE IS ONLY ONE RACE, HUMAN. EVERYTHING ELSE IS BULLSHIT, TO MAKE SOME FEEL INFERIOR OR SUPERIOR. ITS JUST THAT SIMPLE, NOW STOP BEING A DUMBASS AND WORK TO BE A BETTER HUMAN.

TO BE ANTI-RACIST YOU MUST UNDERSTAND THE THERE IS ONLY ONE RACE, HUMAN. EVERYTHING ELSE IS BULLSHIT, TO MAKE SOME FEEL INFERIOR OR SUPERIOR. ITS JUST THAT SIMPLE, NOW STOP BEING A DUMBASS AND WORK TO BE A BETTER HUMAN.

TO BE ANTI-RACIST YOU MUST UNDERSTAND THE THERE IS ONLY ONE RACE, HUMAN. EVERYTHING ELSE IS BULLSHIT, TO MAKE SOME FEEL INFERIOR OR SUPERIOR. ITS JUST THAT SIMPLE, NOW STOP BEING A DUMBASS AND WORK TO BE A BETTER HUMAN.

TO BE ANTI-RACIST YOU MUST UNDERSTAND THE THERE IS ONLY ONE RACE, HUMAN. EVERYTHING ELSE IS BULLSHIT, TO MAKE SOME FEEL INFERIOR OR SUPERIOR. ITS JUST THAT SIMPLE, NOW STOP BEING A DUMBASS AND WORK TO BE A BETTER HUMAN.

JUST THAT SIMPLE, NOW STOP BEING A DUMBASS AND WORK TO BE A BETTER
HUMAN.
TO BE ANTI-RACIST YOU MUST UNDERSTAND THE THERE IS ONLY ONE RACE, HUMAN.
EVERYTHING ELSE IS BULLSHIT, TO MAKE SOME FEEL INFERIOR OR SUPERIOR. ITS
JUST THAT SIMPLE, NOW STOP BEING A DUMBASS AND WORK TO BE A BETTER
HUMAN.
TO BE ANTI-RACIST YOU MUST UNDERSTAND THE THERE IS ONLY ONE RACE, HUMAN.
EVERYTHING ELSE IS BULLSHIT, TO MAKE SOME FEEL INFERIOR OR SUPERIOR. ITS
JUST THAT SIMPLE, NOW STOP BEING A DUMBASS AND WORK TO BE A BETTER
HUMAN.
TO BE ANTI-RACIST YOU MUST UNDERSTAND THE THERE IS ONLY ONE RACE, HUMAN.
EVERYTHING ELSE IS BULLSHIT, TO MAKE SOME FEEL INFERIOR OR SUPERIOR. ITS
JUST THAT SIMPLE, NOW STOP BEING A DUMBASS AND WORK TO BE A BETTER
HUMAN.
TO BE ANTI-RACIST YOU MUST UNDERSTAND THE THERE IS ONLY ONE RACE, HUMAN.
EVERYTHING ELSE IS BULLSHIT, TO MAKE SOME FEEL INFERIOR OR SUPERIOR. ITS
JUST THAT SIMPLE, NOW STOP BEING A DUMBASS AND WORK TO BE A BETTER
HUMAN.
TO BE ANTI-RACIST YOU MUST UNDERSTAND THE THERE IS ONLY ONE RACE, HUMAN.
EVERYTHING ELSE IS BULLSHIT, TO MAKE SOME FEEL INFERIOR OR SUPERIOR. ITS
JUST THAT SIMPLE, NOW STOP BEING A DUMBASS AND WORK TO BE A BETTER
HUMAN.
TO BE ANTI-RACIST YOU MUST UNDERSTAND THE THERE IS ONLY ONE RACE, HUMAN.
EVERYTHING ELSE IS BULLSHIT, TO MAKE SOME FEEL INFERIOR OR SUPERIOR. ITS
JUST THAT SIMPLE, NOW STOP BEING A DUMBASS AND WORK TO BE A BETTER
HUMAN.
TO BE ANTI-RACIST YOU MUST UNDERSTAND THE THERE IS ONLY ONE RACE, HUMAN.
EVERYTHING ELSE IS BULLSHIT, TO MAKE SOME FEEL INFERIOR OR SUPERIOR. ITS
JUST THAT SIMPLE, NOW STOP BEING A DUMBASS AND WORK TO BE A BETTER
HUMAN.
TO BE ANTI-RACIST YOU MUST UNDERSTAND THE THERE IS ONLY ONE RACE, HUMAN.
EVERYTHING ELSE IS BULLSHIT, TO MAKE SOME FEEL INFERIOR OR SUPERIOR. ITS
JUST THAT SIMPLE, NOW STOP BEING A DUMBASS AND WORK TO BE A BETTER
HUMAN.
TO BE ANTI-RACIST YOU MUST UNDERSTAND THE THERE IS ONLY ONE RACE, HUMAN.
EVERYTHING ELSE IS BULLSHIT, TO MAKE SOME FEEL INFERIOR OR SUPERIOR. ITS
JUST THAT SIMPLE, NOW STOP BEING A DUMBASS AND WORK TO BE A BETTER
HUMAN.
TO BE ANTI-RACIST YOU MUST UNDERSTAND THE THERE IS ONLY ONE RACE, HUMAN.
EVERYTHING ELSE IS BULLSHIT, TO MAKE SOME FEEL INFERIOR OR SUPERIOR. ITS

TO BE ANTI-RACIST YOU MUST UNDERSTAND THE THERE IS ONLY ONE RACE, HUMAN. EVERYTHING ELSE IS BULLSHIT, TO MAKE SOME FEEL INFERIOR OR SUPERIOR. ITS JUST THAT SIMPLE, NOW STOP BEING A DUMBASS AND WORK TO BE A BETTER HUMAN.

TO BE ANTI-RACIST YOU MUST UNDERSTAND THE THERE IS ONLY ONE RACE, HUMAN. EVERYTHING ELSE IS BULLSHIT, TO MAKE SOME FEEL INFERIOR OR SUPERIOR. ITS JUST THAT SIMPLE, NOW STOP BEING A DUMBASS AND WORK TO BE A BETTER HUMAN.

TO BE ANTI-RACIST YOU MUST UNDERSTAND THE THERE IS ONLY ONE RACE, HUMAN. EVERYTHING ELSE IS BULLSHIT, TO MAKE SOME FEEL INFERIOR OR SUPERIOR. ITS JUST THAT SIMPLE, NOW STOP BEING A DUMBASS AND WORK TO BE A BETTER HUMAN.

TO BE ANTI-RACIST YOU MUST UNDERSTAND THE THERE IS ONLY ONE RACE, HUMAN. EVERYTHING ELSE IS BULLSHIT, TO MAKE SOME FEEL INFERIOR OR SUPERIOR. ITS JUST THAT SIMPLE, NOW STOP BEING A DUMBASS AND WORK TO BE A BETTER HUMAN.

TO BE ANTI-RACIST YOU MUST UNDERSTAND THE THERE IS ONLY ONE RACE, HUMAN. EVERYTHING ELSE IS BULLSHIT, TO MAKE SOME FEEL INFERIOR OR SUPERIOR. ITS JUST THAT SIMPLE, NOW STOP BEING A DUMBASS AND WORK TO BE A BETTER HUMAN.

TO BE ANTI-RACIST YOU MUST UNDERSTAND THE THERE IS ONLY ONE RACE, HUMAN. EVERYTHING ELSE IS BULLSHIT, TO MAKE SOME FEEL INFERIOR OR SUPERIOR. ITS JUST THAT SIMPLE, NOW STOP BEING A DUMBASS AND WORK TO BE A BETTER HUMAN.

TO BE ANTI-RACIST YOU MUST UNDERSTAND THE THERE IS ONLY ONE RACE, HUMAN. EVERYTHING ELSE IS BULLSHIT, TO MAKE SOME FEEL INFERIOR OR SUPERIOR. ITS JUST THAT SIMPLE, NOW STOP BEING A DUMBASS AND WORK TO BE A BETTER HUMAN.

TO BE ANTI-RACIST YOU MUST UNDERSTAND THE THERE IS ONLY ONE RACE, HUMAN. EVERYTHING ELSE IS BULLSHIT, TO MAKE SOME FEEL INFERIOR OR SUPERIOR. ITS JUST THAT SIMPLE, NOW STOP BEING A DUMBASS AND WORK TO BE A BETTER HUMAN.

TO BE ANTI-RACIST YOU MUST UNDERSTAND THE THERE IS ONLY ONE RACE, HUMAN. EVERYTHING ELSE IS BULLSHIT, TO MAKE SOME FEEL INFERIOR OR SUPERIOR. ITS JUST THAT SIMPLE, NOW STOP BEING A DUMBASS AND WORK TO BE A BETTER HUMAN.

TO BE ANTI-RACIST YOU MUST UNDERSTAND THE THERE IS ONLY ONE RACE, HUMAN. EVERYTHING ELSE IS BULLSHIT, TO MAKE SOME FEEL INFERIOR OR SUPERIOR. ITS JUST THAT SIMPLE, NOW STOP BEING A DUMBASS AND WORK TO BE A BETTER HUMAN.

TO BE ANTI-RACIST YOU MUST UNDERSTAND THE THERE IS ONLY ONE RACE, HUMAN. EVERYTHING ELSE IS BULLSHIT, TO MAKE SOME FEEL INFERIOR OR SUPERIOR. ITS JUST THAT SIMPLE, NOW STOP BEING A DUMBASS AND WORK TO BE A BETTER HUMAN

JUST THAT SIMPLE, NOW STOP BEING A DUMBASS AND WORK TO BE A BETTER HUMAN.

TO BE ANTI-RACIST YOU MUST UNDERSTAND THE THERE IS ONLY ONE RACE, HUMAN. EVERYTHING ELSE IS BULLSHIT, TO MAKE SOME FEEL INFERIOR OR SUPERIOR. ITS JUST THAT SIMPLE, NOW STOP BEING A DUMBASS AND WORK TO BE A BETTER HUMAN.

TO BE ANTI-RACIST YOU MUST UNDERSTAND THE THERE IS ONLY ONE RACE, HUMAN. EVERYTHING ELSE IS BULLSHIT, TO MAKE SOME FEEL INFERIOR OR SUPERIOR. ITS JUST THAT SIMPLE, NOW STOP BEING A DUMBASS AND WORK TO BE A BETTER HUMAN.

TO BE ANTI-RACIST YOU MUST UNDERSTAND THE THERE IS ONLY ONE RACE, HUMAN. EVERYTHING ELSE IS BULLSHIT, TO MAKE SOME FEEL INFERIOR OR SUPERIOR. ITS JUST THAT SIMPLE, NOW STOP BEING A DUMBASS AND WORK TO BE A BETTER HUMAN.

TO BE ANTI-RACIST YOU MUST UNDERSTAND THE THERE IS ONLY ONE RACE, HUMAN. EVERYTHING ELSE IS BULLSHIT, TO MAKE SOME FEEL INFERIOR OR SUPERIOR. ITS JUST THAT SIMPLE, NOW STOP BEING A DUMBASS AND WORK TO BE A BETTER HUMAN.

TO BE ANTI-RACIST YOU MUST UNDERSTAND THE THERE IS ONLY ONE RACE, HUMAN. EVERYTHING ELSE IS BULLSHIT, TO MAKE SOME FEEL INFERIOR OR SUPERIOR. ITS JUST THAT SIMPLE, NOW STOP BEING A DUMBASS AND WORK TO BE A BETTER HUMAN.

TO BE ANTI-RACIST YOU MUST UNDERSTAND THE THERE IS ONLY ONE RACE, HUMAN. EVERYTHING ELSE IS BULLSHIT, TO MAKE SOME FEEL INFERIOR OR SUPERIOR. ITS JUST THAT SIMPLE, NOW STOP BEING A DUMBASS AND WORK TO BE A BETTER HUMAN.

TO BE ANTI-RACIST YOU MUST UNDERSTAND THE THERE IS ONLY ONE RACE, HUMAN. EVERYTHING ELSE IS BULLSHIT, TO MAKE SOME FEEL INFERIOR OR SUPERIOR. ITS JUST THAT SIMPLE, NOW STOP BEING A DUMBASS AND WORK TO BE A BETTER HUMAN.

TO BE ANTI-RACIST YOU MUST UNDERSTAND THE THERE IS ONLY ONE RACE, HUMAN. EVERYTHING ELSE IS BULLSHIT, TO MAKE SOME FEEL INFERIOR OR SUPERIOR. ITS JUST THAT SIMPLE, NOW STOP BEING A DUMBASS AND WORK TO BE A BETTER HUMAN.

TO BE ANTI-RACIST YOU MUST UNDERSTAND THE THERE IS ONLY ONE RACE, HUMAN. EVERYTHING ELSE IS BULLSHIT, TO MAKE SOME FEEL INFERIOR OR SUPERIOR. ITS JUST THAT SIMPLE, NOW STOP BEING A DUMBASS AND WORK TO BE A BETTER HUMAN.

TO BE ANTI-RACIST YOU MUST UNDERSTAND THE THERE IS ONLY ONE RACE, HUMAN. EVERYTHING ELSE IS BULLSHIT, TO MAKE SOME FEEL INFERIOR OR SUPERIOR. ITS

TO BE ANTI-RACIST YOU MUST UNDERSTAND THE THERE IS ONLY ONE RACE, HUMAN. EVERYTHING ELSE IS BULLSHIT, TO MAKE SOME FEEL INFERIOR OR SUPERIOR. ITS JUST THAT SIMPLE, NOW STOP BEING A DUMBASS AND WORK TO BE A BETTER HUMAN.

TO BE ANTI-RACIST YOU MUST UNDERSTAND THE THERE IS ONLY ONE RACE, HUMAN. EVERYTHING ELSE IS BULLSHIT, TO MAKE SOME FEEL INFERIOR OR SUPERIOR. ITS JUST THAT SIMPLE, NOW STOP BEING A DUMBASS AND WORK TO BE A BETTER HUMAN.

TO BE ANTI-RACIST YOU MUST UNDERSTAND THE THERE IS ONLY ONE RACE, HUMAN. EVERYTHING ELSE IS BULLSHIT, TO MAKE SOME FEEL INFERIOR OR SUPERIOR. ITS JUST THAT SIMPLE, NOW STOP BEING A DUMBASS AND WORK TO BE A BETTER HUMAN.

TO BE ANTI-RACIST YOU MUST UNDERSTAND THE THERE IS ONLY ONE RACE, HUMAN. EVERYTHING ELSE IS BULLSHIT, TO MAKE SOME FEEL INFERIOR OR SUPERIOR. ITS JUST THAT SIMPLE, NOW STOP BEING A DUMBASS AND WORK TO BE A BETTER HUMAN.

TO BE ANTI-RACIST YOU MUST UNDERSTAND THE THERE IS ONLY ONE RACE, HUMAN. EVERYTHING ELSE IS BULLSHIT, TO MAKE SOME FEEL INFERIOR OR SUPERIOR. ITS JUST THAT SIMPLE, NOW STOP BEING A DUMBASS AND WORK TO BE A BETTER HUMAN.

TO BE ANTI-RACIST YOU MUST UNDERSTAND THE THERE IS ONLY ONE RACE, HUMAN. EVERYTHING ELSE IS BULLSHIT, TO MAKE SOME FEEL INFERIOR OR SUPERIOR. ITS JUST THAT SIMPLE, NOW STOP BEING A DUMBASS AND WORK TO BE A BETTER HUMAN.

TO BE ANTI-RACIST YOU MUST UNDERSTAND THE THERE IS ONLY ONE RACE, HUMAN. EVERYTHING ELSE IS BULLSHIT, TO MAKE SOME FEEL INFERIOR OR SUPERIOR. ITS JUST THAT SIMPLE, NOW STOP BEING A DUMBASS AND WORK TO BE A BETTER HUMAN.

TO BE ANTI-RACIST YOU MUST UNDERSTAND THE THERE IS ONLY ONE RACE, HUMAN. EVERYTHING ELSE IS BULLSHIT, TO MAKE SOME FEEL INFERIOR OR SUPERIOR. ITS JUST THAT SIMPLE, NOW STOP BEING A DUMBASS AND WORK TO BE A BETTER HUMAN.

TO BE ANTI-RACIST YOU MUST UNDERSTAND THE THERE IS ONLY ONE RACE, HUMAN. EVERYTHING ELSE IS BULLSHIT, TO MAKE SOME FEEL INFERIOR OR SUPERIOR. ITS JUST THAT SIMPLE, NOW STOP BEING A DUMBASS AND WORK TO BE A BETTER HUMAN.

TO BE ANTI-RACIST YOU MUST UNDERSTAND THE THERE IS ONLY ONE RACE, HUMAN. EVERYTHING ELSE IS BULLSHIT, TO MAKE SOME FEEL INFERIOR OR SUPERIOR. ITS JUST THAT SIMPLE, NOW STOP BEING A DUMBASS AND WORK TO BE A BETTER HUMAN.

JUST THAT SIMPLE, NOW STOP BEING A DUMBASS AND WORK TO BE A BETTER
HUMAN.

TO BE ANTI-RACIST YOU MUST UNDERSTAND THE THERE IS ONLY ONE RACE, HUMAN.
EVERYTHING ELSE IS BULLSHIT, TO MAKE SOME FEEL INFERIOR OR SUPERIOR. ITS
JUST THAT SIMPLE, NOW STOP BEING A DUMBASS AND WORK TO BE A BETTER
HUMAN.

TO BE ANTI-RACIST YOU MUST UNDERSTAND THE THERE IS ONLY ONE RACE, HUMAN.
EVERYTHING ELSE IS BULLSHIT, TO MAKE SOME FEEL INFERIOR OR SUPERIOR. ITS
JUST THAT SIMPLE, NOW STOP BEING A DUMBASS AND WORK TO BE A BETTER
HUMAN.

TO BE ANTI-RACIST YOU MUST UNDERSTAND THE THERE IS ONLY ONE RACE, HUMAN.
EVERYTHING ELSE IS BULLSHIT, TO MAKE SOME FEEL INFERIOR OR SUPERIOR. ITS
JUST THAT SIMPLE, NOW STOP BEING A DUMBASS AND WORK TO BE A BETTER
HUMAN.

TO BE ANTI-RACIST YOU MUST UNDERSTAND THE THERE IS ONLY ONE RACE, HUMAN.
EVERYTHING ELSE IS BULLSHIT, TO MAKE SOME FEEL INFERIOR OR SUPERIOR. ITS
JUST THAT SIMPLE, NOW STOP BEING A DUMBASS AND WORK TO BE A BETTER
HUMAN.

TO BE ANTI-RACIST YOU MUST UNDERSTAND THE THERE IS ONLY ONE RACE, HUMAN.
EVERYTHING ELSE IS BULLSHIT, TO MAKE SOME FEEL INFERIOR OR SUPERIOR. ITS
JUST THAT SIMPLE, NOW STOP BEING A DUMBASS AND WORK TO BE A BETTER
HUMAN.

TO BE ANTI-RACIST YOU MUST UNDERSTAND THE THERE IS ONLY ONE RACE, HUMAN.
EVERYTHING ELSE IS BULLSHIT, TO MAKE SOME FEEL INFERIOR OR SUPERIOR. ITS
JUST THAT SIMPLE, NOW STOP BEING A DUMBASS AND WORK TO BE A BETTER
HUMAN.

TO BE ANTI-RACIST YOU MUST UNDERSTAND THE THERE IS ONLY ONE RACE, HUMAN.
EVERYTHING ELSE IS BULLSHIT, TO MAKE SOME FEEL INFERIOR OR SUPERIOR. ITS
JUST THAT SIMPLE, NOW STOP BEING A DUMBASS AND WORK TO BE A BETTER
HUMAN.

TO BE ANTI-RACIST YOU MUST UNDERSTAND THE THERE IS ONLY ONE RACE, HUMAN.
EVERYTHING ELSE IS BULLSHIT, TO MAKE SOME FEEL INFERIOR OR SUPERIOR. ITS
JUST THAT SIMPLE, NOW STOP BEING A DUMBASS AND WORK TO BE A BETTER
HUMAN.

TO BE ANTI-RACIST YOU MUST UNDERSTAND THE THERE IS ONLY ONE RACE, HUMAN.
EVERYTHING ELSE IS BULLSHIT, TO MAKE SOME FEEL INFERIOR OR SUPERIOR. ITS
JUST THAT SIMPLE, NOW STOP BEING A DUMBASS AND WORK TO BE A BETTER
HUMAN.

TO BE ANTI-RACIST YOU MUST UNDERSTAND THE THERE IS ONLY ONE RACE, HUMAN.
EVERYTHING ELSE IS BULLSHIT, TO MAKE SOME FEEL INFERIOR OR SUPERIOR. ITS

TO BE ANTI-RACIST YOU MUST UNDERSTAND THE THERE IS ONLY ONE RACE, HUMAN. EVERYTHING ELSE IS BULLSHIT, TO MAKE SOME FEEL INFERIOR OR SUPERIOR. ITS JUST THAT SIMPLE, NOW STOP BEING A DUMBASS AND WORK TO BE A BETTER HUMAN.

TO BE ANTI-RACIST YOU MUST UNDERSTAND THE THERE IS ONLY ONE RACE, HUMAN. EVERYTHING ELSE IS BULLSHIT, TO MAKE SOME FEEL INFERIOR OR SUPERIOR. ITS JUST THAT SIMPLE, NOW STOP BEING A DUMBASS AND WORK TO BE A BETTER HUMAN.

TO BE ANTI-RACIST YOU MUST UNDERSTAND THE THERE IS ONLY ONE RACE, HUMAN. EVERYTHING ELSE IS BULLSHIT, TO MAKE SOME FEEL INFERIOR OR SUPERIOR. ITS JUST THAT SIMPLE, NOW STOP BEING A DUMBASS AND WORK TO BE A BETTER HUMAN.

TO BE ANTI-RACIST YOU MUST UNDERSTAND THE THERE IS ONLY ONE RACE, HUMAN. EVERYTHING ELSE IS BULLSHIT, TO MAKE SOME FEEL INFERIOR OR SUPERIOR. ITS JUST THAT SIMPLE, NOW STOP BEING A DUMBASS AND WORK TO BE A BETTER HUMAN.

TO BE ANTI-RACIST YOU MUST UNDERSTAND THE THERE IS ONLY ONE RACE, HUMAN. EVERYTHING ELSE IS BULLSHIT, TO MAKE SOME FEEL INFERIOR OR SUPERIOR. ITS JUST THAT SIMPLE, NOW STOP BEING A DUMBASS AND WORK TO BE A BETTER HUMAN.

TO BE ANTI-RACIST YOU MUST UNDERSTAND THE THERE IS ONLY ONE RACE, HUMAN. EVERYTHING ELSE IS BULLSHIT, TO MAKE SOME FEEL INFERIOR OR SUPERIOR. ITS JUST THAT SIMPLE, NOW STOP BEING A DUMBASS AND WORK TO BE A BETTER HUMAN.

TO BE ANTI-RACIST YOU MUST UNDERSTAND THE THERE IS ONLY ONE RACE, HUMAN. EVERYTHING ELSE IS BULLSHIT, TO MAKE SOME FEEL INFERIOR OR SUPERIOR. ITS JUST THAT SIMPLE, NOW STOP BEING A DUMBASS AND WORK TO BE A BETTER HUMAN.

TO BE ANTI-RACIST YOU MUST UNDERSTAND THE THERE IS ONLY ONE RACE, HUMAN. EVERYTHING ELSE IS BULLSHIT, TO MAKE SOME FEEL INFERIOR OR SUPERIOR. ITS JUST THAT SIMPLE, NOW STOP BEING A DUMBASS AND WORK TO BE A BETTER HUMAN.

TO BE ANTI-RACIST YOU MUST UNDERSTAND THE THERE IS ONLY ONE RACE, HUMAN. EVERYTHING ELSE IS BULLSHIT, TO MAKE SOME FEEL INFERIOR OR SUPERIOR. ITS JUST THAT SIMPLE, NOW STOP BEING A DUMBASS AND WORK TO BE A BETTER HUMAN.

TO BE ANTI-RACIST YOU MUST UNDERSTAND THE THERE IS ONLY ONE RACE, HUMAN. EVERYTHING ELSE IS BULLSHIT, TO MAKE SOME FEEL INFERIOR OR SUPERIOR. ITS JUST THAT SIMPLE, NOW STOP BEING A DUMBASS AND WORK TO BE A BETTER HUMAN.

JUST THAT SIMPLE, NOW STOP BEING A DUMBASS AND WORK TO BE A BETTER
HUMAN.

TO BE ANTI-RACIST YOU MUST UNDERSTAND THE THERE IS ONLY ONE RACE, HUMAN.
EVERYTHING ELSE IS BULLSHIT, TO MAKE SOME FEEL INFERIOR OR SUPERIOR. ITS
JUST THAT SIMPLE, NOW STOP BEING A DUMBASS AND WORK TO BE A BETTER
HUMAN.

TO BE ANTI-RACIST YOU MUST UNDERSTAND THE THERE IS ONLY ONE RACE, HUMAN.
EVERYTHING ELSE IS BULLSHIT, TO MAKE SOME FEEL INFERIOR OR SUPERIOR. ITS
JUST THAT SIMPLE, NOW STOP BEING A DUMBASS AND WORK TO BE A BETTER
HUMAN.

TO BE ANTI-RACIST YOU MUST UNDERSTAND THE THERE IS ONLY ONE RACE, HUMAN.
EVERYTHING ELSE IS BULLSHIT, TO MAKE SOME FEEL INFERIOR OR SUPERIOR. ITS
JUST THAT SIMPLE, NOW STOP BEING A DUMBASS AND WORK TO BE A BETTER
HUMAN.

TO BE ANTI-RACIST YOU MUST UNDERSTAND THE THERE IS ONLY ONE RACE, HUMAN.
EVERYTHING ELSE IS BULLSHIT, TO MAKE SOME FEEL INFERIOR OR SUPERIOR. ITS
JUST THAT SIMPLE, NOW STOP BEING A DUMBASS AND WORK TO BE A BETTER
HUMAN.

TO BE ANTI-RACIST YOU MUST UNDERSTAND THE THERE IS ONLY ONE RACE, HUMAN.
EVERYTHING ELSE IS BULLSHIT, TO MAKE SOME FEEL INFERIOR OR SUPERIOR. ITS
JUST THAT SIMPLE, NOW STOP BEING A DUMBASS AND WORK TO BE A BETTER
HUMAN.

TO BE ANTI-RACIST YOU MUST UNDERSTAND THE THERE IS ONLY ONE RACE, HUMAN.
EVERYTHING ELSE IS BULLSHIT, TO MAKE SOME FEEL INFERIOR OR SUPERIOR. ITS
JUST THAT SIMPLE, NOW STOP BEING A DUMBASS AND WORK TO BE A BETTER
HUMAN.

TO BE ANTI-RACIST YOU MUST UNDERSTAND THE THERE IS ONLY ONE RACE, HUMAN.
EVERYTHING ELSE IS BULLSHIT, TO MAKE SOME FEEL INFERIOR OR SUPERIOR. ITS
JUST THAT SIMPLE, NOW STOP BEING A DUMBASS AND WORK TO BE A BETTER
HUMAN.

TO BE ANTI-RACIST YOU MUST UNDERSTAND THE THERE IS ONLY ONE RACE, HUMAN.
EVERYTHING ELSE IS BULLSHIT, TO MAKE SOME FEEL INFERIOR OR SUPERIOR. ITS
JUST THAT SIMPLE, NOW STOP BEING A DUMBASS AND WORK TO BE A BETTER
HUMAN.

TO BE ANTI-RACIST YOU MUST UNDERSTAND THE THERE IS ONLY ONE RACE, HUMAN.
EVERYTHING ELSE IS BULLSHIT, TO MAKE SOME FEEL INFERIOR OR SUPERIOR. ITS

TO BE ANTI-RACIST YOU MUST UNDERSTAND THE THERE IS ONLY ONE RACE, HUMAN. EVERYTHING ELSE IS BULLSHIT, TO MAKE SOME FEEL INFERIOR OR SUPERIOR. ITS JUST THAT SIMPLE, NOW STOP BEING A DUMBASS AND WORK TO BE A BETTER HUMAN.
TO BE ANTI-RACIST YOU MUST UNDERSTAND THE THERE IS ONLY ONE RACE, HUMAN. EVERYTHING ELSE IS BULLSHIT, TO MAKE SOME FEEL INFERIOR OR SUPERIOR. ITS JUST THAT SIMPLE, NOW STOP BEING A DUMBASS AND WORK TO BE A BETTER HUMAN.
TO BE ANTI-RACIST YOU MUST UNDERSTAND THE THERE IS ONLY ONE RACE, HUMAN. EVERYTHING ELSE IS BULLSHIT, TO MAKE SOME FEEL INFERIOR OR SUPERIOR. ITS JUST THAT SIMPLE, NOW STOP BEING A DUMBASS AND WORK TO BE A BETTER HUMAN.
TO BE ANTI-RACIST YOU MUST UNDERSTAND THE THERE IS ONLY ONE RACE, HUMAN. EVERYTHING ELSE IS BULLSHIT, TO MAKE SOME FEEL INFERIOR OR SUPERIOR. ITS JUST THAT SIMPLE, NOW STOP BEING A DUMBASS AND WORK TO BE A BETTER HUMAN.
TO BE ANTI-RACIST YOU MUST UNDERSTAND THE THERE IS ONLY ONE RACE, HUMAN. EVERYTHING ELSE IS BULLSHIT, TO MAKE SOME FEEL INFERIOR OR SUPERIOR. ITS JUST THAT SIMPLE, NOW STOP BEING A DUMBASS AND WORK TO BE A BETTER HUMAN.
TO BE ANTI-RACIST YOU MUST UNDERSTAND THE THERE IS ONLY ONE RACE, HUMAN. EVERYTHING ELSE IS BULLSHIT, TO MAKE SOME FEEL INFERIOR OR SUPERIOR. ITS JUST THAT SIMPLE, NOW STOP BEING A DUMBASS AND WORK TO BE A BETTER HUMAN.
TO BE ANTI-RACIST YOU MUST UNDERSTAND THE THERE IS ONLY ONE RACE, HUMAN. EVERYTHING ELSE IS BULLSHIT, TO MAKE SOME FEEL INFERIOR OR SUPERIOR. ITS JUST THAT SIMPLE, NOW STOP BEING A DUMBASS AND WORK TO BE A BETTER HUMAN.
TO BE ANTI-RACIST YOU MUST UNDERSTAND THE THERE IS ONLY ONE RACE, HUMAN. EVERYTHING ELSE IS BULLSHIT, TO MAKE SOME FEEL INFERIOR OR SUPERIOR. ITS JUST THAT SIMPLE, NOW STOP BEING A DUMBASS AND WORK TO BE A BETTER HUMAN.
TO BE ANTI-RACIST YOU MUST UNDERSTAND THE THERE IS ONLY ONE RACE, HUMAN. EVERYTHING ELSE IS BULLSHIT, TO MAKE SOME FEEL INFERIOR OR SUPERIOR. ITS JUST THAT SIMPLE, NOW STOP BEING A DUMBASS AND WORK TO BE A BETTER HUMAN.
TO BE ANTI-RACIST YOU MUST UNDERSTAND THE THERE IS ONLY ONE RACE, HUMAN. EVERYTHING ELSE IS BULLSHIT, TO MAKE SOME FEEL INFERIOR OR SUPERIOR. ITS JUST THAT SIMPLE, NOW STOP BEING A DUMBASS AND WORK TO BE A BETTER HUMAN.
TO BE ANTI-RACIST YOU MUST UNDERSTAND THE THERE IS ONLY ONE RACE, HUMAN. EVERYTHING ELSE IS BULLSHIT, TO MAKE SOME FEEL INFERIOR OR SUPERIOR. ITS JUST THAT SIMPLE, NOW STOP BEING A DUMBASS AND WORK TO BE A BETTER HUMAN.

JUST THAT SIMPLE, NOW STOP BEING A DUMBASS AND WORK TO BE A BETTER
HUMAN.

TO BE ANTI-RACIST YOU MUST UNDERSTAND THE THERE IS ONLY ONE RACE, HUMAN.
EVERYTHING ELSE IS BULLSHIT, TO MAKE SOME FEEL INFERIOR OR SUPERIOR. ITS
JUST THAT SIMPLE, NOW STOP BEING A DUMBASS AND WORK TO BE A BETTER
HUMAN.

TO BE ANTI-RACIST YOU MUST UNDERSTAND THE THERE IS ONLY ONE RACE, HUMAN.
EVERYTHING ELSE IS BULLSHIT, TO MAKE SOME FEEL INFERIOR OR SUPERIOR. ITS
JUST THAT SIMPLE, NOW STOP BEING A DUMBASS AND WORK TO BE A BETTER
HUMAN.

TO BE ANTI-RACIST YOU MUST UNDERSTAND THE THERE IS ONLY ONE RACE, HUMAN.
EVERYTHING ELSE IS BULLSHIT, TO MAKE SOME FEEL INFERIOR OR SUPERIOR. ITS
JUST THAT SIMPLE, NOW STOP BEING A DUMBASS AND WORK TO BE A BETTER
HUMAN.

TO BE ANTI-RACIST YOU MUST UNDERSTAND THE THERE IS ONLY ONE RACE, HUMAN.
EVERYTHING ELSE IS BULLSHIT, TO MAKE SOME FEEL INFERIOR OR SUPERIOR. ITS
JUST THAT SIMPLE, NOW STOP BEING A DUMBASS AND WORK TO BE A BETTER
HUMAN.

TO BE ANTI-RACIST YOU MUST UNDERSTAND THE THERE IS ONLY ONE RACE, HUMAN.
EVERYTHING ELSE IS BULLSHIT, TO MAKE SOME FEEL INFERIOR OR SUPERIOR. ITS
JUST THAT SIMPLE, NOW STOP BEING A DUMBASS AND WORK TO BE A BETTER
HUMAN.

TO BE ANTI-RACIST YOU MUST UNDERSTAND THE THERE IS ONLY ONE RACE, HUMAN.
EVERYTHING ELSE IS BULLSHIT, TO MAKE SOME FEEL INFERIOR OR SUPERIOR. ITS
JUST THAT SIMPLE, NOW STOP BEING A DUMBASS AND WORK TO BE A BETTER
HUMAN.

TO BE ANTI-RACIST YOU MUST UNDERSTAND THE THERE IS ONLY ONE RACE, HUMAN.
EVERYTHING ELSE IS BULLSHIT, TO MAKE SOME FEEL INFERIOR OR SUPERIOR. ITS
JUST THAT SIMPLE, NOW STOP BEING A DUMBASS AND WORK TO BE A BETTER
HUMAN.

TO BE ANTI-RACIST YOU MUST UNDERSTAND THE THERE IS ONLY ONE RACE, HUMAN.
EVERYTHING ELSE IS BULLSHIT, TO MAKE SOME FEEL INFERIOR OR SUPERIOR. ITS
JUST THAT SIMPLE, NOW STOP BEING A DUMBASS AND WORK TO BE A BETTER
HUMAN.

TO BE ANTI-RACIST YOU MUST UNDERSTAND THE THERE IS ONLY ONE RACE, HUMAN.
EVERYTHING ELSE IS BULLSHIT, TO MAKE SOME FEEL INFERIOR OR SUPERIOR. ITS
JUST THAT SIMPLE, NOW STOP BEING A DUMBASS AND WORK TO BE A BETTER
HUMAN.

TO BE ANTI-RACIST YOU MUST UNDERSTAND THE THERE IS ONLY ONE RACE, HUMAN.
EVERYTHING ELSE IS BULLSHIT, TO MAKE SOME FEEL INFERIOR OR SUPERIOR. ITS

TO BE ANTI-RACIST YOU MUST UNDERSTAND THE THERE IS ONLY ONE RACE, HUMAN. EVERYTHING ELSE IS BULLSHIT, TO MAKE SOME FEEL INFERIOR OR SUPERIOR. ITS JUST THAT SIMPLE, NOW STOP BEING A DUMBASS AND WORK TO BE A BETTER HUMAN.

TO BE ANTI-RACIST YOU MUST UNDERSTAND THE THERE IS ONLY ONE RACE, HUMAN. EVERYTHING ELSE IS BULLSHIT, TO MAKE SOME FEEL INFERIOR OR SUPERIOR. ITS JUST THAT SIMPLE, NOW STOP BEING A DUMBASS AND WORK TO BE A BETTER HUMAN.

TO BE ANTI-RACIST YOU MUST UNDERSTAND THE THERE IS ONLY ONE RACE, HUMAN. EVERYTHING ELSE IS BULLSHIT, TO MAKE SOME FEEL INFERIOR OR SUPERIOR. ITS JUST THAT SIMPLE, NOW STOP BEING A DUMBASS AND WORK TO BE A BETTER HUMAN.

TO BE ANTI-RACIST YOU MUST UNDERSTAND THE THERE IS ONLY ONE RACE, HUMAN. EVERYTHING ELSE IS BULLSHIT, TO MAKE SOME FEEL INFERIOR OR SUPERIOR. ITS JUST THAT SIMPLE, NOW STOP BEING A DUMBASS AND WORK TO BE A BETTER HUMAN.

TO BE ANTI-RACIST YOU MUST UNDERSTAND THE THERE IS ONLY ONE RACE, HUMAN. EVERYTHING ELSE IS BULLSHIT, TO MAKE SOME FEEL INFERIOR OR SUPERIOR. ITS JUST THAT SIMPLE, NOW STOP BEING A DUMBASS AND WORK TO BE A BETTER HUMAN.

TO BE ANTI-RACIST YOU MUST UNDERSTAND THE THERE IS ONLY ONE RACE, HUMAN. EVERYTHING ELSE IS BULLSHIT, TO MAKE SOME FEEL INFERIOR OR SUPERIOR. ITS JUST THAT SIMPLE, NOW STOP BEING A DUMBASS AND WORK TO BE A BETTER HUMAN.

TO BE ANTI-RACIST YOU MUST UNDERSTAND THE THERE IS ONLY ONE RACE, HUMAN. EVERYTHING ELSE IS BULLSHIT, TO MAKE SOME FEEL INFERIOR OR SUPERIOR. ITS JUST THAT SIMPLE, NOW STOP BEING A DUMBASS AND WORK TO BE A BETTER HUMAN.

TO BE ANTI-RACIST YOU MUST UNDERSTAND THE THERE IS ONLY ONE RACE, HUMAN. EVERYTHING ELSE IS BULLSHIT, TO MAKE SOME FEEL INFERIOR OR SUPERIOR. ITS JUST THAT SIMPLE, NOW STOP BEING A DUMBASS AND WORK TO BE A BETTER HUMAN.

TO BE ANTI-RACIST YOU MUST UNDERSTAND THE THERE IS ONLY ONE RACE, HUMAN. EVERYTHING ELSE IS BULLSHIT, TO MAKE SOME FEEL INFERIOR OR SUPERIOR. ITS JUST THAT SIMPLE, NOW STOP BEING A DUMBASS AND WORK TO BE A BETTER HUMAN.

TO BE ANTI-RACIST YOU MUST UNDERSTAND THE THERE IS ONLY ONE RACE, HUMAN. EVERYTHING ELSE IS BULLSHIT, TO MAKE SOME FEEL INFERIOR OR SUPERIOR. ITS JUST THAT SIMPLE, NOW STOP BEING A DUMBASS AND WORK TO BE A BETTER HUMAN.

TO BE ANTI-RACIST YOU MUST UNDERSTAND THE THERE IS ONLY ONE RACE, HUMAN. EVERYTHING ELSE IS BULLSHIT, TO MAKE SOME FEEL INFERIOR OR SUPERIOR. ITS JUST THAT SIMPLE, NOW STOP BEING A DUMBASS AND WORK TO BE A BETTER HUMAN

JUST THAT SIMPLE, NOW STOP BEING A DUMBASS AND WORK TO BE A BETTER HUMAN.

TO BE ANTI-RACIST YOU MUST UNDERSTAND THE THERE IS ONLY ONE RACE, HUMAN. EVERYTHING ELSE IS BULLSHIT, TO MAKE SOME FEEL INFERIOR OR SUPERIOR. ITS JUST THAT SIMPLE, NOW STOP BEING A DUMBASS AND WORK TO BE A BETTER HUMAN.

TO BE ANTI-RACIST YOU MUST UNDERSTAND THE THERE IS ONLY ONE RACE, HUMAN. EVERYTHING ELSE IS BULLSHIT, TO MAKE SOME FEEL INFERIOR OR SUPERIOR. ITS JUST THAT SIMPLE, NOW STOP BEING A DUMBASS AND WORK TO BE A BETTER HUMAN.

TO BE ANTI-RACIST YOU MUST UNDERSTAND THE THERE IS ONLY ONE RACE, HUMAN. EVERYTHING ELSE IS BULLSHIT, TO MAKE SOME FEEL INFERIOR OR SUPERIOR. ITS JUST THAT SIMPLE, NOW STOP BEING A DUMBASS AND WORK TO BE A BETTER HUMAN.

TO BE ANTI-RACIST YOU MUST UNDERSTAND THE THERE IS ONLY ONE RACE, HUMAN. EVERYTHING ELSE IS BULLSHIT, TO MAKE SOME FEEL INFERIOR OR SUPERIOR. ITS JUST THAT SIMPLE, NOW STOP BEING A DUMBASS AND WORK TO BE A BETTER HUMAN.

TO BE ANTI-RACIST YOU MUST UNDERSTAND THE THERE IS ONLY ONE RACE, HUMAN. EVERYTHING ELSE IS BULLSHIT, TO MAKE SOME FEEL INFERIOR OR SUPERIOR. ITS JUST THAT SIMPLE, NOW STOP BEING A DUMBASS AND WORK TO BE A BETTER HUMAN.

TO BE ANTI-RACIST YOU MUST UNDERSTAND THE THERE IS ONLY ONE RACE, HUMAN. EVERYTHING ELSE IS BULLSHIT, TO MAKE SOME FEEL INFERIOR OR SUPERIOR. ITS JUST THAT SIMPLE, NOW STOP BEING A DUMBASS AND WORK TO BE A BETTER HUMAN.

TO BE ANTI-RACIST YOU MUST UNDERSTAND THE THERE IS ONLY ONE RACE, HUMAN. EVERYTHING ELSE IS BULLSHIT, TO MAKE SOME FEEL INFERIOR OR SUPERIOR. ITS JUST THAT SIMPLE, NOW STOP BEING A DUMBASS AND WORK TO BE A BETTER HUMAN.

TO BE ANTI-RACIST YOU MUST UNDERSTAND THE THERE IS ONLY ONE RACE, HUMAN. EVERYTHING ELSE IS BULLSHIT, TO MAKE SOME FEEL INFERIOR OR SUPERIOR. ITS JUST THAT SIMPLE, NOW STOP BEING A DUMBASS AND WORK TO BE A BETTER HUMAN.

TO BE ANTI-RACIST YOU MUST UNDERSTAND THE THERE IS ONLY ONE RACE, HUMAN. EVERYTHING ELSE IS BULLSHIT, TO MAKE SOME FEEL INFERIOR OR SUPERIOR. ITS

TO BE ANTI-RACIST YOU MUST UNDERSTAND THE THERE IS ONLY ONE RACE, HUMAN. EVERYTHING ELSE IS BULLSHIT, TO MAKE SOME FEEL INFERIOR OR SUPERIOR. ITS JUST THAT SIMPLE, NOW STOP BEING A DUMBASS AND WORK TO BE A BETTER HUMAN.

TO BE ANTI-RACIST YOU MUST UNDERSTAND THE THERE IS ONLY ONE RACE, HUMAN. EVERYTHING ELSE IS BULLSHIT, TO MAKE SOME FEEL INFERIOR OR SUPERIOR. ITS JUST THAT SIMPLE, NOW STOP BEING A DUMBASS AND WORK TO BE A BETTER HUMAN.

TO BE ANTI-RACIST YOU MUST UNDERSTAND THE THERE IS ONLY ONE RACE, HUMAN. EVERYTHING ELSE IS BULLSHIT, TO MAKE SOME FEEL INFERIOR OR SUPERIOR. ITS JUST THAT SIMPLE, NOW STOP BEING A DUMBASS AND WORK TO BE A BETTER HUMAN.

TO BE ANTI-RACIST YOU MUST UNDERSTAND THE THERE IS ONLY ONE RACE, HUMAN. EVERYTHING ELSE IS BULLSHIT, TO MAKE SOME FEEL INFERIOR OR SUPERIOR. ITS JUST THAT SIMPLE, NOW STOP BEING A DUMBASS AND WORK TO BE A BETTER HUMAN.

TO BE ANTI-RACIST YOU MUST UNDERSTAND THE THERE IS ONLY ONE RACE, HUMAN. EVERYTHING ELSE IS BULLSHIT, TO MAKE SOME FEEL INFERIOR OR SUPERIOR. ITS JUST THAT SIMPLE, NOW STOP BEING A DUMBASS AND WORK TO BE A BETTER HUMAN.

TO BE ANTI-RACIST YOU MUST UNDERSTAND THE THERE IS ONLY ONE RACE, HUMAN. EVERYTHING ELSE IS BULLSHIT, TO MAKE SOME FEEL INFERIOR OR SUPERIOR. ITS JUST THAT SIMPLE, NOW STOP BEING A DUMBASS AND WORK TO BE A BETTER HUMAN.

TO BE ANTI-RACIST YOU MUST UNDERSTAND THE THERE IS ONLY ONE RACE, HUMAN. EVERYTHING ELSE IS BULLSHIT, TO MAKE SOME FEEL INFERIOR OR SUPERIOR. ITS JUST THAT SIMPLE, NOW STOP BEING A DUMBASS AND WORK TO BE A BETTER HUMAN.

TO BE ANTI-RACIST YOU MUST UNDERSTAND THE THERE IS ONLY ONE RACE, HUMAN. EVERYTHING ELSE IS BULLSHIT, TO MAKE SOME FEEL INFERIOR OR SUPERIOR. ITS JUST THAT SIMPLE, NOW STOP BEING A DUMBASS AND WORK TO BE A BETTER HUMAN.

TO BE ANTI-RACIST YOU MUST UNDERSTAND THE THERE IS ONLY ONE RACE, HUMAN. EVERYTHING ELSE IS BULLSHIT, TO MAKE SOME FEEL INFERIOR OR SUPERIOR. ITS JUST THAT SIMPLE, NOW STOP BEING A DUMBASS AND WORK TO BE A BETTER HUMAN.

TO BE ANTI-RACIST YOU MUST UNDERSTAND THE THERE IS ONLY ONE RACE, HUMAN. EVERYTHING ELSE IS BULLSHIT, TO MAKE SOME FEEL INFERIOR OR SUPERIOR. ITS JUST THAT SIMPLE, NOW STOP BEING A DUMBASS AND WORK TO BE A BETTER HUMAN.

JUST THAT SIMPLE, NOW STOP BEING A DUMBASS AND WORK TO BE A BETTER HUMAN.

TO BE ANTI-RACIST YOU MUST UNDERSTAND THE THERE IS ONLY ONE RACE, HUMAN. EVERYTHING ELSE IS BULLSHIT, TO MAKE SOME FEEL INFERIOR OR SUPERIOR. ITS JUST THAT SIMPLE, NOW STOP BEING A DUMBASS AND WORK TO BE A BETTER HUMAN.

TO BE ANTI-RACIST YOU MUST UNDERSTAND THE THERE IS ONLY ONE RACE, HUMAN. EVERYTHING ELSE IS BULLSHIT, TO MAKE SOME FEEL INFERIOR OR SUPERIOR. ITS JUST THAT SIMPLE, NOW STOP BEING A DUMBASS AND WORK TO BE A BETTER HUMAN.

TO BE ANTI-RACIST YOU MUST UNDERSTAND THE THERE IS ONLY ONE RACE, HUMAN. EVERYTHING ELSE IS BULLSHIT, TO MAKE SOME FEEL INFERIOR OR SUPERIOR. ITS JUST THAT SIMPLE, NOW STOP BEING A DUMBASS AND WORK TO BE A BETTER HUMAN.

TO BE ANTI-RACIST YOU MUST UNDERSTAND THE THERE IS ONLY ONE RACE, HUMAN. EVERYTHING ELSE IS BULLSHIT, TO MAKE SOME FEEL INFERIOR OR SUPERIOR. ITS JUST THAT SIMPLE, NOW STOP BEING A DUMBASS AND WORK TO BE A BETTER HUMAN.

TO BE ANTI-RACIST YOU MUST UNDERSTAND THE THERE IS ONLY ONE RACE, HUMAN. EVERYTHING ELSE IS BULLSHIT, TO MAKE SOME FEEL INFERIOR OR SUPERIOR. ITS JUST THAT SIMPLE, NOW STOP BEING A DUMBASS AND WORK TO BE A BETTER HUMAN.

TO BE ANTI-RACIST YOU MUST UNDERSTAND THE THERE IS ONLY ONE RACE, HUMAN. EVERYTHING ELSE IS BULLSHIT, TO MAKE SOME FEEL INFERIOR OR SUPERIOR. ITS JUST THAT SIMPLE, NOW STOP BEING A DUMBASS AND WORK TO BE A BETTER HUMAN.

TO BE ANTI-RACIST YOU MUST UNDERSTAND THE THERE IS ONLY ONE RACE, HUMAN. EVERYTHING ELSE IS BULLSHIT, TO MAKE SOME FEEL INFERIOR OR SUPERIOR. ITS JUST THAT SIMPLE, NOW STOP BEING A DUMBASS AND WORK TO BE A BETTER HUMAN.

TO BE ANTI-RACIST YOU MUST UNDERSTAND THE THERE IS ONLY ONE RACE, HUMAN. EVERYTHING ELSE IS BULLSHIT, TO MAKE SOME FEEL INFERIOR OR SUPERIOR. ITS JUST THAT SIMPLE, NOW STOP BEING A DUMBASS AND WORK TO BE A BETTER HUMAN.

TO BE ANTI-RACIST YOU MUST UNDERSTAND THE THERE IS ONLY ONE RACE, HUMAN. EVERYTHING ELSE IS BULLSHIT, TO MAKE SOME FEEL INFERIOR OR SUPERIOR. ITS JUST THAT SIMPLE, NOW STOP BEING A DUMBASS AND WORK TO BE A BETTER HUMAN.

TO BE ANTI-RACIST YOU MUST UNDERSTAND THE THERE IS ONLY ONE RACE, HUMAN. EVERYTHING ELSE IS BULLSHIT, TO MAKE SOME FEEL INFERIOR OR SUPERIOR. ITS

TO BE ANTI-RACIST YOU MUST UNDERSTAND THE THERE IS ONLY ONE RACE, HUMAN. EVERYTHING ELSE IS BULLSHIT, TO MAKE SOME FEEL INFERIOR OR SUPERIOR. ITS JUST THAT SIMPLE, NOW STOP BEING A DUMBASS AND WORK TO BE A BETTER HUMAN.

TO BE ANTI-RACIST YOU MUST UNDERSTAND THE THERE IS ONLY ONE RACE, HUMAN. EVERYTHING ELSE IS BULLSHIT, TO MAKE SOME FEEL INFERIOR OR SUPERIOR. ITS JUST THAT SIMPLE, NOW STOP BEING A DUMBASS AND WORK TO BE A BETTER HUMAN.

TO BE ANTI-RACIST YOU MUST UNDERSTAND THE THERE IS ONLY ONE RACE, HUMAN. EVERYTHING ELSE IS BULLSHIT, TO MAKE SOME FEEL INFERIOR OR SUPERIOR. ITS JUST THAT SIMPLE, NOW STOP BEING A DUMBASS AND WORK TO BE A BETTER HUMAN.

TO BE ANTI-RACIST YOU MUST UNDERSTAND THE THERE IS ONLY ONE RACE, HUMAN. EVERYTHING ELSE IS BULLSHIT, TO MAKE SOME FEEL INFERIOR OR SUPERIOR. ITS JUST THAT SIMPLE, NOW STOP BEING A DUMBASS AND WORK TO BE A BETTER HUMAN.

TO BE ANTI-RACIST YOU MUST UNDERSTAND THE THERE IS ONLY ONE RACE, HUMAN. EVERYTHING ELSE IS BULLSHIT, TO MAKE SOME FEEL INFERIOR OR SUPERIOR. ITS JUST THAT SIMPLE, NOW STOP BEING A DUMBASS AND WORK TO BE A BETTER HUMAN.

TO BE ANTI-RACIST YOU MUST UNDERSTAND THE THERE IS ONLY ONE RACE, HUMAN. EVERYTHING ELSE IS BULLSHIT, TO MAKE SOME FEEL INFERIOR OR SUPERIOR. ITS JUST THAT SIMPLE, NOW STOP BEING A DUMBASS AND WORK TO BE A BETTER HUMAN.

TO BE ANTI-RACIST YOU MUST UNDERSTAND THE THERE IS ONLY ONE RACE, HUMAN. EVERYTHING ELSE IS BULLSHIT, TO MAKE SOME FEEL INFERIOR OR SUPERIOR. ITS JUST THAT SIMPLE, NOW STOP BEING A DUMBASS AND WORK TO BE A BETTER HUMAN.

TO BE ANTI-RACIST YOU MUST UNDERSTAND THE THERE IS ONLY ONE RACE, HUMAN. EVERYTHING ELSE IS BULLSHIT, TO MAKE SOME FEEL INFERIOR OR SUPERIOR. ITS JUST THAT SIMPLE, NOW STOP BEING A DUMBASS AND WORK TO BE A BETTER HUMAN.

TO BE ANTI-RACIST YOU MUST UNDERSTAND THE THERE IS ONLY ONE RACE, HUMAN. EVERYTHING ELSE IS BULLSHIT, TO MAKE SOME FEEL INFERIOR OR SUPERIOR. ITS JUST THAT SIMPLE, NOW STOP BEING A DUMBASS AND WORK TO BE A BETTER HUMAN.

TO BE ANTI-RACIST YOU MUST UNDERSTAND THE THERE IS ONLY ONE RACE, HUMAN. EVERYTHING ELSE IS BULLSHIT, TO MAKE SOME FEEL INFERIOR OR SUPERIOR. ITS JUST THAT SIMPLE, NOW STOP BEING A DUMBASS AND WORK TO BE A BETTER HUMAN.

TO BE ANTI-RACIST YOU MUST UNDERSTAND THE THERE IS ONLY ONE RACE, HUMAN. EVERYTHING ELSE IS BULLSHIT, TO MAKE SOME FEEL INFERIOR OR SUPERIOR. ITS JUST THAT SIMPLE, NOW STOP BEING A DUMBASS AND WORK TO BE A BETTER HUMAN.

JUST THAT SIMPLE, NOW STOP BEING A DUMBASS AND WORK TO BE A BETTER HUMAN.

TO BE ANTI-RACIST YOU MUST UNDERSTAND THE THERE IS ONLY ONE RACE, HUMAN. EVERYTHING ELSE IS BULLSHIT, TO MAKE SOME FEEL INFERIOR OR SUPERIOR. ITS JUST THAT SIMPLE, NOW STOP BEING A DUMBASS AND WORK TO BE A BETTER HUMAN.

TO BE ANTI-RACIST YOU MUST UNDERSTAND THE THERE IS ONLY ONE RACE, HUMAN. EVERYTHING ELSE IS BULLSHIT, TO MAKE SOME FEEL INFERIOR OR SUPERIOR. ITS JUST THAT SIMPLE, NOW STOP BEING A DUMBASS AND WORK TO BE A BETTER HUMAN.

TO BE ANTI-RACIST YOU MUST UNDERSTAND THE THERE IS ONLY ONE RACE, HUMAN. EVERYTHING ELSE IS BULLSHIT, TO MAKE SOME FEEL INFERIOR OR SUPERIOR. ITS JUST THAT SIMPLE, NOW STOP BEING A DUMBASS AND WORK TO BE A BETTER HUMAN.

TO BE ANTI-RACIST YOU MUST UNDERSTAND THE THERE IS ONLY ONE RACE, HUMAN. EVERYTHING ELSE IS BULLSHIT, TO MAKE SOME FEEL INFERIOR OR SUPERIOR. ITS JUST THAT SIMPLE, NOW STOP BEING A DUMBASS AND WORK TO BE A BETTER HUMAN.

TO BE ANTI-RACIST YOU MUST UNDERSTAND THE THERE IS ONLY ONE RACE, HUMAN. EVERYTHING ELSE IS BULLSHIT, TO MAKE SOME FEEL INFERIOR OR SUPERIOR. ITS JUST THAT SIMPLE, NOW STOP BEING A DUMBASS AND WORK TO BE A BETTER HUMAN.

TO BE ANTI-RACIST YOU MUST UNDERSTAND THE THERE IS ONLY ONE RACE, HUMAN. EVERYTHING ELSE IS BULLSHIT, TO MAKE SOME FEEL INFERIOR OR SUPERIOR. ITS JUST THAT SIMPLE, NOW STOP BEING A DUMBASS AND WORK TO BE A BETTER HUMAN.

TO BE ANTI-RACIST YOU MUST UNDERSTAND THE THERE IS ONLY ONE RACE, HUMAN. EVERYTHING ELSE IS BULLSHIT, TO MAKE SOME FEEL INFERIOR OR SUPERIOR. ITS JUST THAT SIMPLE, NOW STOP BEING A DUMBASS AND WORK TO BE A BETTER HUMAN.

TO BE ANTI-RACIST YOU MUST UNDERSTAND THE THERE IS ONLY ONE RACE, HUMAN. EVERYTHING ELSE IS BULLSHIT, TO MAKE SOME FEEL INFERIOR OR SUPERIOR. ITS JUST THAT SIMPLE, NOW STOP BEING A DUMBASS AND WORK TO BE A BETTER HUMAN.

TO BE ANTI-RACIST YOU MUST UNDERSTAND THE THERE IS ONLY ONE RACE, HUMAN. EVERYTHING ELSE IS BULLSHIT, TO MAKE SOME FEEL INFERIOR OR SUPERIOR. ITS JUST THAT SIMPLE, NOW STOP BEING A DUMBASS AND WORK TO BE A BETTER HUMAN.

TO BE ANTI-RACIST YOU MUST UNDERSTAND THE THERE IS ONLY ONE RACE, HUMAN. EVERYTHING ELSE IS BULLSHIT, TO MAKE SOME FEEL INFERIOR OR SUPERIOR. ITS

TO BE ANTI-RACIST YOU MUST UNDERSTAND THE THERE IS ONLY ONE RACE, HUMAN. EVERYTHING ELSE IS BULLSHIT, TO MAKE SOME FEEL INFERIOR OR SUPERIOR. ITS JUST THAT SIMPLE, NOW STOP BEING A DUMBASS AND WORK TO BE A BETTER HUMAN.

TO BE ANTI-RACIST YOU MUST UNDERSTAND THE THERE IS ONLY ONE RACE, HUMAN. EVERYTHING ELSE IS BULLSHIT, TO MAKE SOME FEEL INFERIOR OR SUPERIOR. ITS JUST THAT SIMPLE, NOW STOP BEING A DUMBASS AND WORK TO BE A BETTER HUMAN.

TO BE ANTI-RACIST YOU MUST UNDERSTAND THE THERE IS ONLY ONE RACE, HUMAN. EVERYTHING ELSE IS BULLSHIT, TO MAKE SOME FEEL INFERIOR OR SUPERIOR. ITS JUST THAT SIMPLE, NOW STOP BEING A DUMBASS AND WORK TO BE A BETTER HUMAN.

TO BE ANTI-RACIST YOU MUST UNDERSTAND THE THERE IS ONLY ONE RACE, HUMAN. EVERYTHING ELSE IS BULLSHIT, TO MAKE SOME FEEL INFERIOR OR SUPERIOR. ITS JUST THAT SIMPLE, NOW STOP BEING A DUMBASS AND WORK TO BE A BETTER HUMAN.

TO BE ANTI-RACIST YOU MUST UNDERSTAND THE THERE IS ONLY ONE RACE, HUMAN. EVERYTHING ELSE IS BULLSHIT, TO MAKE SOME FEEL INFERIOR OR SUPERIOR. ITS JUST THAT SIMPLE, NOW STOP BEING A DUMBASS AND WORK TO BE A BETTER HUMAN.

TO BE ANTI-RACIST YOU MUST UNDERSTAND THE THERE IS ONLY ONE RACE, HUMAN. EVERYTHING ELSE IS BULLSHIT, TO MAKE SOME FEEL INFERIOR OR SUPERIOR. ITS JUST THAT SIMPLE, NOW STOP BEING A DUMBASS AND WORK TO BE A BETTER HUMAN.

TO BE ANTI-RACIST YOU MUST UNDERSTAND THE THERE IS ONLY ONE RACE, HUMAN. EVERYTHING ELSE IS BULLSHIT, TO MAKE SOME FEEL INFERIOR OR SUPERIOR. ITS JUST THAT SIMPLE, NOW STOP BEING A DUMBASS AND WORK TO BE A BETTER HUMAN.

TO BE ANTI-RACIST YOU MUST UNDERSTAND THE THERE IS ONLY ONE RACE, HUMAN. EVERYTHING ELSE IS BULLSHIT, TO MAKE SOME FEEL INFERIOR OR SUPERIOR. ITS JUST THAT SIMPLE, NOW STOP BEING A DUMBASS AND WORK TO BE A BETTER HUMAN.

TO BE ANTI-RACIST YOU MUST UNDERSTAND THE THERE IS ONLY ONE RACE, HUMAN. EVERYTHING ELSE IS BULLSHIT, TO MAKE SOME FEEL INFERIOR OR SUPERIOR. ITS JUST THAT SIMPLE, NOW STOP BEING A DUMBASS AND WORK TO BE A BETTER HUMAN.

TO BE ANTI-RACIST YOU MUST UNDERSTAND THE THERE IS ONLY ONE RACE, HUMAN. EVERYTHING ELSE IS BULLSHIT, TO MAKE SOME FEEL INFERIOR OR SUPERIOR. ITS JUST THAT SIMPLE, NOW STOP BEING A DUMBASS AND WORK TO BE A BETTER HUMAN.

JUST THAT SIMPLE, NOW STOP BEING A DUMBASS AND WORK TO BE A BETTER HUMAN.

TO BE ANTI-RACIST YOU MUST UNDERSTAND THE THERE IS ONLY ONE RACE, HUMAN. EVERYTHING ELSE IS BULLSHIT, TO MAKE SOME FEEL INFERIOR OR SUPERIOR. ITS JUST THAT SIMPLE, NOW STOP BEING A DUMBASS AND WORK TO BE A BETTER HUMAN.

TO BE ANTI-RACIST YOU MUST UNDERSTAND THE THERE IS ONLY ONE RACE, HUMAN. EVERYTHING ELSE IS BULLSHIT, TO MAKE SOME FEEL INFERIOR OR SUPERIOR. ITS JUST THAT SIMPLE, NOW STOP BEING A DUMBASS AND WORK TO BE A BETTER HUMAN.

TO BE ANTI-RACIST YOU MUST UNDERSTAND THE THERE IS ONLY ONE RACE, HUMAN. EVERYTHING ELSE IS BULLSHIT, TO MAKE SOME FEEL INFERIOR OR SUPERIOR. ITS JUST THAT SIMPLE, NOW STOP BEING A DUMBASS AND WORK TO BE A BETTER HUMAN.

TO BE ANTI-RACIST YOU MUST UNDERSTAND THE THERE IS ONLY ONE RACE, HUMAN. EVERYTHING ELSE IS BULLSHIT, TO MAKE SOME FEEL INFERIOR OR SUPERIOR. ITS JUST THAT SIMPLE, NOW STOP BEING A DUMBASS AND WORK TO BE A BETTER HUMAN.

TO BE ANTI-RACIST YOU MUST UNDERSTAND THE THERE IS ONLY ONE RACE, HUMAN. EVERYTHING ELSE IS BULLSHIT, TO MAKE SOME FEEL INFERIOR OR SUPERIOR. ITS JUST THAT SIMPLE, NOW STOP BEING A DUMBASS AND WORK TO BE A BETTER HUMAN.

TO BE ANTI-RACIST YOU MUST UNDERSTAND THE THERE IS ONLY ONE RACE, HUMAN. EVERYTHING ELSE IS BULLSHIT, TO MAKE SOME FEEL INFERIOR OR SUPERIOR. ITS JUST THAT SIMPLE, NOW STOP BEING A DUMBASS AND WORK TO BE A BETTER HUMAN.

TO BE ANTI-RACIST YOU MUST UNDERSTAND THE THERE IS ONLY ONE RACE, HUMAN. EVERYTHING ELSE IS BULLSHIT, TO MAKE SOME FEEL INFERIOR OR SUPERIOR. ITS JUST THAT SIMPLE, NOW STOP BEING A DUMBASS AND WORK TO BE A BETTER HUMAN.

TO BE ANTI-RACIST YOU MUST UNDERSTAND THE THERE IS ONLY ONE RACE, HUMAN. EVERYTHING ELSE IS BULLSHIT, TO MAKE SOME FEEL INFERIOR OR SUPERIOR. ITS JUST THAT SIMPLE, NOW STOP BEING A DUMBASS AND WORK TO BE A BETTER HUMAN.

TO BE ANTI-RACIST YOU MUST UNDERSTAND THE THERE IS ONLY ONE RACE, HUMAN. EVERYTHING ELSE IS BULLSHIT, TO MAKE SOME FEEL INFERIOR OR SUPERIOR. ITS JUST THAT SIMPLE, NOW STOP BEING A DUMBASS AND WORK TO BE A BETTER HUMAN.

TO BE ANTI-RACIST YOU MUST UNDERSTAND THE THERE IS ONLY ONE RACE, HUMAN. EVERYTHING ELSE IS BULLSHIT, TO MAKE SOME FEEL INFERIOR OR SUPERIOR. ITS

TO BE ANTI-RACIST YOU MUST UNDERSTAND THE THERE IS ONLY ONE RACE, HUMAN. EVERYTHING ELSE IS BULLSHIT, TO MAKE SOME FEEL INFERIOR OR SUPERIOR. ITS JUST THAT SIMPLE, NOW STOP BEING A DUMBASS AND WORK TO BE A BETTER HUMAN.

TO BE ANTI-RACIST YOU MUST UNDERSTAND THE THERE IS ONLY ONE RACE, HUMAN. EVERYTHING ELSE IS BULLSHIT, TO MAKE SOME FEEL INFERIOR OR SUPERIOR. ITS JUST THAT SIMPLE, NOW STOP BEING A DUMBASS AND WORK TO BE A BETTER HUMAN.

TO BE ANTI-RACIST YOU MUST UNDERSTAND THE THERE IS ONLY ONE RACE, HUMAN. EVERYTHING ELSE IS BULLSHIT, TO MAKE SOME FEEL INFERIOR OR SUPERIOR. ITS JUST THAT SIMPLE, NOW STOP BEING A DUMBASS AND WORK TO BE A BETTER HUMAN.

TO BE ANTI-RACIST YOU MUST UNDERSTAND THE THERE IS ONLY ONE RACE, HUMAN. EVERYTHING ELSE IS BULLSHIT, TO MAKE SOME FEEL INFERIOR OR SUPERIOR. ITS JUST THAT SIMPLE, NOW STOP BEING A DUMBASS AND WORK TO BE A BETTER HUMAN.

TO BE ANTI-RACIST YOU MUST UNDERSTAND THE THERE IS ONLY ONE RACE, HUMAN. EVERYTHING ELSE IS BULLSHIT, TO MAKE SOME FEEL INFERIOR OR SUPERIOR. ITS JUST THAT SIMPLE, NOW STOP BEING A DUMBASS AND WORK TO BE A BETTER HUMAN.

TO BE ANTI-RACIST YOU MUST UNDERSTAND THE THERE IS ONLY ONE RACE, HUMAN. EVERYTHING ELSE IS BULLSHIT, TO MAKE SOME FEEL INFERIOR OR SUPERIOR. ITS JUST THAT SIMPLE, NOW STOP BEING A DUMBASS AND WORK TO BE A BETTER HUMAN.

TO BE ANTI-RACIST YOU MUST UNDERSTAND THE THERE IS ONLY ONE RACE, HUMAN. EVERYTHING ELSE IS BULLSHIT, TO MAKE SOME FEEL INFERIOR OR SUPERIOR. ITS JUST THAT SIMPLE, NOW STOP BEING A DUMBASS AND WORK TO BE A BETTER HUMAN.

TO BE ANTI-RACIST YOU MUST UNDERSTAND THE THERE IS ONLY ONE RACE, HUMAN. EVERYTHING ELSE IS BULLSHIT, TO MAKE SOME FEEL INFERIOR OR SUPERIOR. ITS JUST THAT SIMPLE, NOW STOP BEING A DUMBASS AND WORK TO BE A BETTER HUMAN.

TO BE ANTI-RACIST YOU MUST UNDERSTAND THE THERE IS ONLY ONE RACE, HUMAN. EVERYTHING ELSE IS BULLSHIT, TO MAKE SOME FEEL INFERIOR OR SUPERIOR. ITS JUST THAT SIMPLE, NOW STOP BEING A DUMBASS AND WORK TO BE A BETTER HUMAN.

TO BE ANTI-RACIST YOU MUST UNDERSTAND THE THERE IS ONLY ONE RACE, HUMAN. EVERYTHING ELSE IS BULLSHIT, TO MAKE SOME FEEL INFERIOR OR SUPERIOR. ITS JUST THAT SIMPLE, NOW STOP BEING A DUMBASS AND WORK TO BE A BETTER HUMAN.

TO BE ANTI-RACIST YOU MUST UNDERSTAND THE THERE IS ONLY ONE RACE, HUMAN. EVERYTHING ELSE IS BULLSHIT, TO MAKE SOME FEEL INFERIOR OR SUPERIOR. ITS JUST THAT SIMPLE, NOW STOP BEING A DUMBASS AND WORK TO BE A BETTER HUMAN.

JUST THAT SIMPLE, NOW STOP BEING A DUMBASS AND WORK TO BE A BETTER HUMAN.

TO BE ANTI-RACIST YOU MUST UNDERSTAND THE THERE IS ONLY ONE RACE, HUMAN. EVERYTHING ELSE IS BULLSHIT, TO MAKE SOME FEEL INFERIOR OR SUPERIOR. ITS JUST THAT SIMPLE, NOW STOP BEING A DUMBASS AND WORK TO BE A BETTER HUMAN.

TO BE ANTI-RACIST YOU MUST UNDERSTAND THE THERE IS ONLY ONE RACE, HUMAN. EVERYTHING ELSE IS BULLSHIT, TO MAKE SOME FEEL INFERIOR OR SUPERIOR. ITS JUST THAT SIMPLE, NOW STOP BEING A DUMBASS AND WORK TO BE A BETTER HUMAN.

TO BE ANTI-RACIST YOU MUST UNDERSTAND THE THERE IS ONLY ONE RACE, HUMAN. EVERYTHING ELSE IS BULLSHIT, TO MAKE SOME FEEL INFERIOR OR SUPERIOR. ITS JUST THAT SIMPLE, NOW STOP BEING A DUMBASS AND WORK TO BE A BETTER HUMAN.

TO BE ANTI-RACIST YOU MUST UNDERSTAND THE THERE IS ONLY ONE RACE, HUMAN. EVERYTHING ELSE IS BULLSHIT, TO MAKE SOME FEEL INFERIOR OR SUPERIOR. ITS JUST THAT SIMPLE, NOW STOP BEING A DUMBASS AND WORK TO BE A BETTER HUMAN.

TO BE ANTI-RACIST YOU MUST UNDERSTAND THE THERE IS ONLY ONE RACE, HUMAN. EVERYTHING ELSE IS BULLSHIT, TO MAKE SOME FEEL INFERIOR OR SUPERIOR. ITS JUST THAT SIMPLE, NOW STOP BEING A DUMBASS AND WORK TO BE A BETTER HUMAN.

TO BE ANTI-RACIST YOU MUST UNDERSTAND THE THERE IS ONLY ONE RACE, HUMAN. EVERYTHING ELSE IS BULLSHIT, TO MAKE SOME FEEL INFERIOR OR SUPERIOR. ITS JUST THAT SIMPLE, NOW STOP BEING A DUMBASS AND WORK TO BE A BETTER HUMAN.

TO BE ANTI-RACIST YOU MUST UNDERSTAND THE THERE IS ONLY ONE RACE, HUMAN. EVERYTHING ELSE IS BULLSHIT, TO MAKE SOME FEEL INFERIOR OR SUPERIOR. ITS JUST THAT SIMPLE, NOW STOP BEING A DUMBASS AND WORK TO BE A BETTER HUMAN.

TO BE ANTI-RACIST YOU MUST UNDERSTAND THE THERE IS ONLY ONE RACE, HUMAN. EVERYTHING ELSE IS BULLSHIT, TO MAKE SOME FEEL INFERIOR OR SUPERIOR. ITS JUST THAT SIMPLE, NOW STOP BEING A DUMBASS AND WORK TO BE A BETTER HUMAN.

TO BE ANTI-RACIST YOU MUST UNDERSTAND THE THERE IS ONLY ONE RACE, HUMAN. EVERYTHING ELSE IS BULLSHIT, TO MAKE SOME FEEL INFERIOR OR SUPERIOR. ITS

TO BE ANTI-RACIST YOU MUST UNDERSTAND THE THERE IS ONLY ONE RACE, HUMAN. EVERYTHING ELSE IS BULLSHIT, TO MAKE SOME FEEL INFERIOR OR SUPERIOR. ITS JUST THAT SIMPLE, NOW STOP BEING A DUMBASS AND WORK TO BE A BETTER HUMAN.

TO BE ANTI-RACIST YOU MUST UNDERSTAND THE THERE IS ONLY ONE RACE, HUMAN. EVERYTHING ELSE IS BULLSHIT, TO MAKE SOME FEEL INFERIOR OR SUPERIOR. ITS JUST THAT SIMPLE, NOW STOP BEING A DUMBASS AND WORK TO BE A BETTER HUMAN.

TO BE ANTI-RACIST YOU MUST UNDERSTAND THE THERE IS ONLY ONE RACE, HUMAN. EVERYTHING ELSE IS BULLSHIT, TO MAKE SOME FEEL INFERIOR OR SUPERIOR. ITS JUST THAT SIMPLE, NOW STOP BEING A DUMBASS AND WORK TO BE A BETTER HUMAN.

TO BE ANTI-RACIST YOU MUST UNDERSTAND THE THERE IS ONLY ONE RACE, HUMAN. EVERYTHING ELSE IS BULLSHIT, TO MAKE SOME FEEL INFERIOR OR SUPERIOR. ITS JUST THAT SIMPLE, NOW STOP BEING A DUMBASS AND WORK TO BE A BETTER HUMAN.

TO BE ANTI-RACIST YOU MUST UNDERSTAND THE THERE IS ONLY ONE RACE, HUMAN. EVERYTHING ELSE IS BULLSHIT, TO MAKE SOME FEEL INFERIOR OR SUPERIOR. ITS JUST THAT SIMPLE, NOW STOP BEING A DUMBASS AND WORK TO BE A BETTER HUMAN.

TO BE ANTI-RACIST YOU MUST UNDERSTAND THE THERE IS ONLY ONE RACE, HUMAN. EVERYTHING ELSE IS BULLSHIT, TO MAKE SOME FEEL INFERIOR OR SUPERIOR. ITS JUST THAT SIMPLE, NOW STOP BEING A DUMBASS AND WORK TO BE A BETTER HUMAN.

TO BE ANTI-RACIST YOU MUST UNDERSTAND THE THERE IS ONLY ONE RACE, HUMAN. EVERYTHING ELSE IS BULLSHIT, TO MAKE SOME FEEL INFERIOR OR SUPERIOR. ITS JUST THAT SIMPLE, NOW STOP BEING A DUMBASS AND WORK TO BE A BETTER HUMAN.

TO BE ANTI-RACIST YOU MUST UNDERSTAND THE THERE IS ONLY ONE RACE, HUMAN. EVERYTHING ELSE IS BULLSHIT, TO MAKE SOME FEEL INFERIOR OR SUPERIOR. ITS JUST THAT SIMPLE, NOW STOP BEING A DUMBASS AND WORK TO BE A BETTER HUMAN.

TO BE ANTI-RACIST YOU MUST UNDERSTAND THE THERE IS ONLY ONE RACE, HUMAN. EVERYTHING ELSE IS BULLSHIT, TO MAKE SOME FEEL INFERIOR OR SUPERIOR. ITS JUST THAT SIMPLE, NOW STOP BEING A DUMBASS AND WORK TO BE A BETTER HUMAN.

TO BE ANTI-RACIST YOU MUST UNDERSTAND THE THERE IS ONLY ONE RACE, HUMAN. EVERYTHING ELSE IS BULLSHIT, TO MAKE SOME FEEL INFERIOR OR SUPERIOR. ITS JUST THAT SIMPLE, NOW STOP BEING A DUMBASS AND WORK TO BE A BETTER HUMAN.

JUST THAT SIMPLE, NOW STOP BEING A DUMBASS AND WORK TO BE A BETTER
HUMAN.
TO BE ANTI-RACIST YOU MUST UNDERSTAND THE THERE IS ONLY ONE RACE, HUMAN.
EVERYTHING ELSE IS BULLSHIT, TO MAKE SOME FEEL INFERIOR OR SUPERIOR. ITS
JUST THAT SIMPLE, NOW STOP BEING A DUMBASS AND WORK TO BE A BETTER
HUMAN.
TO BE ANTI-RACIST YOU MUST UNDERSTAND THE THERE IS ONLY ONE RACE, HUMAN.
EVERYTHING ELSE IS BULLSHIT, TO MAKE SOME FEEL INFERIOR OR SUPERIOR. ITS
JUST THAT SIMPLE, NOW STOP BEING A DUMBASS AND WORK TO BE A BETTER
HUMAN.
TO BE ANTI-RACIST YOU MUST UNDERSTAND THE THERE IS ONLY ONE RACE, HUMAN.
EVERYTHING ELSE IS BULLSHIT, TO MAKE SOME FEEL INFERIOR OR SUPERIOR. ITS
JUST THAT SIMPLE, NOW STOP BEING A DUMBASS AND WORK TO BE A BETTER
HUMAN.
TO BE ANTI-RACIST YOU MUST UNDERSTAND THE THERE IS ONLY ONE RACE, HUMAN.
EVERYTHING ELSE IS BULLSHIT, TO MAKE SOME FEEL INFERIOR OR SUPERIOR. ITS
JUST THAT SIMPLE, NOW STOP BEING A DUMBASS AND WORK TO BE A BETTER
HUMAN.
TO BE ANTI-RACIST YOU MUST UNDERSTAND THE THERE IS ONLY ONE RACE, HUMAN.
EVERYTHING ELSE IS BULLSHIT, TO MAKE SOME FEEL INFERIOR OR SUPERIOR. ITS
JUST THAT SIMPLE, NOW STOP BEING A DUMBASS AND WORK TO BE A BETTER
HUMAN.
TO BE ANTI-RACIST YOU MUST UNDERSTAND THE THERE IS ONLY ONE RACE, HUMAN.
EVERYTHING ELSE IS BULLSHIT, TO MAKE SOME FEEL INFERIOR OR SUPERIOR. ITS
JUST THAT SIMPLE, NOW STOP BEING A DUMBASS AND WORK TO BE A BETTER
HUMAN.
TO BE ANTI-RACIST YOU MUST UNDERSTAND THE THERE IS ONLY ONE RACE, HUMAN.
EVERYTHING ELSE IS BULLSHIT, TO MAKE SOME FEEL INFERIOR OR SUPERIOR. ITS
JUST THAT SIMPLE, NOW STOP BEING A DUMBASS AND WORK TO BE A BETTER
HUMAN.
TO BE ANTI-RACIST YOU MUST UNDERSTAND THE THERE IS ONLY ONE RACE, HUMAN.
EVERYTHING ELSE IS BULLSHIT, TO MAKE SOME FEEL INFERIOR OR SUPERIOR. ITS
JUST THAT SIMPLE, NOW STOP BEING A DUMBASS AND WORK TO BE A BETTER
HUMAN.
TO BE ANTI-RACIST YOU MUST UNDERSTAND THE THERE IS ONLY ONE RACE, HUMAN.
EVERYTHING ELSE IS BULLSHIT, TO MAKE SOME FEEL INFERIOR OR SUPERIOR. ITS
JUST THAT SIMPLE, NOW STOP BEING A DUMBASS AND WORK TO BE A BETTER
HUMAN.
TO BE ANTI-RACIST YOU MUST UNDERSTAND THE THERE IS ONLY ONE RACE, HUMAN.
EVERYTHING ELSE IS BULLSHIT, TO MAKE SOME FEEL INFERIOR OR SUPERIOR. ITS

TO BE ANTI-RACIST YOU MUST UNDERSTAND THE THERE IS ONLY ONE RACE, HUMAN. EVERYTHING ELSE IS BULLSHIT, TO MAKE SOME FEEL INFERIOR OR SUPERIOR. ITS JUST THAT SIMPLE, NOW STOP BEING A DUMBASS AND WORK TO BE A BETTER HUMAN.

TO BE ANTI-RACIST YOU MUST UNDERSTAND THE THERE IS ONLY ONE RACE, HUMAN. EVERYTHING ELSE IS BULLSHIT, TO MAKE SOME FEEL INFERIOR OR SUPERIOR. ITS JUST THAT SIMPLE, NOW STOP BEING A DUMBASS AND WORK TO BE A BETTER HUMAN.

TO BE ANTI-RACIST YOU MUST UNDERSTAND THE THERE IS ONLY ONE RACE, HUMAN. EVERYTHING ELSE IS BULLSHIT, TO MAKE SOME FEEL INFERIOR OR SUPERIOR. ITS JUST THAT SIMPLE, NOW STOP BEING A DUMBASS AND WORK TO BE A BETTER HUMAN.

TO BE ANTI-RACIST YOU MUST UNDERSTAND THE THERE IS ONLY ONE RACE, HUMAN. EVERYTHING ELSE IS BULLSHIT, TO MAKE SOME FEEL INFERIOR OR SUPERIOR. ITS JUST THAT SIMPLE, NOW STOP BEING A DUMBASS AND WORK TO BE A BETTER HUMAN.

TO BE ANTI-RACIST YOU MUST UNDERSTAND THE THERE IS ONLY ONE RACE, HUMAN. EVERYTHING ELSE IS BULLSHIT, TO MAKE SOME FEEL INFERIOR OR SUPERIOR. ITS JUST THAT SIMPLE, NOW STOP BEING A DUMBASS AND WORK TO BE A BETTER HUMAN.

TO BE ANTI-RACIST YOU MUST UNDERSTAND THE THERE IS ONLY ONE RACE, HUMAN. EVERYTHING ELSE IS BULLSHIT, TO MAKE SOME FEEL INFERIOR OR SUPERIOR. ITS JUST THAT SIMPLE, NOW STOP BEING A DUMBASS AND WORK TO BE A BETTER HUMAN.

TO BE ANTI-RACIST YOU MUST UNDERSTAND THE THERE IS ONLY ONE RACE, HUMAN. EVERYTHING ELSE IS BULLSHIT, TO MAKE SOME FEEL INFERIOR OR SUPERIOR. ITS JUST THAT SIMPLE, NOW STOP BEING A DUMBASS AND WORK TO BE A BETTER HUMAN.

TO BE ANTI-RACIST YOU MUST UNDERSTAND THE THERE IS ONLY ONE RACE, HUMAN. EVERYTHING ELSE IS BULLSHIT, TO MAKE SOME FEEL INFERIOR OR SUPERIOR. ITS JUST THAT SIMPLE, NOW STOP BEING A DUMBASS AND WORK TO BE A BETTER HUMAN.

TO BE ANTI-RACIST YOU MUST UNDERSTAND THE THERE IS ONLY ONE RACE, HUMAN. EVERYTHING ELSE IS BULLSHIT, TO MAKE SOME FEEL INFERIOR OR SUPERIOR. ITS JUST THAT SIMPLE, NOW STOP BEING A DUMBASS AND WORK TO BE A BETTER HUMAN.

TO BE ANTI-RACIST YOU MUST UNDERSTAND THE THERE IS ONLY ONE RACE, HUMAN. EVERYTHING ELSE IS BULLSHIT, TO MAKE SOME FEEL INFERIOR OR SUPERIOR. ITS JUST THAT SIMPLE, NOW STOP BEING A DUMBASS AND WORK TO BE A BETTER HUMAN.

TO BE ANTI-RACIST YOU MUST UNDERSTAND THE THERE IS ONLY ONE RACE, HUMAN. EVERYTHING ELSE IS BULLSHIT, TO MAKE SOME FEEL INFERIOR OR SUPERIOR. ITS JUST THAT SIMPLE, NOW STOP BEING A DUMBASS AND WORK TO BE A BETTER HUMAN.

JUST THAT SIMPLE, NOW STOP BEING A DUMBASS AND WORK TO BE A BETTER HUMAN.

TO BE ANTI-RACIST YOU MUST UNDERSTAND THE THERE IS ONLY ONE RACE, HUMAN. EVERYTHING ELSE IS BULLSHIT, TO MAKE SOME FEEL INFERIOR OR SUPERIOR. ITS JUST THAT SIMPLE, NOW STOP BEING A DUMBASS AND WORK TO BE A BETTER HUMAN.

TO BE ANTI-RACIST YOU MUST UNDERSTAND THE THERE IS ONLY ONE RACE, HUMAN. EVERYTHING ELSE IS BULLSHIT, TO MAKE SOME FEEL INFERIOR OR SUPERIOR. ITS JUST THAT SIMPLE, NOW STOP BEING A DUMBASS AND WORK TO BE A BETTER HUMAN.

TO BE ANTI-RACIST YOU MUST UNDERSTAND THE THERE IS ONLY ONE RACE, HUMAN. EVERYTHING ELSE IS BULLSHIT, TO MAKE SOME FEEL INFERIOR OR SUPERIOR. ITS JUST THAT SIMPLE, NOW STOP BEING A DUMBASS AND WORK TO BE A BETTER HUMAN.

TO BE ANTI-RACIST YOU MUST UNDERSTAND THE THERE IS ONLY ONE RACE, HUMAN. EVERYTHING ELSE IS BULLSHIT, TO MAKE SOME FEEL INFERIOR OR SUPERIOR. ITS JUST THAT SIMPLE, NOW STOP BEING A DUMBASS AND WORK TO BE A BETTER HUMAN.

TO BE ANTI-RACIST YOU MUST UNDERSTAND THE THERE IS ONLY ONE RACE, HUMAN. EVERYTHING ELSE IS BULLSHIT, TO MAKE SOME FEEL INFERIOR OR SUPERIOR. ITS JUST THAT SIMPLE, NOW STOP BEING A DUMBASS AND WORK TO BE A BETTER HUMAN.

TO BE ANTI-RACIST YOU MUST UNDERSTAND THE THERE IS ONLY ONE RACE, HUMAN. EVERYTHING ELSE IS BULLSHIT, TO MAKE SOME FEEL INFERIOR OR SUPERIOR. ITS JUST THAT SIMPLE, NOW STOP BEING A DUMBASS AND WORK TO BE A BETTER HUMAN.

TO BE ANTI-RACIST YOU MUST UNDERSTAND THE THERE IS ONLY ONE RACE, HUMAN. EVERYTHING ELSE IS BULLSHIT, TO MAKE SOME FEEL INFERIOR OR SUPERIOR. ITS JUST THAT SIMPLE, NOW STOP BEING A DUMBASS AND WORK TO BE A BETTER HUMAN.

TO BE ANTI-RACIST YOU MUST UNDERSTAND THE THERE IS ONLY ONE RACE, HUMAN. EVERYTHING ELSE IS BULLSHIT, TO MAKE SOME FEEL INFERIOR OR SUPERIOR. ITS JUST THAT SIMPLE, NOW STOP BEING A DUMBASS AND WORK TO BE A BETTER HUMAN.

TO BE ANTI-RACIST YOU MUST UNDERSTAND THE THERE IS ONLY ONE RACE, HUMAN. EVERYTHING ELSE IS BULLSHIT, TO MAKE SOME FEEL INFERIOR OR SUPERIOR. ITS JUST THAT SIMPLE, NOW STOP BEING A DUMBASS AND WORK TO BE A BETTER HUMAN.

TO BE ANTI-RACIST YOU MUST UNDERSTAND THE THERE IS ONLY ONE RACE, HUMAN. EVERYTHING ELSE IS BULLSHIT, TO MAKE SOME FEEL INFERIOR OR SUPERIOR. ITS

TO BE ANTI-RACIST YOU MUST UNDERSTAND THE THERE IS ONLY ONE RACE, HUMAN. EVERYTHING ELSE IS BULLSHIT, TO MAKE SOME FEEL INFERIOR OR SUPERIOR. ITS JUST THAT SIMPLE, NOW STOP BEING A DUMBASS AND WORK TO BE A BETTER HUMAN.

TO BE ANTI-RACIST YOU MUST UNDERSTAND THE THERE IS ONLY ONE RACE, HUMAN. EVERYTHING ELSE IS BULLSHIT, TO MAKE SOME FEEL INFERIOR OR SUPERIOR. ITS JUST THAT SIMPLE, NOW STOP BEING A DUMBASS AND WORK TO BE A BETTER HUMAN.

TO BE ANTI-RACIST YOU MUST UNDERSTAND THE THERE IS ONLY ONE RACE, HUMAN. EVERYTHING ELSE IS BULLSHIT, TO MAKE SOME FEEL INFERIOR OR SUPERIOR. ITS JUST THAT SIMPLE, NOW STOP BEING A DUMBASS AND WORK TO BE A BETTER HUMAN.

TO BE ANTI-RACIST YOU MUST UNDERSTAND THE THERE IS ONLY ONE RACE, HUMAN. EVERYTHING ELSE IS BULLSHIT, TO MAKE SOME FEEL INFERIOR OR SUPERIOR. ITS JUST THAT SIMPLE, NOW STOP BEING A DUMBASS AND WORK TO BE A BETTER HUMAN.

TO BE ANTI-RACIST YOU MUST UNDERSTAND THE THERE IS ONLY ONE RACE, HUMAN. EVERYTHING ELSE IS BULLSHIT, TO MAKE SOME FEEL INFERIOR OR SUPERIOR. ITS JUST THAT SIMPLE, NOW STOP BEING A DUMBASS AND WORK TO BE A BETTER HUMAN.

TO BE ANTI-RACIST YOU MUST UNDERSTAND THE THERE IS ONLY ONE RACE, HUMAN. EVERYTHING ELSE IS BULLSHIT, TO MAKE SOME FEEL INFERIOR OR SUPERIOR. ITS JUST THAT SIMPLE, NOW STOP BEING A DUMBASS AND WORK TO BE A BETTER HUMAN.

TO BE ANTI-RACIST YOU MUST UNDERSTAND THE THERE IS ONLY ONE RACE, HUMAN. EVERYTHING ELSE IS BULLSHIT, TO MAKE SOME FEEL INFERIOR OR SUPERIOR. ITS JUST THAT SIMPLE, NOW STOP BEING A DUMBASS AND WORK TO BE A BETTER HUMAN.

TO BE ANTI-RACIST YOU MUST UNDERSTAND THE THERE IS ONLY ONE RACE, HUMAN. EVERYTHING ELSE IS BULLSHIT, TO MAKE SOME FEEL INFERIOR OR SUPERIOR. ITS JUST THAT SIMPLE, NOW STOP BEING A DUMBASS AND WORK TO BE A BETTER HUMAN.

TO BE ANTI-RACIST YOU MUST UNDERSTAND THE THERE IS ONLY ONE RACE, HUMAN. EVERYTHING ELSE IS BULLSHIT, TO MAKE SOME FEEL INFERIOR OR SUPERIOR. ITS JUST THAT SIMPLE, NOW STOP BEING A DUMBASS AND WORK TO BE A BETTER HUMAN.

TO BE ANTI-RACIST YOU MUST UNDERSTAND THE THERE IS ONLY ONE RACE, HUMAN. EVERYTHING ELSE IS BULLSHIT, TO MAKE SOME FEEL INFERIOR OR SUPERIOR. ITS JUST THAT SIMPLE, NOW STOP BEING A DUMBASS AND WORK TO BE A BETTER HUMAN.

TO BE ANTI-RACIST YOU MUST UNDERSTAND THE THERE IS ONLY ONE RACE, HUMAN. EVERYTHING ELSE IS BULLSHIT, TO MAKE SOME FEEL INFERIOR OR SUPERIOR. ITS JUST THAT SIMPLE, NOW STOP BEING A DUMBASS AND WORK TO BE A BETTER HUMAN.

JUST THAT SIMPLE, NOW STOP BEING A DUMBASS AND WORK TO BE A BETTER
HUMAN.
TO BE ANTI-RACIST YOU MUST UNDERSTAND THE THERE IS ONLY ONE RACE, HUMAN.
EVERYTHING ELSE IS BULLSHIT, TO MAKE SOME FEEL INFERIOR OR SUPERIOR. ITS
JUST THAT SIMPLE, NOW STOP BEING A DUMBASS AND WORK TO BE A BETTER
HUMAN.
TO BE ANTI-RACIST YOU MUST UNDERSTAND THE THERE IS ONLY ONE RACE, HUMAN.
EVERYTHING ELSE IS BULLSHIT, TO MAKE SOME FEEL INFERIOR OR SUPERIOR. ITS
JUST THAT SIMPLE, NOW STOP BEING A DUMBASS AND WORK TO BE A BETTER
HUMAN.
TO BE ANTI-RACIST YOU MUST UNDERSTAND THE THERE IS ONLY ONE RACE, HUMAN.
EVERYTHING ELSE IS BULLSHIT, TO MAKE SOME FEEL INFERIOR OR SUPERIOR. ITS
JUST THAT SIMPLE, NOW STOP BEING A DUMBASS AND WORK TO BE A BETTER
HUMAN.
TO BE ANTI-RACIST YOU MUST UNDERSTAND THE THERE IS ONLY ONE RACE, HUMAN.
EVERYTHING ELSE IS BULLSHIT, TO MAKE SOME FEEL INFERIOR OR SUPERIOR. ITS
JUST THAT SIMPLE, NOW STOP BEING A DUMBASS AND WORK TO BE A BETTER
HUMAN.
TO BE ANTI-RACIST YOU MUST UNDERSTAND THE THERE IS ONLY ONE RACE, HUMAN.
EVERYTHING ELSE IS BULLSHIT, TO MAKE SOME FEEL INFERIOR OR SUPERIOR. ITS
JUST THAT SIMPLE, NOW STOP BEING A DUMBASS AND WORK TO BE A BETTER
HUMAN.
TO BE ANTI-RACIST YOU MUST UNDERSTAND THE THERE IS ONLY ONE RACE, HUMAN.
EVERYTHING ELSE IS BULLSHIT, TO MAKE SOME FEEL INFERIOR OR SUPERIOR. ITS
JUST THAT SIMPLE, NOW STOP BEING A DUMBASS AND WORK TO BE A BETTER
HUMAN.
TO BE ANTI-RACIST YOU MUST UNDERSTAND THE THERE IS ONLY ONE RACE, HUMAN.
EVERYTHING ELSE IS BULLSHIT, TO MAKE SOME FEEL INFERIOR OR SUPERIOR. ITS
JUST THAT SIMPLE, NOW STOP BEING A DUMBASS AND WORK TO BE A BETTER
HUMAN.
TO BE ANTI-RACIST YOU MUST UNDERSTAND THE THERE IS ONLY ONE RACE, HUMAN.
EVERYTHING ELSE IS BULLSHIT, TO MAKE SOME FEEL INFERIOR OR SUPERIOR. ITS
JUST THAT SIMPLE, NOW STOP BEING A DUMBASS AND WORK TO BE A BETTER
HUMAN.
TO BE ANTI-RACIST YOU MUST UNDERSTAND THE THERE IS ONLY ONE RACE, HUMAN.
EVERYTHING ELSE IS BULLSHIT, TO MAKE SOME FEEL INFERIOR OR SUPERIOR. ITS
JUST THAT SIMPLE, NOW STOP BEING A DUMBASS AND WORK TO BE A BETTER
HUMAN.
TO BE ANTI-RACIST YOU MUST UNDERSTAND THE THERE IS ONLY ONE RACE, HUMAN.
EVERYTHING ELSE IS BULLSHIT, TO MAKE SOME FEEL INFERIOR OR SUPERIOR. ITS

TO BE ANTI-RACIST YOU MUST UNDERSTAND THE THERE IS ONLY ONE RACE, HUMAN. EVERYTHING ELSE IS BULLSHIT, TO MAKE SOME FEEL INFERIOR OR SUPERIOR. ITS JUST THAT SIMPLE, NOW STOP BEING A DUMBASS AND WORK TO BE A BETTER HUMAN.

TO BE ANTI-RACIST YOU MUST UNDERSTAND THE THERE IS ONLY ONE RACE, HUMAN. EVERYTHING ELSE IS BULLSHIT, TO MAKE SOME FEEL INFERIOR OR SUPERIOR. ITS JUST THAT SIMPLE, NOW STOP BEING A DUMBASS AND WORK TO BE A BETTER HUMAN.

TO BE ANTI-RACIST YOU MUST UNDERSTAND THE THERE IS ONLY ONE RACE, HUMAN. EVERYTHING ELSE IS BULLSHIT, TO MAKE SOME FEEL INFERIOR OR SUPERIOR. ITS JUST THAT SIMPLE, NOW STOP BEING A DUMBASS AND WORK TO BE A BETTER HUMAN.

TO BE ANTI-RACIST YOU MUST UNDERSTAND THE THERE IS ONLY ONE RACE, HUMAN. EVERYTHING ELSE IS BULLSHIT, TO MAKE SOME FEEL INFERIOR OR SUPERIOR. ITS JUST THAT SIMPLE, NOW STOP BEING A DUMBASS AND WORK TO BE A BETTER HUMAN.

TO BE ANTI-RACIST YOU MUST UNDERSTAND THE THERE IS ONLY ONE RACE, HUMAN. EVERYTHING ELSE IS BULLSHIT, TO MAKE SOME FEEL INFERIOR OR SUPERIOR. ITS JUST THAT SIMPLE, NOW STOP BEING A DUMBASS AND WORK TO BE A BETTER HUMAN.

TO BE ANTI-RACIST YOU MUST UNDERSTAND THE THERE IS ONLY ONE RACE, HUMAN. EVERYTHING ELSE IS BULLSHIT, TO MAKE SOME FEEL INFERIOR OR SUPERIOR. ITS JUST THAT SIMPLE, NOW STOP BEING A DUMBASS AND WORK TO BE A BETTER HUMAN.

TO BE ANTI-RACIST YOU MUST UNDERSTAND THE THERE IS ONLY ONE RACE, HUMAN. EVERYTHING ELSE IS BULLSHIT, TO MAKE SOME FEEL INFERIOR OR SUPERIOR. ITS JUST THAT SIMPLE, NOW STOP BEING A DUMBASS AND WORK TO BE A BETTER HUMAN.

TO BE ANTI-RACIST YOU MUST UNDERSTAND THE THERE IS ONLY ONE RACE, HUMAN. EVERYTHING ELSE IS BULLSHIT, TO MAKE SOME FEEL INFERIOR OR SUPERIOR. ITS JUST THAT SIMPLE, NOW STOP BEING A DUMBASS AND WORK TO BE A BETTER HUMAN.

TO BE ANTI-RACIST YOU MUST UNDERSTAND THE THERE IS ONLY ONE RACE, HUMAN. EVERYTHING ELSE IS BULLSHIT, TO MAKE SOME FEEL INFERIOR OR SUPERIOR. ITS JUST THAT SIMPLE, NOW STOP BEING A DUMBASS AND WORK TO BE A BETTER HUMAN.

TO BE ANTI-RACIST YOU MUST UNDERSTAND THE THERE IS ONLY ONE RACE, HUMAN. EVERYTHING ELSE IS BULLSHIT, TO MAKE SOME FEEL INFERIOR OR SUPERIOR. ITS JUST THAT SIMPLE, NOW STOP BEING A DUMBASS AND WORK TO BE A BETTER HUMAN.

TO BE ANTI-RACIST YOU MUST UNDERSTAND THE THERE IS ONLY ONE RACE, HUMAN. EVERYTHING ELSE IS BULLSHIT, TO MAKE SOME FEEL INFERIOR OR SUPERIOR. ITS JUST THAT SIMPLE, NOW STOP BEING A DUMBASS AND WORK TO BE A BETTER HUMAN.

TO BE ANTI-RACIST YOU MUST UNDERSTAND THE THERE IS ONLY ONE RACE, HUMAN. EVERYTHING ELSE IS BULLSHIT, TO MAKE SOME FEEL INFERIOR OR SUPERIOR. ITS JUST THAT SIMPLE, NOW STOP BEING A DUMBASS AND WORK TO BE A BETTER HUMAN.

JUST THAT SIMPLE, NOW STOP BEING A DUMBASS AND WORK TO BE A BETTER
HUMAN.

TO BE ANTI-RACIST YOU MUST UNDERSTAND THE THERE IS ONLY ONE RACE, HUMAN.
EVERYTHING ELSE IS BULLSHIT, TO MAKE SOME FEEL INFERIOR OR SUPERIOR. ITS
JUST THAT SIMPLE, NOW STOP BEING A DUMBASS AND WORK TO BE A BETTER
HUMAN.

TO BE ANTI-RACIST YOU MUST UNDERSTAND THE THERE IS ONLY ONE RACE, HUMAN.
EVERYTHING ELSE IS BULLSHIT, TO MAKE SOME FEEL INFERIOR OR SUPERIOR. ITS
JUST THAT SIMPLE, NOW STOP BEING A DUMBASS AND WORK TO BE A BETTER
HUMAN.

TO BE ANTI-RACIST YOU MUST UNDERSTAND THE THERE IS ONLY ONE RACE, HUMAN.
EVERYTHING ELSE IS BULLSHIT, TO MAKE SOME FEEL INFERIOR OR SUPERIOR. ITS
JUST THAT SIMPLE, NOW STOP BEING A DUMBASS AND WORK TO BE A BETTER
HUMAN.

TO BE ANTI-RACIST YOU MUST UNDERSTAND THE THERE IS ONLY ONE RACE, HUMAN.
EVERYTHING ELSE IS BULLSHIT, TO MAKE SOME FEEL INFERIOR OR SUPERIOR. ITS
JUST THAT SIMPLE, NOW STOP BEING A DUMBASS AND WORK TO BE A BETTER
HUMAN.

TO BE ANTI-RACIST YOU MUST UNDERSTAND THE THERE IS ONLY ONE RACE, HUMAN.
EVERYTHING ELSE IS BULLSHIT, TO MAKE SOME FEEL INFERIOR OR SUPERIOR. ITS
JUST THAT SIMPLE, NOW STOP BEING A DUMBASS AND WORK TO BE A BETTER
HUMAN.

TO BE ANTI-RACIST YOU MUST UNDERSTAND THE THERE IS ONLY ONE RACE, HUMAN.
EVERYTHING ELSE IS BULLSHIT, TO MAKE SOME FEEL INFERIOR OR SUPERIOR. ITS
JUST THAT SIMPLE, NOW STOP BEING A DUMBASS AND WORK TO BE A BETTER
HUMAN.

TO BE ANTI-RACIST YOU MUST UNDERSTAND THE THERE IS ONLY ONE RACE, HUMAN.
EVERYTHING ELSE IS BULLSHIT, TO MAKE SOME FEEL INFERIOR OR SUPERIOR. ITS
JUST THAT SIMPLE, NOW STOP BEING A DUMBASS AND WORK TO BE A BETTER
HUMAN.

TO BE ANTI-RACIST YOU MUST UNDERSTAND THE THERE IS ONLY ONE RACE, HUMAN.
EVERYTHING ELSE IS BULLSHIT, TO MAKE SOME FEEL INFERIOR OR SUPERIOR. ITS
JUST THAT SIMPLE, NOW STOP BEING A DUMBASS AND WORK TO BE A BETTER
HUMAN.

TO BE ANTI-RACIST YOU MUST UNDERSTAND THE THERE IS ONLY ONE RACE, HUMAN.
EVERYTHING ELSE IS BULLSHIT, TO MAKE SOME FEEL INFERIOR OR SUPERIOR. ITS

TO BE ANTI-RACIST YOU MUST UNDERSTAND THE THERE IS ONLY ONE RACE, HUMAN. EVERYTHING ELSE IS BULLSHIT, TO MAKE SOME FEEL INFERIOR OR SUPERIOR. ITS JUST THAT SIMPLE, NOW STOP BEING A DUMBASS AND WORK TO BE A BETTER HUMAN.

TO BE ANTI-RACIST YOU MUST UNDERSTAND THE THERE IS ONLY ONE RACE, HUMAN. EVERYTHING ELSE IS BULLSHIT, TO MAKE SOME FEEL INFERIOR OR SUPERIOR. ITS JUST THAT SIMPLE, NOW STOP BEING A DUMBASS AND WORK TO BE A BETTER HUMAN.

TO BE ANTI-RACIST YOU MUST UNDERSTAND THE THERE IS ONLY ONE RACE, HUMAN. EVERYTHING ELSE IS BULLSHIT, TO MAKE SOME FEEL INFERIOR OR SUPERIOR. ITS JUST THAT SIMPLE, NOW STOP BEING A DUMBASS AND WORK TO BE A BETTER HUMAN.

TO BE ANTI-RACIST YOU MUST UNDERSTAND THE THERE IS ONLY ONE RACE, HUMAN. EVERYTHING ELSE IS BULLSHIT, TO MAKE SOME FEEL INFERIOR OR SUPERIOR. ITS JUST THAT SIMPLE, NOW STOP BEING A DUMBASS AND WORK TO BE A BETTER HUMAN.

TO BE ANTI-RACIST YOU MUST UNDERSTAND THE THERE IS ONLY ONE RACE, HUMAN. EVERYTHING ELSE IS BULLSHIT, TO MAKE SOME FEEL INFERIOR OR SUPERIOR. ITS JUST THAT SIMPLE, NOW STOP BEING A DUMBASS AND WORK TO BE A BETTER HUMAN.

TO BE ANTI-RACIST YOU MUST UNDERSTAND THE THERE IS ONLY ONE RACE, HUMAN. EVERYTHING ELSE IS BULLSHIT, TO MAKE SOME FEEL INFERIOR OR SUPERIOR. ITS JUST THAT SIMPLE, NOW STOP BEING A DUMBASS AND WORK TO BE A BETTER HUMAN.

TO BE ANTI-RACIST YOU MUST UNDERSTAND THE THERE IS ONLY ONE RACE, HUMAN. EVERYTHING ELSE IS BULLSHIT, TO MAKE SOME FEEL INFERIOR OR SUPERIOR. ITS JUST THAT SIMPLE, NOW STOP BEING A DUMBASS AND WORK TO BE A BETTER HUMAN.

TO BE ANTI-RACIST YOU MUST UNDERSTAND THE THERE IS ONLY ONE RACE, HUMAN. EVERYTHING ELSE IS BULLSHIT, TO MAKE SOME FEEL INFERIOR OR SUPERIOR. ITS JUST THAT SIMPLE, NOW STOP BEING A DUMBASS AND WORK TO BE A BETTER HUMAN.

TO BE ANTI-RACIST YOU MUST UNDERSTAND THE THERE IS ONLY ONE RACE, HUMAN. EVERYTHING ELSE IS BULLSHIT, TO MAKE SOME FEEL INFERIOR OR SUPERIOR. ITS JUST THAT SIMPLE, NOW STOP BEING A DUMBASS AND WORK TO BE A BETTER HUMAN.

TO BE ANTI-RACIST YOU MUST UNDERSTAND THE THERE IS ONLY ONE RACE, HUMAN. EVERYTHING ELSE IS BULLSHIT, TO MAKE SOME FEEL INFERIOR OR SUPERIOR. ITS JUST THAT SIMPLE, NOW STOP BEING A DUMBASS AND WORK TO BE A BETTER HUMAN.

TO BE ANTI-RACIST YOU MUST UNDERSTAND THE THERE IS ONLY ONE RACE, HUMAN. EVERYTHING ELSE IS BULLSHIT, TO MAKE SOME FEEL INFERIOR OR SUPERIOR. ITS JUST THAT SIMPLE, NOW STOP BEING A DUMBASS AND WORK TO BE A BETTER HUMAN

JUST THAT SIMPLE, NOW STOP BEING A DUMBASS AND WORK TO BE A BETTER
HUMAN.

TO BE ANTI-RACIST YOU MUST UNDERSTAND THE THERE IS ONLY ONE RACE, HUMAN.
EVERYTHING ELSE IS BULLSHIT, TO MAKE SOME FEEL INFERIOR OR SUPERIOR. ITS
JUST THAT SIMPLE, NOW STOP BEING A DUMBASS AND WORK TO BE A BETTER
HUMAN.

TO BE ANTI-RACIST YOU MUST UNDERSTAND THE THERE IS ONLY ONE RACE, HUMAN.
EVERYTHING ELSE IS BULLSHIT, TO MAKE SOME FEEL INFERIOR OR SUPERIOR. ITS
JUST THAT SIMPLE, NOW STOP BEING A DUMBASS AND WORK TO BE A BETTER
HUMAN.

TO BE ANTI-RACIST YOU MUST UNDERSTAND THE THERE IS ONLY ONE RACE, HUMAN.
EVERYTHING ELSE IS BULLSHIT, TO MAKE SOME FEEL INFERIOR OR SUPERIOR. ITS
JUST THAT SIMPLE, NOW STOP BEING A DUMBASS AND WORK TO BE A BETTER
HUMAN.

TO BE ANTI-RACIST YOU MUST UNDERSTAND THE THERE IS ONLY ONE RACE, HUMAN.
EVERYTHING ELSE IS BULLSHIT, TO MAKE SOME FEEL INFERIOR OR SUPERIOR. ITS
JUST THAT SIMPLE, NOW STOP BEING A DUMBASS AND WORK TO BE A BETTER
HUMAN.

TO BE ANTI-RACIST YOU MUST UNDERSTAND THE THERE IS ONLY ONE RACE, HUMAN.
EVERYTHING ELSE IS BULLSHIT, TO MAKE SOME FEEL INFERIOR OR SUPERIOR. ITS
JUST THAT SIMPLE, NOW STOP BEING A DUMBASS AND WORK TO BE A BETTER
HUMAN.

TO BE ANTI-RACIST YOU MUST UNDERSTAND THE THERE IS ONLY ONE RACE, HUMAN.
EVERYTHING ELSE IS BULLSHIT, TO MAKE SOME FEEL INFERIOR OR SUPERIOR. ITS
JUST THAT SIMPLE, NOW STOP BEING A DUMBASS AND WORK TO BE A BETTER
HUMAN.

TO BE ANTI-RACIST YOU MUST UNDERSTAND THE THERE IS ONLY ONE RACE, HUMAN.
EVERYTHING ELSE IS BULLSHIT, TO MAKE SOME FEEL INFERIOR OR SUPERIOR. ITS
JUST THAT SIMPLE, NOW STOP BEING A DUMBASS AND WORK TO BE A BETTER
HUMAN.

TO BE ANTI-RACIST YOU MUST UNDERSTAND THE THERE IS ONLY ONE RACE, HUMAN.
EVERYTHING ELSE IS BULLSHIT, TO MAKE SOME FEEL INFERIOR OR SUPERIOR. ITS
JUST THAT SIMPLE, NOW STOP BEING A DUMBASS AND WORK TO BE A BETTER
HUMAN.

TO BE ANTI-RACIST YOU MUST UNDERSTAND THE THERE IS ONLY ONE RACE, HUMAN.
EVERYTHING ELSE IS BULLSHIT, TO MAKE SOME FEEL INFERIOR OR SUPERIOR. ITS
JUST THAT SIMPLE, NOW STOP BEING A DUMBASS AND WORK TO BE A BETTER
HUMAN.

TO BE ANTI-RACIST YOU MUST UNDERSTAND THE THERE IS ONLY ONE RACE, HUMAN.
EVERYTHING ELSE IS BULLSHIT, TO MAKE SOME FEEL INFERIOR OR SUPERIOR. ITS

TO BE ANTI-RACIST YOU MUST UNDERSTAND THE THERE IS ONLY ONE RACE, HUMAN. EVERYTHING ELSE IS BULLSHIT, TO MAKE SOME FEEL INFERIOR OR SUPERIOR. ITS JUST THAT SIMPLE, NOW STOP BEING A DUMBASS AND WORK TO BE A BETTER HUMAN.

TO BE ANTI-RACIST YOU MUST UNDERSTAND THE THERE IS ONLY ONE RACE, HUMAN. EVERYTHING ELSE IS BULLSHIT, TO MAKE SOME FEEL INFERIOR OR SUPERIOR. ITS JUST THAT SIMPLE, NOW STOP BEING A DUMBASS AND WORK TO BE A BETTER HUMAN.

TO BE ANTI-RACIST YOU MUST UNDERSTAND THE THERE IS ONLY ONE RACE, HUMAN. EVERYTHING ELSE IS BULLSHIT, TO MAKE SOME FEEL INFERIOR OR SUPERIOR. ITS JUST THAT SIMPLE, NOW STOP BEING A DUMBASS AND WORK TO BE A BETTER HUMAN.

TO BE ANTI-RACIST YOU MUST UNDERSTAND THE THERE IS ONLY ONE RACE, HUMAN. EVERYTHING ELSE IS BULLSHIT, TO MAKE SOME FEEL INFERIOR OR SUPERIOR. ITS JUST THAT SIMPLE, NOW STOP BEING A DUMBASS AND WORK TO BE A BETTER HUMAN.

TO BE ANTI-RACIST YOU MUST UNDERSTAND THE THERE IS ONLY ONE RACE, HUMAN. EVERYTHING ELSE IS BULLSHIT, TO MAKE SOME FEEL INFERIOR OR SUPERIOR. ITS JUST THAT SIMPLE, NOW STOP BEING A DUMBASS AND WORK TO BE A BETTER HUMAN.

TO BE ANTI-RACIST YOU MUST UNDERSTAND THE THERE IS ONLY ONE RACE, HUMAN. EVERYTHING ELSE IS BULLSHIT, TO MAKE SOME FEEL INFERIOR OR SUPERIOR. ITS JUST THAT SIMPLE, NOW STOP BEING A DUMBASS AND WORK TO BE A BETTER HUMAN.

TO BE ANTI-RACIST YOU MUST UNDERSTAND THE THERE IS ONLY ONE RACE, HUMAN. EVERYTHING ELSE IS BULLSHIT, TO MAKE SOME FEEL INFERIOR OR SUPERIOR. ITS JUST THAT SIMPLE, NOW STOP BEING A DUMBASS AND WORK TO BE A BETTER HUMAN.

TO BE ANTI-RACIST YOU MUST UNDERSTAND THE THERE IS ONLY ONE RACE, HUMAN. EVERYTHING ELSE IS BULLSHIT, TO MAKE SOME FEEL INFERIOR OR SUPERIOR. ITS JUST THAT SIMPLE, NOW STOP BEING A DUMBASS AND WORK TO BE A BETTER HUMAN.

TO BE ANTI-RACIST YOU MUST UNDERSTAND THE THERE IS ONLY ONE RACE, HUMAN. EVERYTHING ELSE IS BULLSHIT, TO MAKE SOME FEEL INFERIOR OR SUPERIOR. ITS JUST THAT SIMPLE, NOW STOP BEING A DUMBASS AND WORK TO BE A BETTER HUMAN.

TO BE ANTI-RACIST YOU MUST UNDERSTAND THE THERE IS ONLY ONE RACE, HUMAN. EVERYTHING ELSE IS BULLSHIT, TO MAKE SOME FEEL INFERIOR OR SUPERIOR. ITS JUST THAT SIMPLE, NOW STOP BEING A DUMBASS AND WORK TO BE A BETTER HUMAN.

TO BE ANTI-RACIST YOU MUST UNDERSTAND THE THERE IS ONLY ONE RACE, HUMAN. EVERYTHING ELSE IS BULLSHIT, TO MAKE SOME FEEL INFERIOR OR SUPERIOR. ITS JUST THAT SIMPLE, NOW STOP BEING A DUMBASS AND WORK TO BE A BETTER HUMAN

JUST THAT SIMPLE, NOW STOP BEING A DUMBASS AND WORK TO BE A BETTER
HUMAN.
TO BE ANTI-RACIST YOU MUST UNDERSTAND THE THERE IS ONLY ONE RACE, HUMAN.
EVERYTHING ELSE IS BULLSHIT, TO MAKE SOME FEEL INFERIOR OR SUPERIOR. ITS
JUST THAT SIMPLE, NOW STOP BEING A DUMBASS AND WORK TO BE A BETTER
HUMAN.
TO BE ANTI-RACIST YOU MUST UNDERSTAND THE THERE IS ONLY ONE RACE, HUMAN.
EVERYTHING ELSE IS BULLSHIT, TO MAKE SOME FEEL INFERIOR OR SUPERIOR. ITS
JUST THAT SIMPLE, NOW STOP BEING A DUMBASS AND WORK TO BE A BETTER
HUMAN.
TO BE ANTI-RACIST YOU MUST UNDERSTAND THE THERE IS ONLY ONE RACE, HUMAN.
EVERYTHING ELSE IS BULLSHIT, TO MAKE SOME FEEL INFERIOR OR SUPERIOR. ITS
JUST THAT SIMPLE, NOW STOP BEING A DUMBASS AND WORK TO BE A BETTER
HUMAN.
TO BE ANTI-RACIST YOU MUST UNDERSTAND THE THERE IS ONLY ONE RACE, HUMAN.
EVERYTHING ELSE IS BULLSHIT, TO MAKE SOME FEEL INFERIOR OR SUPERIOR. ITS
JUST THAT SIMPLE, NOW STOP BEING A DUMBASS AND WORK TO BE A BETTER
HUMAN.
TO BE ANTI-RACIST YOU MUST UNDERSTAND THE THERE IS ONLY ONE RACE, HUMAN.
EVERYTHING ELSE IS BULLSHIT, TO MAKE SOME FEEL INFERIOR OR SUPERIOR. ITS
JUST THAT SIMPLE, NOW STOP BEING A DUMBASS AND WORK TO BE A BETTER
HUMAN.
TO BE ANTI-RACIST YOU MUST UNDERSTAND THE THERE IS ONLY ONE RACE, HUMAN.
EVERYTHING ELSE IS BULLSHIT, TO MAKE SOME FEEL INFERIOR OR SUPERIOR. ITS
JUST THAT SIMPLE, NOW STOP BEING A DUMBASS AND WORK TO BE A BETTER
HUMAN.
TO BE ANTI-RACIST YOU MUST UNDERSTAND THE THERE IS ONLY ONE RACE, HUMAN.
EVERYTHING ELSE IS BULLSHIT, TO MAKE SOME FEEL INFERIOR OR SUPERIOR. ITS
JUST THAT SIMPLE, NOW STOP BEING A DUMBASS AND WORK TO BE A BETTER
HUMAN.
TO BE ANTI-RACIST YOU MUST UNDERSTAND THE THERE IS ONLY ONE RACE, HUMAN.
EVERYTHING ELSE IS BULLSHIT, TO MAKE SOME FEEL INFERIOR OR SUPERIOR. ITS
JUST THAT SIMPLE, NOW STOP BEING A DUMBASS AND WORK TO BE A BETTER
HUMAN.
TO BE ANTI-RACIST YOU MUST UNDERSTAND THE THERE IS ONLY ONE RACE, HUMAN.
EVERYTHING ELSE IS BULLSHIT, TO MAKE SOME FEEL INFERIOR OR SUPERIOR. ITS
JUST THAT SIMPLE, NOW STOP BEING A DUMBASS AND WORK TO BE A BETTER
HUMAN.
TO BE ANTI-RACIST YOU MUST UNDERSTAND THE THERE IS ONLY ONE RACE, HUMAN.
EVERYTHING ELSE IS BULLSHIT, TO MAKE SOME FEEL INFERIOR OR SUPERIOR. ITS

TO BE ANTI-RACIST YOU MUST UNDERSTAND THE THERE IS ONLY ONE RACE, HUMAN. EVERYTHING ELSE IS BULLSHIT, TO MAKE SOME FEEL INFERIOR OR SUPERIOR. ITS JUST THAT SIMPLE, NOW STOP BEING A DUMBASS AND WORK TO BE A BETTER HUMAN.

TO BE ANTI-RACIST YOU MUST UNDERSTAND THE THERE IS ONLY ONE RACE, HUMAN. EVERYTHING ELSE IS BULLSHIT, TO MAKE SOME FEEL INFERIOR OR SUPERIOR. ITS JUST THAT SIMPLE, NOW STOP BEING A DUMBASS AND WORK TO BE A BETTER HUMAN.

TO BE ANTI-RACIST YOU MUST UNDERSTAND THE THERE IS ONLY ONE RACE, HUMAN. EVERYTHING ELSE IS BULLSHIT, TO MAKE SOME FEEL INFERIOR OR SUPERIOR. ITS JUST THAT SIMPLE, NOW STOP BEING A DUMBASS AND WORK TO BE A BETTER HUMAN.

TO BE ANTI-RACIST YOU MUST UNDERSTAND THE THERE IS ONLY ONE RACE, HUMAN. EVERYTHING ELSE IS BULLSHIT, TO MAKE SOME FEEL INFERIOR OR SUPERIOR. ITS JUST THAT SIMPLE, NOW STOP BEING A DUMBASS AND WORK TO BE A BETTER HUMAN.

TO BE ANTI-RACIST YOU MUST UNDERSTAND THE THERE IS ONLY ONE RACE, HUMAN. EVERYTHING ELSE IS BULLSHIT, TO MAKE SOME FEEL INFERIOR OR SUPERIOR. ITS JUST THAT SIMPLE, NOW STOP BEING A DUMBASS AND WORK TO BE A BETTER HUMAN.

TO BE ANTI-RACIST YOU MUST UNDERSTAND THE THERE IS ONLY ONE RACE, HUMAN. EVERYTHING ELSE IS BULLSHIT, TO MAKE SOME FEEL INFERIOR OR SUPERIOR. ITS JUST THAT SIMPLE, NOW STOP BEING A DUMBASS AND WORK TO BE A BETTER HUMAN.

TO BE ANTI-RACIST YOU MUST UNDERSTAND THE THERE IS ONLY ONE RACE, HUMAN. EVERYTHING ELSE IS BULLSHIT, TO MAKE SOME FEEL INFERIOR OR SUPERIOR. ITS JUST THAT SIMPLE, NOW STOP BEING A DUMBASS AND WORK TO BE A BETTER HUMAN.

TO BE ANTI-RACIST YOU MUST UNDERSTAND THE THERE IS ONLY ONE RACE, HUMAN. EVERYTHING ELSE IS BULLSHIT, TO MAKE SOME FEEL INFERIOR OR SUPERIOR. ITS JUST THAT SIMPLE, NOW STOP BEING A DUMBASS AND WORK TO BE A BETTER HUMAN.

TO BE ANTI-RACIST YOU MUST UNDERSTAND THE THERE IS ONLY ONE RACE, HUMAN. EVERYTHING ELSE IS BULLSHIT, TO MAKE SOME FEEL INFERIOR OR SUPERIOR. ITS JUST THAT SIMPLE, NOW STOP BEING A DUMBASS AND WORK TO BE A BETTER HUMAN.

TO BE ANTI-RACIST YOU MUST UNDERSTAND THE THERE IS ONLY ONE RACE, HUMAN. EVERYTHING ELSE IS BULLSHIT, TO MAKE SOME FEEL INFERIOR OR SUPERIOR. ITS JUST THAT SIMPLE, NOW STOP BEING A DUMBASS AND WORK TO BE A BETTER HUMAN.

TO BE ANTI-RACIST YOU MUST UNDERSTAND THE THERE IS ONLY ONE RACE, HUMAN. EVERYTHING ELSE IS BULLSHIT, TO MAKE SOME FEEL INFERIOR OR SUPERIOR. ITS JUST THAT SIMPLE, NOW STOP BEING A DUMBASS AND WORK TO BE A BETTER HUMAN.

JUST THAT SIMPLE, NOW STOP BEING A DUMBASS AND WORK TO BE A BETTER HUMAN.

TO BE ANTI-RACIST YOU MUST UNDERSTAND THE THERE IS ONLY ONE RACE, HUMAN. EVERYTHING ELSE IS BULLSHIT, TO MAKE SOME FEEL INFERIOR OR SUPERIOR. ITS JUST THAT SIMPLE, NOW STOP BEING A DUMBASS AND WORK TO BE A BETTER HUMAN.

TO BE ANTI-RACIST YOU MUST UNDERSTAND THE THERE IS ONLY ONE RACE, HUMAN. EVERYTHING ELSE IS BULLSHIT, TO MAKE SOME FEEL INFERIOR OR SUPERIOR. ITS JUST THAT SIMPLE, NOW STOP BEING A DUMBASS AND WORK TO BE A BETTER HUMAN.

TO BE ANTI-RACIST YOU MUST UNDERSTAND THE THERE IS ONLY ONE RACE, HUMAN. EVERYTHING ELSE IS BULLSHIT, TO MAKE SOME FEEL INFERIOR OR SUPERIOR. ITS JUST THAT SIMPLE, NOW STOP BEING A DUMBASS AND WORK TO BE A BETTER HUMAN.

TO BE ANTI-RACIST YOU MUST UNDERSTAND THE THERE IS ONLY ONE RACE, HUMAN. EVERYTHING ELSE IS BULLSHIT, TO MAKE SOME FEEL INFERIOR OR SUPERIOR. ITS JUST THAT SIMPLE, NOW STOP BEING A DUMBASS AND WORK TO BE A BETTER HUMAN.

TO BE ANTI-RACIST YOU MUST UNDERSTAND THE THERE IS ONLY ONE RACE, HUMAN. EVERYTHING ELSE IS BULLSHIT, TO MAKE SOME FEEL INFERIOR OR SUPERIOR. ITS JUST THAT SIMPLE, NOW STOP BEING A DUMBASS AND WORK TO BE A BETTER HUMAN.

TO BE ANTI-RACIST YOU MUST UNDERSTAND THE THERE IS ONLY ONE RACE, HUMAN. EVERYTHING ELSE IS BULLSHIT, TO MAKE SOME FEEL INFERIOR OR SUPERIOR. ITS JUST THAT SIMPLE, NOW STOP BEING A DUMBASS AND WORK TO BE A BETTER HUMAN.

TO BE ANTI-RACIST YOU MUST UNDERSTAND THE THERE IS ONLY ONE RACE, HUMAN. EVERYTHING ELSE IS BULLSHIT, TO MAKE SOME FEEL INFERIOR OR SUPERIOR. ITS JUST THAT SIMPLE, NOW STOP BEING A DUMBASS AND WORK TO BE A BETTER HUMAN.

TO BE ANTI-RACIST YOU MUST UNDERSTAND THE THERE IS ONLY ONE RACE, HUMAN. EVERYTHING ELSE IS BULLSHIT, TO MAKE SOME FEEL INFERIOR OR SUPERIOR. ITS JUST THAT SIMPLE, NOW STOP BEING A DUMBASS AND WORK TO BE A BETTER HUMAN.

TO BE ANTI-RACIST YOU MUST UNDERSTAND THE THERE IS ONLY ONE RACE, HUMAN. EVERYTHING ELSE IS BULLSHIT, TO MAKE SOME FEEL INFERIOR OR SUPERIOR. ITS JUST THAT SIMPLE, NOW STOP BEING A DUMBASS AND WORK TO BE A BETTER HUMAN.

TO BE ANTI-RACIST YOU MUST UNDERSTAND THE THERE IS ONLY ONE RACE, HUMAN. EVERYTHING ELSE IS BULLSHIT, TO MAKE SOME FEEL INFERIOR OR SUPERIOR. ITS

TO BE ANTI-RACIST YOU MUST UNDERSTAND THE THERE IS ONLY ONE RACE, HUMAN. EVERYTHING ELSE IS BULLSHIT, TO MAKE SOME FEEL INFERIOR OR SUPERIOR. ITS JUST THAT SIMPLE, NOW STOP BEING A DUMBASS AND WORK TO BE A BETTER HUMAN.

TO BE ANTI-RACIST YOU MUST UNDERSTAND THE THERE IS ONLY ONE RACE, HUMAN. EVERYTHING ELSE IS BULLSHIT, TO MAKE SOME FEEL INFERIOR OR SUPERIOR. ITS JUST THAT SIMPLE, NOW STOP BEING A DUMBASS AND WORK TO BE A BETTER HUMAN.

TO BE ANTI-RACIST YOU MUST UNDERSTAND THE THERE IS ONLY ONE RACE, HUMAN. EVERYTHING ELSE IS BULLSHIT, TO MAKE SOME FEEL INFERIOR OR SUPERIOR. ITS JUST THAT SIMPLE, NOW STOP BEING A DUMBASS AND WORK TO BE A BETTER HUMAN.

TO BE ANTI-RACIST YOU MUST UNDERSTAND THE THERE IS ONLY ONE RACE, HUMAN. EVERYTHING ELSE IS BULLSHIT, TO MAKE SOME FEEL INFERIOR OR SUPERIOR. ITS JUST THAT SIMPLE, NOW STOP BEING A DUMBASS AND WORK TO BE A BETTER HUMAN.

TO BE ANTI-RACIST YOU MUST UNDERSTAND THE THERE IS ONLY ONE RACE, HUMAN. EVERYTHING ELSE IS BULLSHIT, TO MAKE SOME FEEL INFERIOR OR SUPERIOR. ITS JUST THAT SIMPLE, NOW STOP BEING A DUMBASS AND WORK TO BE A BETTER HUMAN.

TO BE ANTI-RACIST YOU MUST UNDERSTAND THE THERE IS ONLY ONE RACE, HUMAN. EVERYTHING ELSE IS BULLSHIT, TO MAKE SOME FEEL INFERIOR OR SUPERIOR. ITS JUST THAT SIMPLE, NOW STOP BEING A DUMBASS AND WORK TO BE A BETTER HUMAN.

TO BE ANTI-RACIST YOU MUST UNDERSTAND THE THERE IS ONLY ONE RACE, HUMAN. EVERYTHING ELSE IS BULLSHIT, TO MAKE SOME FEEL INFERIOR OR SUPERIOR. ITS JUST THAT SIMPLE, NOW STOP BEING A DUMBASS AND WORK TO BE A BETTER HUMAN.

TO BE ANTI-RACIST YOU MUST UNDERSTAND THE THERE IS ONLY ONE RACE, HUMAN. EVERYTHING ELSE IS BULLSHIT, TO MAKE SOME FEEL INFERIOR OR SUPERIOR. ITS JUST THAT SIMPLE, NOW STOP BEING A DUMBASS AND WORK TO BE A BETTER HUMAN.

TO BE ANTI-RACIST YOU MUST UNDERSTAND THE THERE IS ONLY ONE RACE, HUMAN. EVERYTHING ELSE IS BULLSHIT, TO MAKE SOME FEEL INFERIOR OR SUPERIOR. ITS JUST THAT SIMPLE, NOW STOP BEING A DUMBASS AND WORK TO BE A BETTER HUMAN.

TO BE ANTI-RACIST YOU MUST UNDERSTAND THE THERE IS ONLY ONE RACE, HUMAN. EVERYTHING ELSE IS BULLSHIT, TO MAKE SOME FEEL INFERIOR OR SUPERIOR. ITS JUST THAT SIMPLE, NOW STOP BEING A DUMBASS AND WORK TO BE A BETTER HUMAN.

TO BE ANTI-RACIST YOU MUST UNDERSTAND THE THERE IS ONLY ONE RACE, HUMAN. EVERYTHING ELSE IS BULLSHIT, TO MAKE SOME FEEL INFERIOR OR SUPERIOR. ITS JUST THAT SIMPLE, NOW STOP BEING A DUMBASS AND WORK TO BE A BETTER HUMAN

JUST THAT SIMPLE, NOW STOP BEING A DUMBASS AND WORK TO BE A BETTER HUMAN.
TO BE ANTI-RACIST YOU MUST UNDERSTAND THE THERE IS ONLY ONE RACE, HUMAN. EVERYTHING ELSE IS BULLSHIT, TO MAKE SOME FEEL INFERIOR OR SUPERIOR. ITS JUST THAT SIMPLE, NOW STOP BEING A DUMBASS AND WORK TO BE A BETTER HUMAN.
TO BE ANTI-RACIST YOU MUST UNDERSTAND THE THERE IS ONLY ONE RACE, HUMAN. EVERYTHING ELSE IS BULLSHIT, TO MAKE SOME FEEL INFERIOR OR SUPERIOR. ITS JUST THAT SIMPLE, NOW STOP BEING A DUMBASS AND WORK TO BE A BETTER HUMAN.
TO BE ANTI-RACIST YOU MUST UNDERSTAND THE THERE IS ONLY ONE RACE, HUMAN. EVERYTHING ELSE IS BULLSHIT, TO MAKE SOME FEEL INFERIOR OR SUPERIOR. ITS JUST THAT SIMPLE, NOW STOP BEING A DUMBASS AND WORK TO BE A BETTER HUMAN.
TO BE ANTI-RACIST YOU MUST UNDERSTAND THE THERE IS ONLY ONE RACE, HUMAN. EVERYTHING ELSE IS BULLSHIT, TO MAKE SOME FEEL INFERIOR OR SUPERIOR. ITS JUST THAT SIMPLE, NOW STOP BEING A DUMBASS AND WORK TO BE A BETTER HUMAN.
TO BE ANTI-RACIST YOU MUST UNDERSTAND THE THERE IS ONLY ONE RACE, HUMAN. EVERYTHING ELSE IS BULLSHIT, TO MAKE SOME FEEL INFERIOR OR SUPERIOR. ITS JUST THAT SIMPLE, NOW STOP BEING A DUMBASS AND WORK TO BE A BETTER HUMAN.
TO BE ANTI-RACIST YOU MUST UNDERSTAND THE THERE IS ONLY ONE RACE, HUMAN. EVERYTHING ELSE IS BULLSHIT, TO MAKE SOME FEEL INFERIOR OR SUPERIOR. ITS JUST THAT SIMPLE, NOW STOP BEING A DUMBASS AND WORK TO BE A BETTER HUMAN.
TO BE ANTI-RACIST YOU MUST UNDERSTAND THE THERE IS ONLY ONE RACE, HUMAN. EVERYTHING ELSE IS BULLSHIT, TO MAKE SOME FEEL INFERIOR OR SUPERIOR. ITS JUST THAT SIMPLE, NOW STOP BEING A DUMBASS AND WORK TO BE A BETTER HUMAN.
TO BE ANTI-RACIST YOU MUST UNDERSTAND THE THERE IS ONLY ONE RACE, HUMAN. EVERYTHING ELSE IS BULLSHIT, TO MAKE SOME FEEL INFERIOR OR SUPERIOR. ITS JUST THAT SIMPLE, NOW STOP BEING A DUMBASS AND WORK TO BE A BETTER HUMAN.
TO BE ANTI-RACIST YOU MUST UNDERSTAND THE THERE IS ONLY ONE RACE, HUMAN. EVERYTHING ELSE IS BULLSHIT, TO MAKE SOME FEEL INFERIOR OR SUPERIOR. ITS JUST THAT SIMPLE, NOW STOP BEING A DUMBASS AND WORK TO BE A BETTER HUMAN.
TO BE ANTI-RACIST YOU MUST UNDERSTAND THE THERE IS ONLY ONE RACE, HUMAN. EVERYTHING ELSE IS BULLSHIT, TO MAKE SOME FEEL INFERIOR OR SUPERIOR. ITS

TO BE ANTI-RACIST YOU MUST UNDERSTAND THE THERE IS ONLY ONE RACE, HUMAN. EVERYTHING ELSE IS BULLSHIT, TO MAKE SOME FEEL INFERIOR OR SUPERIOR. ITS JUST THAT SIMPLE, NOW STOP BEING A DUMBASS AND WORK TO BE A BETTER HUMAN.

TO BE ANTI-RACIST YOU MUST UNDERSTAND THE THERE IS ONLY ONE RACE, HUMAN. EVERYTHING ELSE IS BULLSHIT, TO MAKE SOME FEEL INFERIOR OR SUPERIOR. ITS JUST THAT SIMPLE, NOW STOP BEING A DUMBASS AND WORK TO BE A BETTER HUMAN.

TO BE ANTI-RACIST YOU MUST UNDERSTAND THE THERE IS ONLY ONE RACE, HUMAN. EVERYTHING ELSE IS BULLSHIT, TO MAKE SOME FEEL INFERIOR OR SUPERIOR. ITS JUST THAT SIMPLE, NOW STOP BEING A DUMBASS AND WORK TO BE A BETTER HUMAN.

TO BE ANTI-RACIST YOU MUST UNDERSTAND THE THERE IS ONLY ONE RACE, HUMAN. EVERYTHING ELSE IS BULLSHIT, TO MAKE SOME FEEL INFERIOR OR SUPERIOR. ITS JUST THAT SIMPLE, NOW STOP BEING A DUMBASS AND WORK TO BE A BETTER HUMAN.

TO BE ANTI-RACIST YOU MUST UNDERSTAND THE THERE IS ONLY ONE RACE, HUMAN. EVERYTHING ELSE IS BULLSHIT, TO MAKE SOME FEEL INFERIOR OR SUPERIOR. ITS JUST THAT SIMPLE, NOW STOP BEING A DUMBASS AND WORK TO BE A BETTER HUMAN.

TO BE ANTI-RACIST YOU MUST UNDERSTAND THE THERE IS ONLY ONE RACE, HUMAN. EVERYTHING ELSE IS BULLSHIT, TO MAKE SOME FEEL INFERIOR OR SUPERIOR. ITS JUST THAT SIMPLE, NOW STOP BEING A DUMBASS AND WORK TO BE A BETTER HUMAN.

TO BE ANTI-RACIST YOU MUST UNDERSTAND THE THERE IS ONLY ONE RACE, HUMAN. EVERYTHING ELSE IS BULLSHIT, TO MAKE SOME FEEL INFERIOR OR SUPERIOR. ITS JUST THAT SIMPLE, NOW STOP BEING A DUMBASS AND WORK TO BE A BETTER HUMAN.

TO BE ANTI-RACIST YOU MUST UNDERSTAND THE THERE IS ONLY ONE RACE, HUMAN. EVERYTHING ELSE IS BULLSHIT, TO MAKE SOME FEEL INFERIOR OR SUPERIOR. ITS JUST THAT SIMPLE, NOW STOP BEING A DUMBASS AND WORK TO BE A BETTER HUMAN.

TO BE ANTI-RACIST YOU MUST UNDERSTAND THE THERE IS ONLY ONE RACE, HUMAN. EVERYTHING ELSE IS BULLSHIT, TO MAKE SOME FEEL INFERIOR OR SUPERIOR. ITS JUST THAT SIMPLE, NOW STOP BEING A DUMBASS AND WORK TO BE A BETTER HUMAN.

TO BE ANTI-RACIST YOU MUST UNDERSTAND THE THERE IS ONLY ONE RACE, HUMAN. EVERYTHING ELSE IS BULLSHIT, TO MAKE SOME FEEL INFERIOR OR SUPERIOR. ITS JUST THAT SIMPLE, NOW STOP BEING A DUMBASS AND WORK TO BE A BETTER HUMAN.

TO BE ANTI-RACIST YOU MUST UNDERSTAND THE THERE IS ONLY ONE RACE, HUMAN. EVERYTHING ELSE IS BULLSHIT, TO MAKE SOME FEEL INFERIOR OR SUPERIOR. ITS JUST THAT SIMPLE, NOW STOP BEING A DUMBASS AND WORK TO BE A BETTER HUMAN.

JUST THAT SIMPLE, NOW STOP BEING A DUMBASS AND WORK TO BE A BETTER HUMAN.

TO BE ANTI-RACIST YOU MUST UNDERSTAND THE THERE IS ONLY ONE RACE, HUMAN. EVERYTHING ELSE IS BULLSHIT, TO MAKE SOME FEEL INFERIOR OR SUPERIOR. ITS JUST THAT SIMPLE, NOW STOP BEING A DUMBASS AND WORK TO BE A BETTER HUMAN.

TO BE ANTI-RACIST YOU MUST UNDERSTAND THE THERE IS ONLY ONE RACE, HUMAN. EVERYTHING ELSE IS BULLSHIT, TO MAKE SOME FEEL INFERIOR OR SUPERIOR. ITS JUST THAT SIMPLE, NOW STOP BEING A DUMBASS AND WORK TO BE A BETTER HUMAN.

TO BE ANTI-RACIST YOU MUST UNDERSTAND THE THERE IS ONLY ONE RACE, HUMAN. EVERYTHING ELSE IS BULLSHIT, TO MAKE SOME FEEL INFERIOR OR SUPERIOR. ITS JUST THAT SIMPLE, NOW STOP BEING A DUMBASS AND WORK TO BE A BETTER HUMAN.

TO BE ANTI-RACIST YOU MUST UNDERSTAND THE THERE IS ONLY ONE RACE, HUMAN. EVERYTHING ELSE IS BULLSHIT, TO MAKE SOME FEEL INFERIOR OR SUPERIOR. ITS JUST THAT SIMPLE, NOW STOP BEING A DUMBASS AND WORK TO BE A BETTER HUMAN.

TO BE ANTI-RACIST YOU MUST UNDERSTAND THE THERE IS ONLY ONE RACE, HUMAN. EVERYTHING ELSE IS BULLSHIT, TO MAKE SOME FEEL INFERIOR OR SUPERIOR. ITS JUST THAT SIMPLE, NOW STOP BEING A DUMBASS AND WORK TO BE A BETTER HUMAN.

TO BE ANTI-RACIST YOU MUST UNDERSTAND THE THERE IS ONLY ONE RACE, HUMAN. EVERYTHING ELSE IS BULLSHIT, TO MAKE SOME FEEL INFERIOR OR SUPERIOR. ITS JUST THAT SIMPLE, NOW STOP BEING A DUMBASS AND WORK TO BE A BETTER HUMAN.

TO BE ANTI-RACIST YOU MUST UNDERSTAND THE THERE IS ONLY ONE RACE, HUMAN. EVERYTHING ELSE IS BULLSHIT, TO MAKE SOME FEEL INFERIOR OR SUPERIOR. ITS JUST THAT SIMPLE, NOW STOP BEING A DUMBASS AND WORK TO BE A BETTER HUMAN.

TO BE ANTI-RACIST YOU MUST UNDERSTAND THE THERE IS ONLY ONE RACE, HUMAN. EVERYTHING ELSE IS BULLSHIT, TO MAKE SOME FEEL INFERIOR OR SUPERIOR. ITS JUST THAT SIMPLE, NOW STOP BEING A DUMBASS AND WORK TO BE A BETTER HUMAN.

TO BE ANTI-RACIST YOU MUST UNDERSTAND THE THERE IS ONLY ONE RACE, HUMAN. EVERYTHING ELSE IS BULLSHIT, TO MAKE SOME FEEL INFERIOR OR SUPERIOR. ITS JUST THAT SIMPLE, NOW STOP BEING A DUMBASS AND WORK TO BE A BETTER HUMAN.

TO BE ANTI-RACIST YOU MUST UNDERSTAND THE THERE IS ONLY ONE RACE, HUMAN. EVERYTHING ELSE IS BULLSHIT, TO MAKE SOME FEEL INFERIOR OR SUPERIOR. ITS

TO BE ANTI-RACIST YOU MUST UNDERSTAND THE THERE IS ONLY ONE RACE, HUMAN. EVERYTHING ELSE IS BULLSHIT, TO MAKE SOME FEEL INFERIOR OR SUPERIOR. ITS JUST THAT SIMPLE, NOW STOP BEING A DUMBASS AND WORK TO BE A BETTER HUMAN.

TO BE ANTI-RACIST YOU MUST UNDERSTAND THE THERE IS ONLY ONE RACE, HUMAN. EVERYTHING ELSE IS BULLSHIT, TO MAKE SOME FEEL INFERIOR OR SUPERIOR. ITS JUST THAT SIMPLE, NOW STOP BEING A DUMBASS AND WORK TO BE A BETTER HUMAN.

TO BE ANTI-RACIST YOU MUST UNDERSTAND THE THERE IS ONLY ONE RACE, HUMAN. EVERYTHING ELSE IS BULLSHIT, TO MAKE SOME FEEL INFERIOR OR SUPERIOR. ITS JUST THAT SIMPLE, NOW STOP BEING A DUMBASS AND WORK TO BE A BETTER HUMAN.

TO BE ANTI-RACIST YOU MUST UNDERSTAND THE THERE IS ONLY ONE RACE, HUMAN. EVERYTHING ELSE IS BULLSHIT, TO MAKE SOME FEEL INFERIOR OR SUPERIOR. ITS JUST THAT SIMPLE, NOW STOP BEING A DUMBASS AND WORK TO BE A BETTER HUMAN.

TO BE ANTI-RACIST YOU MUST UNDERSTAND THE THERE IS ONLY ONE RACE, HUMAN. EVERYTHING ELSE IS BULLSHIT, TO MAKE SOME FEEL INFERIOR OR SUPERIOR. ITS JUST THAT SIMPLE, NOW STOP BEING A DUMBASS AND WORK TO BE A BETTER HUMAN.

TO BE ANTI-RACIST YOU MUST UNDERSTAND THE THERE IS ONLY ONE RACE, HUMAN. EVERYTHING ELSE IS BULLSHIT, TO MAKE SOME FEEL INFERIOR OR SUPERIOR. ITS JUST THAT SIMPLE, NOW STOP BEING A DUMBASS AND WORK TO BE A BETTER HUMAN.

TO BE ANTI-RACIST YOU MUST UNDERSTAND THE THERE IS ONLY ONE RACE, HUMAN. EVERYTHING ELSE IS BULLSHIT, TO MAKE SOME FEEL INFERIOR OR SUPERIOR. ITS JUST THAT SIMPLE, NOW STOP BEING A DUMBASS AND WORK TO BE A BETTER HUMAN.

TO BE ANTI-RACIST YOU MUST UNDERSTAND THE THERE IS ONLY ONE RACE, HUMAN. EVERYTHING ELSE IS BULLSHIT, TO MAKE SOME FEEL INFERIOR OR SUPERIOR. ITS JUST THAT SIMPLE, NOW STOP BEING A DUMBASS AND WORK TO BE A BETTER HUMAN.

TO BE ANTI-RACIST YOU MUST UNDERSTAND THE THERE IS ONLY ONE RACE, HUMAN. EVERYTHING ELSE IS BULLSHIT, TO MAKE SOME FEEL INFERIOR OR SUPERIOR. ITS JUST THAT SIMPLE, NOW STOP BEING A DUMBASS AND WORK TO BE A BETTER HUMAN.

TO BE ANTI-RACIST YOU MUST UNDERSTAND THE THERE IS ONLY ONE RACE, HUMAN. EVERYTHING ELSE IS BULLSHIT, TO MAKE SOME FEEL INFERIOR OR SUPERIOR. ITS JUST THAT SIMPLE, NOW STOP BEING A DUMBASS AND WORK TO BE A BETTER HUMAN.

TO BE ANTI-RACIST YOU MUST UNDERSTAND THE THERE IS ONLY ONE RACE, HUMAN. EVERYTHING ELSE IS BULLSHIT, TO MAKE SOME FEEL INFERIOR OR SUPERIOR. ITS JUST THAT SIMPLE, NOW STOP BEING A DUMBASS AND WORK TO BE A BETTER HUMAN.

JUST THAT SIMPLE, NOW STOP BEING A DUMBASS AND WORK TO BE A BETTER HUMAN.

TO BE ANTI-RACIST YOU MUST UNDERSTAND THE THERE IS ONLY ONE RACE, HUMAN. EVERYTHING ELSE IS BULLSHIT, TO MAKE SOME FEEL INFERIOR OR SUPERIOR. ITS JUST THAT SIMPLE, NOW STOP BEING A DUMBASS AND WORK TO BE A BETTER HUMAN.

TO BE ANTI-RACIST YOU MUST UNDERSTAND THE THERE IS ONLY ONE RACE, HUMAN. EVERYTHING ELSE IS BULLSHIT, TO MAKE SOME FEEL INFERIOR OR SUPERIOR. ITS JUST THAT SIMPLE, NOW STOP BEING A DUMBASS AND WORK TO BE A BETTER HUMAN.

TO BE ANTI-RACIST YOU MUST UNDERSTAND THE THERE IS ONLY ONE RACE, HUMAN. EVERYTHING ELSE IS BULLSHIT, TO MAKE SOME FEEL INFERIOR OR SUPERIOR. ITS JUST THAT SIMPLE, NOW STOP BEING A DUMBASS AND WORK TO BE A BETTER HUMAN.

TO BE ANTI-RACIST YOU MUST UNDERSTAND THE THERE IS ONLY ONE RACE, HUMAN. EVERYTHING ELSE IS BULLSHIT, TO MAKE SOME FEEL INFERIOR OR SUPERIOR. ITS JUST THAT SIMPLE, NOW STOP BEING A DUMBASS AND WORK TO BE A BETTER HUMAN.

TO BE ANTI-RACIST YOU MUST UNDERSTAND THE THERE IS ONLY ONE RACE, HUMAN. EVERYTHING ELSE IS BULLSHIT, TO MAKE SOME FEEL INFERIOR OR SUPERIOR. ITS JUST THAT SIMPLE, NOW STOP BEING A DUMBASS AND WORK TO BE A BETTER HUMAN.

TO BE ANTI-RACIST YOU MUST UNDERSTAND THE THERE IS ONLY ONE RACE, HUMAN. EVERYTHING ELSE IS BULLSHIT, TO MAKE SOME FEEL INFERIOR OR SUPERIOR. ITS JUST THAT SIMPLE, NOW STOP BEING A DUMBASS AND WORK TO BE A BETTER HUMAN.

TO BE ANTI-RACIST YOU MUST UNDERSTAND THE THERE IS ONLY ONE RACE, HUMAN. EVERYTHING ELSE IS BULLSHIT, TO MAKE SOME FEEL INFERIOR OR SUPERIOR. ITS JUST THAT SIMPLE, NOW STOP BEING A DUMBASS AND WORK TO BE A BETTER HUMAN.

TO BE ANTI-RACIST YOU MUST UNDERSTAND THE THERE IS ONLY ONE RACE, HUMAN. EVERYTHING ELSE IS BULLSHIT, TO MAKE SOME FEEL INFERIOR OR SUPERIOR. ITS JUST THAT SIMPLE, NOW STOP BEING A DUMBASS AND WORK TO BE A BETTER HUMAN.

TO BE ANTI-RACIST YOU MUST UNDERSTAND THE THERE IS ONLY ONE RACE, HUMAN. EVERYTHING ELSE IS BULLSHIT, TO MAKE SOME FEEL INFERIOR OR SUPERIOR. ITS JUST THAT SIMPLE, NOW STOP BEING A DUMBASS AND WORK TO BE A BETTER HUMAN.

TO BE ANTI-RACIST YOU MUST UNDERSTAND THE THERE IS ONLY ONE RACE, HUMAN. EVERYTHING ELSE IS BULLSHIT, TO MAKE SOME FEEL INFERIOR OR SUPERIOR. ITS

IF AFTER READING A 100 PAGES OF THE SAME THING YOU STILL DON'T GET IT, YOU'RE A SUPER DUMBASS, AND NOTHING CAN HELP YOU.

IF AFTER READING A 100 PAGES OF THE SAME THING YOU STILL DON'T GET IT, YOU'RE A SUPER DUMBASS, AND NOTHING CAN HELP YOU.

If you liked booked please check out my other products
https://bit.ly/VoteDemocratsOut

https://bit.ly/3yrsdontknowgender

https://bit.ly/NipTuck1

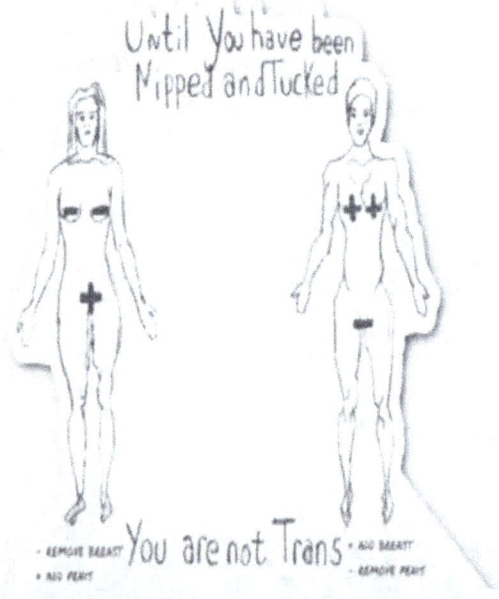

IF YOU BELIVE
THE

OF YOUR SKIN
MAKES YOU
SURPERIOR
YOU'RE A
DUMBASS